Praise for Fugitive Days

"With considerable wit, no small amount of remorse, and an anger that smolders still across the decades, Bill Ayers tells the story of his quintessentially American trip through the 1960s. That it is written in a consistently absorbing style with many passages of undiluted brilliance only adds to its appeal.
—Thomas Frank, author of *One Market Under God* and *What's the Matter with Kansas?*

"A gripping account . . . Ayers describes well the deep emotions that inflamed the '60s."
—John Patrick Diggins, *Los Angeles Times*

"This is a precious book, not simply because it offers a gripping personal account of the primal American suspense story of life on the run, but, more important, because it re-creates a critical point of view and way of thinking that we seem, even a few decades later, barely able to recall."
—Scott Turow, author of *Ordinary Heroes* and *Ultimate Punishment*

"It's been a long time since American political culture last tilted left-ward . . . Extremists of the left have all but disappeared, while extremists of the right are as common as mushrooms after rain . . . Ayers has a knack for capturing the spirit of his times . . . It's a fascinating story."
—Jean Dubail, *Cleveland Plain Dealer*

"Finally, here is an irresistibly readable book that answers the question, How did a nice suburban boy go from the ordinary pleasures of his class to the Days of Rage and beyond? Bill Ayers not only makes this exalting and painful journey comprehensible, he peoples it with sympathetic family, friends, and lovers, and moves us with his candor."
—Rosellen Brown, author of *Before and After* and *Half a Heart*

D0950770

"Terrific . . . This memoir rings of hard-learned truth and integrity and is an important contribution to literature on 1960s culture and American radicalism."

—*Publishers Weekly*

"What makes *Fugitive Days* unique is its unsparing detail and its marvelous human coherence and integrity. Bill Ayers's America and his family background, his education, his political awakening, his anger and involvement, his anguished re-emergence from the shadows: all these are rendered in their truth without a trace of nostalgia or 'second thinking.' For anyone who cares about the sorry mess we are in, this book is essential, indeed necessary, reading."

—EDWARD W. SAID, author of *Reflections on Exile* and *Out of Place*

"This remarkable memoir gives us the visceral experience of being on the run. Ayers writes with eloquence and irony. This is one man's amazingly honest, authentic, and gripping testament—and a helluva story it makes."

—PHILLIP LOPATE, author of *Portrait of My Body*

"A wild and painful ride in the savage years of the late sixties. A very good book about a terrifying time in America."

—HUNTER S. THOMPSON, author of *Fear and Loathing in Las Vegas* and *Hell's Angels*

Fugitive Days

Also by William Ayers

Fugitive Days

Memoirs of an Antiwar Activist

Bill Ayers

Beacon Press

Boston

WITHDRAWN

CONTRA COSTA COUNTY LIBRARY

3 1901 04434 8193

Beacon Press
25 Beacon Street
Boston, Massachusetts 02108-2892
www.beacon.org

Beacon Press books
are published under the auspices of
the Unitarian Universalist Association of Congregations.

© 2001 by William Ayers, © 2009 afterword by William Ayers
All rights reserved
Printed in the United States of America

"In Those Years" from *Dark Fields of the Republic: Poems 1991–1995* by Adrienne
Rich. Copyright © 1995 by Adrienne Rich. Used by permission of the author and W.
W. Norton & Company, Inc.

I've written these stories as I recall them, making only minor changes, including
some names and details to protect privacy.

12 11 10 09   8 7 6 5 4 3 2 1

This book is printed on acid-free paper that meets the uncoated paper ANSI/NISO
specifications for permanence as revised in 1992.

Text design by Sara Eisenman
Composition by Wilsted & Taylor Publishing Services

Library of Congress Cataloging-in-Publication Data
Ayers, Bill.
    Fugitive days: memoirs of an antiwar activist / Bill Ayers.
    p. cm.
    ISBN 978-0-8070-3277-0 (paperback : alk. paper)
    1. Ayers, Bill. 2. Left-wing extremists—United States—Biography. 3. Left-wing
extremists—Michigan—Ann Arbor—Biography. 4. Vietnamese Conflict,
1961–1975—Protest movements—United States. 5. Radicalism—United States—
History—20th century. 6. Radicalism—Michigan—Ann Arbor—History—20th century. 7. United States—Social conditions—1960–1980.1. Title.
    HN90.R3 A96 2001
    973.92'092–dc21   2001000362

For Bernardine

contents

Fugitive Days

Prelude

Wait a minute. This can't be happening now. Wait.

The fuse is already lit, little sparks flickering forward in a desperate, deadly dance. The steel hands on the big clock tick-tick-tick relentlessly onward as the world spins further and further out of control. My whole life is about to blow up.

In a minute I'll be staggering down a dusty stretch of road alone, wobbling into the night, everything torn to pieces, but I don't know it yet, not yet. The hints and the clues, the doubts, the fears, have been trampled down and banished to the far edges of my mind, and so I simply sit here looking dumbly toward this deserted little telephone booth, wondering for the third night in a row in the gathering dusk if the damn thing is ever going to ring. Everything will collapse in a minute. But not yet. Sixty seconds to chaos.

The faded blue sign invites neither scrutiny nor confidence: "PUBLIC" it announces uneasily, "TELEPHONE." The phone works—I've checked and then rechecked a hundred times—but the red paint along its borders has bleached to pink, the dull fluorescent light flutters frantically, and the black wire slouches uncertainly toward the main line. Any sensible traveler, even the most desperate, will, I hope, push on to a more promising spot; here there's no food, no gas, no toilet, nothing but a solitary smudgy telephone booth and a broken-down picnic table. It's my own private line by now, just as I want it.

I'd nicknamed this place the Spider's Palace, from a children's book I knew long ago, and it's true, the black spiders are living large, collecting luminous flies in frail-looking but intractable cobwebs. Diana and the others all have my number—I'll be at the Spider's Palace at eight, I'd said as we synchronized our watches and split up days ago—and here I've been since eight o'clock exactly, waiting.

The phone booth reeks of ancient piss, baked daily I imagine in this accidental solar oven. Who would pee here? I wonder aloud, looking away toward the horizon, wide as a church door. Maybe the sight of an abandoned phone booth is like the bells of Pavlov's dogs. My mind is wandering now. Where is everybody? I groan into the night, into myself. Five minutes after eight. I'll wait till quarter past, I think, no longer.

I slide off the table and walk a few steps away, scooping up a handful of stones, pitching them one by one at a godforsaken wooden gate across the road.

Two nights, no call. What if there's nothing again tonight? I'll be back at the Spider's Palace at eight tomorrow night, I think, eight the next night, and the next, and the next, forever, I guess. I've felt my courage flicker in recent months, and my confidence choke, but I hold tight to this one small hard thing: discipline. I was supposed to be right here starting Saturday, and here I am. It's like a death grip, this phone and me; I can't let go. The chilly air is turning bitter, and I shiver slightly. Come on, I say, breaking the silence again, feeling cold and forlorn. Call me. Please call me.

A dark sedan appears as a dot in the distance making tracks down the road, accelerating thunderously past me toward the far horizon, and is, like a mirage, quickly gone, and my phone roars suddenly to life, erupts like a shotgun. Two loud rings, both barrels. I leap to snatch it as at a life jacket before going over the side of a sinking ship. Hey, babe—a friend's voice, but not Diana's. Something's wrong—the closeness, her urgency, the intimate embrace, I think, of the desperate. Are you OK? she asks. Are you alone?

What's up? I say, my frustration pushed roughly aside by simple fear, larger and more imposing. What is it? I could picture her then, standing at her own isolated phone booth, tough and sure, not like me at all. But she hesitates; there's an unexpected catch in her breath, the sound of suppressed sobs, perhaps, and a surprising sadness tempering her steely will. Alarms are going off up in my head.

You've got to leave now, she says firmly. Tomorrow at the latest. We'll meet up in a week at the shore. There's been a terrible accident.

What the hell? An accident? What the hell is she talking about?

Dadadada . . . She sounds weirdly incoherent now, chattering like a monkey, and I can't make any of it out.

Wait a minute, I say. This can't be happening now. Wait.

Diana is dead, she says again, the sound of breaking glass rising up in her throat. And some of the others . . . dead as well.

My mind stutters.

Diana is dead, she repeats slowly, and then I'm running wildly, the abandoned phone swinging side to side. Diana is dead—those three shrill words rebounding off the wall of my skull in a continuous loop—Diana is dead. Stumbling, I drop down, bob back up, scratched and covered with gravel, running again. Where do I think I'm going?

A voice, not one I recognize, comes ripping from afar, rising and gathering into a long scream propelled from some unknown place inside me—NO! And then, a deathly quiet, just the rushing of air and the pumping of blood, the echo of escape. I can hear the drum beating in my ears, my heart hammering through my chest, and I feel my muscles flexing from a distance, working automatically now. I am running for my life, but I don't know where I'm going.

In a minute I'll be making lists—ditch the cars, they'll say, hide the evidence. In a minute I'll be panting to repair, struggling to understand where things went so awfully wrong. But not yet. Now my mind is exploding and I'm running all alone, virtually on empty.

That was March 1970, and the American war in Viet Nam was half done, though we didn't know it yet. The woman on the other end of the phone would save me soon, and soon after that we would plunge together into a subterranean river, the strong, swift brown god of life pulling us forward for decades to come, but we didn't know that yet, either. All that was certain was this: Diana was suddenly dead and I was—in a flash—unhinged and going under.

Part I 1965-1970

1.

Memory is a motherfucker.

I myself remember almost nothing. I don't remember the places I've been in the last year, where I've stayed, or the people I've met. It's all a blur, really, all that traveling, all that work, for what?

I spent a week in Taos. I had coffee each morning at Tazza, dinner at Orlando's. And still I remember nothing.

I spent time in New Orleans—the Camellia Grill, the Atlas Oyster Bar—and in Roanoke—Carlo's New Brazil, the Old Vietnam—but it's all, finally, a blank. Spaces and vacant lots.

I don't remember names. Hardly ever. Even names I ought to remember—the names of my students when they look at me expectantly, of my colleagues' husbands at social occasions, of my old teachers. The names I do remember are entirely unremarkable: Jacob Pearle sold me a car in New Jersey once; Sylvan Esperanza rented us a flat above his café.

I remember faces vividly—a woman I saw in a bar months ago, her mysterious black eyes pitched close together, now coming out of a restaurant; I smile and she frowns and looks away as if to say, You don't know me, motherfucker—but I do remember her, I really do. Or this tattered, tired-looking young man selling Streetwise on the corner—he was several blocks north last winter, and here he is now, a familiar face and I'm happy to buy a paper from him for a dollar, and even happier that I don't have to know his name. I wouldn't anyway.

I never remember presents: Who gave me this gray vest? My earrings? This notebook? I have no idea. What did I get for my last birthday?

I routinely forget birthdays. Already this year I've missed my father's, one of my sons', a niece's. And there are many, many months to go, more to forget.

My mom doesn't remember even more than I. I mean she barely remembers me, and the scope and scale of her obliviousness is huge. I at least remember to brush my teeth and to eat and to put on my clothes. These things now elude her. I remember to recoil from pain, not to pick at my skin, to cover a cut or a troubled scab with a Band-Aid so that the blood doesn't gush all over the place and the bleeding will stop. And I remember to breathe, to swallow, to move. So while I admit that I don't remember much, my mom points out that there's even more to forget. In the end, I know I'll forget it all. Oblivion trumps memory.

I remember the overdrawn story of my birth. I do.

On the day I was born my family was bundled beneath a heavy blanket of snow in their neat little bungalow in Glen Ellyn, a promising Chicago suburb, they thought—the schools, of course, the space to grow, the affordable property. At thirty, Tom was already a rising executive, and Mary was raising the kids. They had neither aspirations nor pretensions for the Gold Coast and, though they would outgrow house after house in the years ahead, this midmost of midwestern suburbs was where they chose to be.

That December morning was cold, cold, cold outside, while inside everything was hot and glowing—the flickering red and green lights on the little Christmas tree, the butter cookies fresh from the oven cooling on a rack, the chestnuts, the steaming cider. And, of course, Mom herself, two weeks past her due date, swollen to explosive proportions and absolutely ablaze. The aroma of roasting turkey and sweet potatoes splitting their skins mixed with the close and pungent scent from the nursery, and the air crackled expectantly.

The presents had all been opened, wrapping paper and ribbon littering the living room, when Mom felt me stir and stretch. Here it is, she said, the last unopened present.

A neighbor watched over my brother and sister while Tom and

Mary drove off to Oak Park Hospital, twenty miles east along North Avenue, covered now with slush and ice. Tom maneuvered the car through the snow blurries, struggling to stay toward the center line.

As the journey to my birth was told and retold, stretched and exaggerated, it was as if the young couple had arrived by dogsled having crossed the Alps in a blinding blizzard. Would they arrive in time? Would they survive? Would there be a bed prepared? It blended easily with the story of Christmas and became a story of peril, precariousness, lives in the balance, and, yes, miracle, which is, properly narrated, the story of every birth. In reality mine was strictly middle-of-the-road, routine, par-for-the-miracle course. I missed Christmas by minutes, but that never diminished the intensity of this foundational myth—I was the best Christmas present ever, my life achieved against great danger and risk. And I believed it for years and decades to come.

I was the third baby, Cathy leading the way, followed by Tim a couple of years later, and then—boom!—eighteen months and there I was, scrambling, I imagine now, for space and food in the hatchery, angling for rank in this rapidly expanding household. It didn't take long for me to move up in the kiddyarchy—Rick came along directly, with Juan still a decade off, a kind of blessed mistake or wondrous afterthought.

Juan was not his given name, of course—no, that would be John Steven. He acquired Juan in late adolescence when, as a school dropout, he went to work as a dishwasher and busboy in a cafeteria in California. John Ayers, he saw right away, was not a good fit here, and so he reinvented and rechristened himself. He's been Juan Chicago to friends and family ever since.

Being the middle child forever stamped me. Cathy and Tim forged the way, set the agendas, pushed some of the bigger boulders aside, while leaving other obstacles in their wakes. Rick and Juan nudged from below and behind, and I learned to look simultaneously up and down, forward and backward. Cathy was the brains of the outfit, a consistent straight-A student, and Tim the most popular in anything he did. Rick was the true intellectual, wide-ranging and perceptive, with a searching and curious disposition of mind, and Juan was always the most likable. I was faithfully midship, dead center, and from my earliest memories I made friends with the older and the younger generations, moved easily both ways, became larger and smaller as required, dilated and contracted by the hour, comfortably stretching above myself in one moment, and in the next happily coming down.

There were memorable advantages to be sure. When I was little, Tim's bed was inches from mine, and he was under strict orders to face me until I fell asleep—along with my nightlight, which had the power of a sunlamp, Tim's face kept the monsters at bay. Of course, if Tim was in a mood to torment, he would show me a gleeful face and then turn over before my eyes closed. I would howl in protest until he turned back, grinning wickedly. Tim had that power over me, and I was forever awed.

When I was older, Miss Alexander, my frail and venerable Latin teacher, who, it was said, was old enough to have spoken Latin before it became a dead language, simply refused to believe that I was as stupid as I appeared. You're Cathy's brother, she smiled benevolently, showing sharp little yellow teeth as she remembered her star student, winner of the coveted Latin Prize, and I wanted to throw up. But I escaped with a low B. Cathy was, as always, a bit horrified as I trailed her through school, diminishing the family reputation for academic excellence every year, stumbling happily along, but to an indifferent student like me, a low B was pure gold.

There were distinct disadvantages as well. Ken Nardella, an Italian kid from above North Avenue, with his long DA greased up and the shiny fenders of his pompadour swooping suggestively over and down his forehead, had a little gang of hoods and he hated Tim, who was, of course, president of the junior class. Ken was old to be in high school; his family had moved out from Chicago a few years ago and he'd been put back a couple of grades. I knew him from football, and from hanging out at the pool hall next to the Glen Theater. Ken acknowledged me only grudgingly.

I was fourteen, but I'd been playing football since I could walk—I was a chunky kid and my earliest memories include a constant chorus of adults looking me over, smiling broadly, and saying, Oh, you're the football player of the family. The Skinnerian reinforcement worked: I felt destined to the game and threw myself into it, although baby fat proved a poor substitute for skill, strength, and size.

I'd been shooting pool and smoking cigarettes for a couple of years. I knew how to put wicked English on a cue ball, and take a lit butt in my teeth, flip it into my mouth with my tongue, and push two puffy plumes of white smoke out of my nostrils while banking the eight ball into the corner pocket. I could also blow three perfect smoke rings through one another, the first large and lazy and then smaller and tighter and faster, the rings exploding into an impressive cloud, and I was working on the Olympic symbol, five interconnected circles. I practiced at the pool hall on Saturdays, or after football practice. It was an edgy place to hang out, the pool hall, for Glen Ellyn kids in the scrubbed and spongy fifties.

The football field and the pool hall were the only places the hoods and a few of the straight kids met as equals, but most of the kids I knew well stuck to football. Safer that way. I, on the other hand, adored the pool hall—shades of James Dean and Marlon Brando. And, of course, shooting pool beat doing homework.

One afternoon Ken asked me if I'd ever seen a zip gun. It felt like a test. Sure, I said.

Want to see mine? he asked.

OK. I wasn't so sure, but what could I say? It was a test.

I'll go get it. Meet me in the alley behind the Glen in fifteen minutes.

Oh shit, I thought. I was supposed to be home by seven on school nights, and it was almost seven now. Oh shit, I thought. Sure, I said.

I finished my rack, called home to say I'd be just a little late, and then headed over to the alley, trying to amble. Ken was sitting on a loading dock in the dusk, a brown lunch bag in his lap with what looked to be something hefty inside. And, oh shit, he was with his cousin, Bob Napolito, who was my age, and their buddy Dave

Salerno. I knew them all from the football field and from the pool hall. All three had deep voices and shaved regularly, and although Ken had a pretty face like Sal Mineo's, Dave was huge with dead eyes and a square head like Frankenstein's monster—I could imagine him with a bolt through his neck. Shit, shit, shit. Hey, they said simultaneously, smirking a little. Hey, I said, a little shaky.

Ken pulled a heavy piece of pipe, about a foot long, from the bag. He showed me how one end was open, but the other had a bolt threaded into it, sealing the end tight. A tiny hole had been drilled into the bolt, big enough for a fuse. Ken had firecracker fuses in his pocket, a jar full of match heads meticulously cut from their stems, some paper and cotton wadding, and a ball bearing as big as a marble. He also had a rod that fit the pipe perfectly.

Here's how it works, he said, demonstrating. First you fix a length of fuse in this hole, and then you pour in about two inches of match heads. His comrades and I leaned in toward Ken's subversive seminar. Some gunpowder would be nice, but, what the hell, matches work OK. Then you push some cotton and paper in and use this rod to really punch it down. A match is a lazy explosion because the gases expand so slowly, and everything has time to get away. But when I tighten it up like this, it's an overly excited explosion, and it can wreak havoc.

Shit, I thought. Ken's like a D student or something, but he's a damn good halfback, a clever pool shark, and, good God, a scientific genius in zip guns to boot. Who knew?

If I close both ends securely, he continued, it's a pipe bomb. Real damage. One end open, with a ball bearing packed neatly in, it's a single-shot zip gun. And it can kill a guy at close range. Watch.

We watched. Ken held the thing at arm's length, aiming at a large windowpane across the alley, and told me to stand back and a few feet to his left. Bob and Frankenstein faded to the right as Ken scraped his Zippo across his jeans and lit the little fuse. As the fire danced and sputtered toward the bolt Ken wheeled suddenly and, with big smiles on all of them—shit, shit, shit—aimed the fucking thing right at me. Shit!

There was no time to do a goddamn thing; I never even heard the explosion. But I cried out and, alive, started running in tight circles, feeling myself in flames. And it's true—Ken had not packed the ball bearing in and the joke was to make me think I was being shot, while shooting me only with harmless cotton and paper. But Ken, his scientific IQ predictably falling short, failed to account for the fact that some of the match heads would still be igniting lazily, some of the bits of cotton still flaming wildly. I was ablaze, my chest and stomach and arms lit up.

Bob grabbed me in an instant and smothered the little flames with his jacket. All of them looked mortified. Oh, man, Ken said, red and suddenly sweating. That wasn't supposed to happen. Oh, man, I'm so sorry, man. His voice cracking, he looked like a big whining baby about to cry. Don't tell your parents, man. Please. Oh shit. Don't tell Tim. He was pretty miserable.

My shirt had little black holes all over it, and under each was a blister or a welt on my skin. Bob helped me off with my shirt while Frankenstein ran around the corner to the store for butter and bandages. Oh, man, I'm so very sorry, man, Ken spluttered again and again. That wasn't supposed to happen. I was just pretending to kill you.

Bob dressed my wounds and gave me his shirt. Ken lit a Camel and we passed it around like a peace pipe. Then we piled into Frankenstein's beat-up Plymouth and they drove me home. I never told, and that was an unexpected bit of heroism. Soon Bob became my best friend—he introduced me to the joys of smoking cigars on the sly with a bottle of dago red, and of eating homemade spaghetti with meatballs and whole garlic cloves on stale bread soaked in burgundy. We hunted pheasants together in the fields near his house, and played bumper tag along St. Charles Road with our parents' cars. Soon we called each other Wop, and in our junior years we each left home, me for prep school, Bob for military academy. And I was one of them. I wanted to become Italian. I peeped at my profile reflected in the classroom windows—head up, chin out, not-so-Roman nose pointing like a hood ornament, lips in a superior sneer, DA growing long and provocative. I practiced the stance and the posture fiercely.

My first love in high school was Katie Blue, small and dark and daz-zling, a junior when I was a freshman. I was playing up. We enjoyed hanging out as buddies and, like a lot of Tim's friends, she treated me like a cute little toy. But, surprise, returning late from a school trip one night, she asked me if I'd walk her home.

Sure, I said.

And when we get there, she said, will you kiss me good night?

Sure, I said, suddenly a little wobbly.

And when you kiss me good night, she pressed on, will you kiss me like a freshman?

What the hell did that mean? I thought, a little frantic.

Never! I said firmly, recovering just in time, trying now to sound convincing. Of course not. How does a freshman kiss? I wondered. And, of course, I was a freshman, so did I have any choice?

Standing at her door, she showed me exactly what she meant, her mouth opening slightly, our tongues touching secretly, sending a sweet shock through my whole body. I gave way to warm joy. The surprise over, I felt the insistent pull of a kind of calling. I drew "Katie Blue" on my hand every day in thick letters with a black pen—a tem-porary tattoo—and wanted only to be her sex slave, her eager and intense apprentice. I practiced that fiercely, too.

My little brothers were their own gift and challenge. I could play down with them. Juan was cute and cuddly and fun. He's still—now that he's grown up and middle-aged—cute as hell, but he was pure and delicious then. When I was still learning how to change his dia-per, I was shocked to discover that he often had a little hard-on, which looked too weird to tell my mom about, even though it made changing him a lot tougher. But I figured out how to bend it up toward his belly button and pin the diaper tight. My friends and I baby-sat for him a lot. Sometimes we'd put him in his crib or playpen and forget about him for hours. No problem. I adored him.

When he was nine or ten and visiting me at college, I sat him on the back of my 1948 Indian motorcycle for a tour of Ann Arbor and the surrounding countryside. My parents, needless to say, had no idea I owned a motorcycle, let alone a classic Indian. I swore Juan to secrecy, and off we went. At Packard and State a car blew through the light and I slammed on the brakes, skidding sideways along the pavement to a rough and terrifying stop. What flooded through my mind at that moment—besides that I loved him—was how pissed off Mom would be that I hadn't told them I owned a motorcycle, and pissed, too, that I'd killed Juan. I was certain she'd look on the bright side, but still. Luckily, Juan was just a little scraped and bruised, and he already knew how to keep a secret.

Years earlier Tim and I almost finished Rick off in another bizarre accident. We'd removed the cover to a floor vent next to the kitchen —Mom was in there somewhere, doing something—and we were taking turns lowering ourselves down, pretending to work in a sewer. The vent and pipe were large, but we could squeeze our big bodies only partway in. When we tired of the game, we simply walked off, forgetting to replace the cover. Rick, about two, strolled out of the kitchen carrying a large wooden bowl in front of him and, just as I looked up, disappeared into the sewer. He was a perfect fit. Tim and I followed Mom as she raced down the cellar stairs in horror, knowing she'd be pissed at us, visions of Rick feeding the old coal-burning furnace, only to find him crawling from a large piece of pipe he'd broken with his weight, filthy but smiling.

Rick was my filthy, smiling sidekick for many years, but by high school he'd taken his own distinct path. He actually liked Latin, and he was the first kid I'd ever known who read the newspaper every morning—not the comics or the sports page, but the entire goddamn thing—who wore black turtlenecks, and who drank coffee when he was thirteen. He's going through a stage, Mom said cheerily as he went six straight years without saying a single word to either Dad or her.

Rick introduced me to the Gate of Horn, a legendary Chicago folk club, where we saw Lenny Bruce and Peter, Paul and Mary. He took me to a James Brown concert at 47th Street and State where four of us from the suburbs were embraced in a large bronze rock 'n' roll bosom. He uncovered the Second City improvisational theater, the Art Institute, and Studs Terkel. In a way he introduced me to politics.

Years later he would emigrate to Canada to escape the draft, return and enlist with the intention of organizing a servicemen's union, only to desert after Diana was killed. We were underground together all those years. But I'm getting ahead of myself.

There were five of us, then, and I was in the middle, a little dreamy and trying on the possibilities presented to me. I was blond in a crowd of brunettes, chubby in a family of beanpoles. There were always friends over for dinner or the night, and there was always noise, romance, crises, comedy, projects, possibilities. I remember distinctly the new baby-sitter who said after dinner one night, You'll have to go home now, Bill, the Ayers kids are going to bed.

2.

There's something about a good bomb.

I am just an infant at my mother's breast when the United States drops the Big One on Japan and President Harry S. Truman tells a blinking, uncomprehending public that this selfless act of innocence and wonder and science and progress is a particularly American moment. This is, he tells the world, a very good bomb:

> **Sixteen hours ago an American airplane dropped one bomb on Hiroshima. That bomb had more power than 20,000 tons of TNT. It had more than two thousand times the blast power of the largest bomb ever yet used in the history of warfare. With this bomb we have now added a new and revolutionary increase in destruction. It is an atomic bomb. It is a harnessing of the basic power of the universe. The force from which the sun draws its power has been loosed.**

Harry Truman is drooling now. He's excited. He's fetishizing and eroticizing. And why not? Explosive power, newborn, stirring, dangerous, and overwhelming. A breathtaking discharge. He loves this bomb, loves it more than life, more than words can ever convey, but still he tries. It turns out, he tells the wide world against the naive judgment of ordinary eyes and minds, that this one good bomb saved millions of lives, that we won the battle of the laboratories—our beneficent scientists outperforming the evil geniuses in all the other labs—and prevented the bomb from falling into the hands of bad people who would put the bomb to their own abhorrent purposes, killing and maiming indiscriminately, for example. "Having found the atomic bomb," he says modestly, "we have used it. It is an awful responsibility that has come to us. We thank God that it has come to us and not to our enemies. And we pray that He may guide us to use it in His ways and for His purposes." What? What did he say? Can you rewind that? Yabadabadaba . . . "And we pray that He may guide us to use it in His way and for His purposes."

Harry S. Truman likes to be thought of as a straight-talking, no bullshit, midwestern American guy. The buck stops here, he says. Show me, he says. I won't mince my words.

The Bomb, dubbed Fat Man by its crew and keepers (ordinary American good guys all), is 10½ feet long and 29 inches in diameter, equal in explosive power to a stick of dynamite 12 yards in diameter and the length of a football field. It kills 71,379 people in Hiroshima outright. A few days later its baby brother, Little Boy, annihilates 49,308 at Nagasaki. Months earlier American bombs with cute and inoffensive names had killed 83,783 people in massive raids over Tokyo. The saturation bombing of Dresden—still secret—incinerated 135,000 more. And Harry Truman says, The end is not yet. Show me, he says. The buck stops here, he adds. Harry Truman is swelling. He's also mincing. A million American lives were saved by this one humanitarian act, he says, that fantastic figure drawn from thin air by McGeorge Bundy, a smart-ass young speech writer who would grow old as an architect of the coming Viet Nam War, and then repeated ever after as the truth. Bombs away.

I don't remember America dropping the Bomb, of course, because as I said I was just a baby at my mother's breast. But I've lived my whole life in its thick and sticky shadow, and I grew up on the noble story of this most excellent and worthy A-bomb: A for American; A for Atomic; A for Amnesia. I was born into an orgy of explosions.

The Russians stole the secret of the Bomb from us just before I went to kindergarten, and I learned then that the whole world could blow up at any moment. My first-grade teacher, Miss Loving, taught us that wherever we were—at home with our families, on a picnic, or right here in our classroom—we should stay alert to the possibility of a nuclear attack. It could come at any time. Once, as a group of us boys wrestled across the playground, Miss Loving reprimanded us for being too rowdy, adding that we weren't in any position to respond properly to a nuclear attack. We all knew the response by now: Duck! And cover! Whenever we saw the bright flash, wherever we were, we were supposed to drop everything, duck and cover. Under our desks, beneath a beach towel, below our beds—the key was to close our eyes, cover our heads, and wait for the blast to pass over us. And then, when it was all over, Miss Loving told us, we should always wash thoroughly.

I knew what supplies we were supposed to keep in our basements—tuna, dry fruit, evaporated milk, canned chicken, tomato juice—and I was a little bothered about why Mom frowned and said not to worry, we didn't need it. In Cub Scouts we were taught to encourage everyone in our neighborhood to stock up, so that those of us who were prepared wouldn't be in the uncomfortable position of denying canned chicken to our less responsible neighbors, but Mom wouldn't budge. I kept quiet on the subject at Cub Scout meetings. That was OK, because it wasn't long before Dad and I went to an award ceremony and heard a man from the national Cub Scouts tell a confusing story about a boy from Boise, Idaho, who had found out that his parents were soft on the Russians and that the boy had turned them in to the police—I didn't know if that was a good thing or a bad thing—and Dad said I couldn't go to Cub Scout meetings anymore. I was baffled.

When I was young, five or six and for years after, we went with friends to their grandparents' farm in nearby Woodstock, Illinois, for the Fourth of July. Glanmuzzie, her eyes twinkling, her long hair wrapped into a bun, made fresh lemonade from scratch, and served us homemade rhubarb pie right out of the oven. She shook her head and clucked disapprovingly, her jowls shaking, as Paw Paw reached a long, sinewy arm into his huge duffel bag filled with the highly prized illicit goods—we each got tiny glowing punks to light the little cracking bombs, a handful of sparklers, some buzzers and thumpers, and long packages of sweet firecrackers with their fuses woven together. We pulled them off the braid individually and pop! pop! pop! most of the morning until my big brother fashioned a way to hang the whole load to a tree and light the bottom fuse—a sudden dance of fire and smoke unraveled just beneath the branch, a chaos of deafening charges, the exciting smell of gunpowder everywhere, and Paw Paw, inspired, drooled slightly and laughed out loud as he adjusted his hearing aid. He looked a lot like Harry Truman, but taller and a little stooped.

Paw Paw gave us a cherished Big One only now and then, and only if we begged a little. A Big One was treasured because it was rare and because it was huge and because it made a concussion that rattled the windows in the farmhouse and made a thunderous impact that shook Glanmuzzie to her toes. That excited Paw Paw every time. But we were only worthy of a Big One if we could walk a fine line, demonstrating proper awe and reverence, but never slipping into groveling or whimpering. Stop your bellyaching, said Paw Paw sternly if more than two of us approached at once. Stop your whining. We had to demonstrate our courage in the asking, I suppose, or we were unlikely to have the required courage in the bombing. Look a man in the eye when you make a request, Paw Paw instructed. Stand up straight, and don't mince your words.

My older brother was a bomb thrower. Big Ones are cool, he said forcefully, displaying his competence and, again, his power. When he held a lit M-80 in his hand—the casing said DO NOT HOLD IN HAND, DO NOT HOLD IN HAND over and over—and heaved it into the middle of the pond, a waterspout leapt into the air high above the trees. Minutes later, little lifeless goldfish bodies floated to the surface. When he put a cherry bomb under a can away from the house, shrapnel whizzed past us into the woods. He was the absolute master of the Big One.

We drove home in time to see the giant fireworks display over Lake Ellyn. We waved our flaming sticks in the night, and we sang along with the crowd and the amplified recording as the sun went down: "And the rockets red glare, the bombs bursting in air . . . " Mom loved the flowers of fire, the colorful starbursts, the pinwheels, and the ladyfingers, and my sister liked the golden spiderwebs rushing upward to fill the night sky. My brothers and I loved everything about the wild displays of noise and color, the flares, the surprising candle bombs, but we trembled mostly for the Big Ones, the loud concussions, especially those crashing near the end in quick succession. BOOM! BOOM! BOOM! We went ecstatic. The bigger the better.

The Fourth of July bombs were all good bombs, except sometimes. The bomb that took off a neighbor kid's little finger in Woodstock one year was a pretty bad bomb. And the bomb that killed a man accidentally at Lake Ellyn years later was a very bad bomb. Could there ever be a really good bomb? It could not be built to hurt or kill. Maybe it could extract minerals from the ground. Maybe it could knock over an abandoned building, or maybe the Pentagon after everyone goes home. Simple earthworks, performance art, everyone standing back. Bombs away.

3.

It'll be fine, my mom cooed, leaning over my bruised and bleeding knee and my crumpled bicycle. Let's get this cleaned up and then it will be just fine. Mom was right, as usual, and I remember her chirpy watchword, applied routinely to a steady stream of calamities and misfortunes, always adding to her burgeoning status as clairvoyant. It was fine, after all.

Mom, bless her heart, was famous in our family for holding fast to a personal motto perfectly fitted to the tone and temperament of her circumstances and her times: It'll be fine. It was the childlike fifties in the privileged and padded suburbs of America, and a kind of willed blindness had afflicted the people. The impending threat of nuclear annihilation? Not here on Forest Avenue. The unfolding battle for equal access to education? Not at Forest Glen School. The Army-McCarthy hearings on TV? Let's just watch Jack Benny. Crisis, war, the lynching of fourteen-year-old Emmett Till, his skull crushed in, his eye gouged out, barbed wire wrapped around his neck? All of it approached from the margins, and Mom steadily pushed it all away. Not, not, not, not in Glen Ellyn, Illinois.

Why is Celeste brown? I asked Mom one morning. Celeste cleaned our house and I had just noticed something interesting. Shush, my mother scolded. We don't talk that way. Growing up I learned that race is unspeakable. We don't talk that way, or we don't talk at all.

Mom called me Billy or Little Bill, and it happened that Commonwealth Edison's logo and mascot at that time was a tiny animated bird made from a lightbulb whose name was also Little Bill. He sang a little jingle:

> *E-lec-tricity costs less today you know,*
> *Than it did twenty-five years ago.*
> *A little birdie told me so,*
> *Tweet! Tweet! Little Bill.*

My dad worked for Edison and for years I believed—and friends and family fed the delusion—that the famous ad campaign was named for me.

At the end of summer—after Y camp and a week on Cape Cod with my family—I packed peanut butter sandwiches on Wonderbread with a) mayonnaise and lettuce; b) mustard; c) marshmallows; or d) bacon, and explored the Du Page River with my brothers, finding crayfish and frogs—some weirdly misshapen—skipping stones and struggling for days to assemble a leaking raft out of driftwood and old logs. We were the captains of our dreams, the masters of our destinies, even though our raft sank ingloriously a quarter-mile downriver that year and the crew had to swim for the safety of the shore.

This is the life, we said, meaning the good and the happy life. And I said it believing that happiness was affordable and easy to accept, effortless and without risk. The world of the happy is a happy world, we told each other.

For dinner we always had corn on the cob from a farmer's stand just north of town, potato salad, fried chicken, or sloppy joes. Then came spirited games with a gaggle of kids, ranging over the entire neighborhood. On clear nights Mom spread blankets and pillows on the lawn and we watched for shooting stars, making secret wishes on each one. I wished for happiness, and that everything would be just fine.

Wednesday nights, as dusk deepened, we always heard the fogger truck lumbering up our street, humming steadily, white plumes billowing from silver tanks on either side filling the bushes and trees and trimmed lawns along Forest Avenue. We rushed to see the fogger truck before it heaved right on Elm Street, the driver's orange face filling the windshield like a moonbeam, his gleaming smile and reassuring white coat and cap illuminating the twilight. He looked just like Howdy Doody's buddy Uncle Bob, but in surgical scrubs. We raised our fists and pumped the air up and down, and Uncle Bob laughed and honked his horn; he sounded just like Clarabell.

Sometimes we jumped on our bikes and followed in the wake of the fogger truck, holding our breath as we dashed in and out of DDT clouds. When we returned to our blankets we didn't have to slather on the insect repellant, because nothing crawled or flew on Forest Avenue on Wednesday nights. The fogger truck held the promise of a mosquito-free world. It'll be fine.

The going world of my parents was full of people, friends, neighbors, clubs and cliques and all the trappings of suburban social life. They hosted dinner parties, card parties, and cocktail parties, organized noisy weekend picnics, and orchestrated intimate late-night dances. I fell asleep to the sounds of Louis Armstrong and Benny Goodman, laughter and grown-up talk, and then woke up to my mother's voice on the telephone.

My parents lived through the crushing experiences of the Depression and World War II, events that burned permanent marks deep inside each of them. Those were not nice things, however, and so they were not fit for us kids, and they remained forever in the background, never actually discussed. The nice things were all now, nothing too much from before. We were modern people determined to be happy, always looking ahead with white smiles fixed and in place. History was finished—the past is past, my dad would say—and our job was to create ourselves anew. Mom's script was already written as a simple smiley face, but I wanted more than that relentlessly sunny atmosphere, the enveloping gleam of an untroubled narrative. I was optimistic and friendly, like the rest, naive and filled with an ingenuous enthusiasm, but like every kid, I suppose, I wanted something darker and more soulful. I longed to run away and write my own story.

I was a reader, and the books that held me were all tales of escape and reinvention: *The Runaway Bunny, Oliver Twist, Huckleberry Finn, A Farewell to Arms, The Catcher in the Rye, The Invisible Man, On the Road.* I was a literalist and books were as real to me as anything else; I felt a kinship with Jim and Huck, Jack and Holden. I breathed the air of deliverance through books, and through books I leapt over the walls of confinement long before I was sixteen.

Memory is a house of mirrors, a land of make-believe—instead of remembering the bad things, Mom said, remember what happened immediately before the bad things. Only the good things. That way everything will turn out to be just fine.

"It'll be fine" was her wellspring and principal channel, but Mom had endless brooks and streams, creeks and trickles that flowed directly from it. Isn't that interesting? she remarked as a disagreeable tick burrowed busily into her thigh on a beach one morning. From that day forward, any despicable or odious encounter, any repulsive or loathsome event, anything at all that was hateful or horrendous was foretold in my family with our own neat little maxim: This is about as interesting as a tick bite.

Mom's excessive joy, unbounded optimism, generous good cheer, and surplus happiness were gift and curse. She was the captain of her own ship—the captain of ours in those early years as well—and it was a ship of high expectation for the good, of confidence to act in happiness for ourselves and for the world. She never let up, and sometimes the cheeriness felt forced, a kind of willful naivete. Then our ship seemed a homemade raft on the Du Page River, a ragged thing with fatal leaks.

Every human being, of course, is thrust into the world by chance, as it were, the recipient of unearned privilege or undeserved suffering, or both. We were born on a ship of hope and a world of privilege, a ship of fools and a sea of carelessness. Whatever we would become, whatever we would make of ourselves, we would launch from this certain deck.

What's this greenhouse effect I've been hearing so much about? Mom asked me one day years later, and I gave her a pretty painless rundown. She fixed me with a cold, unhappy glare—Well, I'm sorry I asked, she said disapprovingly. Optimism at any cost was up, up, up. Skepticism and doubt—down. And much later Mom said to me, Well, I know you kids don't like war, but you have to admit, this one turned out well. She was thinking of smart bombs and surgical strikes, quick conclusions and a friendly dictator, our onetime ally, who everyone suddenly agreed was insane. I think of the mosquitoes and the baby sparrows in the bushes during the gas attacks. I think of the Kurds and the Iraqi children. And then there is Mom's voice, my whole upbringing, the genetic gift.

Where we lived, it's true, the grass was always green, the moms were always smiling, and seldom was heard a discouraging word—the skies were not cloudy all day. Our kitchen was sparkling: white cabinets and countertops, gleaming linoleum and Formica, white-bread sandwiches with Velveeta cheese and lunch meat. Our house was all electric and you could practically hear it humming: electric garage door and stove, electric water heater and garbage disposal. We were the guinea pigs for the gadgets any quack might dream up long before they hit the market—we had the earliest electric knife, a lethal thing in my father's hands, a thing to flay a turkey or decimate a chicken, the first electric toothbrushes, electric door locks and shoe-horns and dog brushes. My friends would sometimes come by just to see what was new and noisy. We were totally wired.

We always looked nice, and we tried to always sound nice, too. Nice was crucially important. When Doug Anderson, my girlfriend's brother, knocked up Lizzie Egg, my best friend's sister, and they ran off for two weeks and were found in Door County, Wisconsin, and Lizzie was sent away in disgrace, we were bursting to know the details. Especially things like how do you go to the bathroom when you're with a girl all day, and what if you have to fart. Practical things. We whispered among ourselves, of course, but nothing was ever mentioned out loud over dinner in our house. We couldn't say something nice, so we didn't say anything at all.

And when Dan Lundy and three other high school football heroes talked Anne Cookson into doing a striptease at his lake house, and after they'd all had a few beers too many and ran a train on her and she met the same fate as Lizzie, well, we didn't say anything at all. Not a goddamn thing.

The family legacy.

The movies swallowed me when I was a kid, and I was an eager victim. I got into the movies and the movies got into me. My lowest personal rating for a film was "Worth Seeing," and it had to be pretty dismal to sink that far. With my uncritical mind, my enthusiastic eye, and the inevitable box of popcorn perched on my lap, I was at the movies each and every week.

Because I grew up in the late forties and fifties, a lot of what I remember of those Saturday afternoons are war films. *Flying Leathernecks, Sahara, The African Queen, The Bridge on the River Kwai, Casablanca, From Here to Eternity, The Audie Murphy Story, Mister Roberts*—these were among my favorites, each a "Must See," and each making hyper-impressions on my understanding of people and the world. World War II was a large part of growing up, and the reality of war was brought to me exclusively on film. War was, to my mind, what the movies said war was: heroic, romantic, sometimes difficult, sometimes funny, but always *exciting*.

From the ordinariness of my life, war was a vivid and welcomed event. After I was swallowed by war at the movies, I played at war with my friends on a dirt hill near my house or, later, in an elaborate variation of "capture the flag," a team game that ranged from the lake by the high school to the forest preserve on the other side of town. I carried my gun, a short stout stick, across my chest as I ran to battle, and I heard echoes of the movies as I dived for cover or overwhelmed an enemy machine-gun nest. I was powerful in war, just like the heroes in those movies, and killing and being killed was sanitized and safe, just like on those Saturday afternoons.

The movies shaped the play, and the play became a lens through which to view the films. With John Wayne, Old Blood-and-Guts, I fired my machine gun at "Japs" as I raced up a hill on some obscure Pacific island to plant a shredded but proud American flag. With Montgomery Clift, the working-class hero, I surveyed the wreckage at Pearl Harbor with a troubled look in my eyes and said, "They're pickin' trouble with the best army in the world." And with the regal Henry Fonda—Mister Roberts—I ached to be riding west across the Pacific, into the action.

I shared Mr. Roberts's pain when he felt that the war was ending and he couldn't get to it. What could be worse? Without war he could never prove himself, and we could never prove ourselves. We could never really experience the fullness of life, never fall in love, have buddies, overcome adversity. We needed war. Poor, sweet Mr. Roberts, the most decent guy in the navy, but not yet a real man, not until he had the opportunity to kill. I choked and cheered with millions of other boys when Mr. Roberts finally got his wish: he went to war and became a man—a dead man.

One summer morning when I was about ten, at an age when war play was fading as a central preoccupation but becoming a man was more an obsession than ever, the calm and quiet of our neighborhood was shattered by the sound of sirens. Ambulances and fire trucks rushed up our street, converging on the house directly across from ours, and I ran barefoot with my brothers and sister to see what was happening. Kids from everywhere crowded the lawn and we were thrilled to have serious-looking police officers telling us to stay back. I was giddy, excited, and happy, joking and roughhousing with friends, and I was gripped by a fresh, tingling feeling at the expectant scene. Within moments a surge of firefighters spilled through the front door hoisting a stretcher with a bloody body flung upon it. It was Jimmy, a boy just eight years older than I, and he had blown his brains out with a handgun. I got sick and became drained and weak. Jimmy, I found out, didn't want to go to Korea. He felt like a misfit. Plus, he was high-strung, I was told, and must have been temporarily insane.

We kidded Mom for years about being a Pollyanna, a person entangled in her own optimism, blinded by her hopes. She laughed along, of course. But we also learned with her to call this happiness life, to claim it and demand it for others and for ourselves, to hold on to it fiercely, even as it passes. She was always good to us—and we didn't always deserve it—and she instructed us to be good to others always. She could have no idea where we might take her dictum.

4.

Memory is a delicate dance of desire and faith, a shadow of a shadow,
an echo of a sigh. We cheat. We steal. We remember in our favor.

When Tim and my sweetheart Katie Blue went off to college, I
remember so clearly the cold touch of abandonment. I didn't want to
stay at home anymore. Dad and Mom were, luckily it turned out,
alarmed by my lackluster academic commitment, and we found a
common ground in searching for a proper prep school for me to
attend. For them, remediation; for me, a timely escape.

Lake Forest Academy, an hour north of Chicago, spread easily over
acres and acres of woods, lovely lakes and formal gardens, rolling
lawns and spacious athletic fields. The main hall was the former
Armor Estate, and we took our meals in the shadow of the grand
staircase on the first floor. Our classrooms were little garrets and
grottos hidden here and there on the floors above, turned now to
seminar spaces with the imposition of a small table and a few chairs.
All of this was then home to 180 favored teenage boys, me included,
crowded incongruously together.

The place felt to me at times like an exotic and exclusive reforma-
tory, incarcerating the scrubbed-up children of successful mobsters
and the deviant progeny of the well-to-do. Meyer Katzman's dad and
uncle were in federal prison in our junior year, but that didn't stop
him from managing a thriving business making book for a downtown organization. Dirck Benton would no doubt follow his patriarch

into the restaurant business as his brothers had before him, and I figured selling bootleg liquor was part of the training.

Pandy Parker's extensive collection of antique and one-of-a-kind pens was worth a look, but only once, because the next time he'd offer not only the history of each but an update on the kinky doings and offbeat dippings of each erotic or deadly instrument. His roommate Denny Darrow, heir to General Dynamics, trapped small animals in the woods and blew them up with candle bombs late at night. Their next-door neighbor, Elijah Smith III, had an unspeakable physical deformity observable in the showers after gym class that we talked about endlessly, and Stinky Stolowitz, too, made me ponder the dangers of multigenerational inbreeding.

We were damaged and destructive, the dim-witted and the depressed, some of us dangerous, some of us nuts, all of us trapped. I was the only normal kid there, I thought, me and a kid named Kerry Eisenstein.

At football camp Kerry Eisenstein and I decided to room together. Kerry was a popular guy, a class officer, our quarterback. He was also brilliant, the son of a small jewelry store owner from Iowa, and he encouraged me to study hard after playing hard, to read, read, read, and to take ideas seriously. He was the first person I'd ever met who got depressed. Why are you sad, I asked when I knew him well, and he'd tell me he wasn't sad, but depressed. He also taught me about Yom Kippur and Chanukah, matzo brei and bagels and goyim. If you don't know what a goy is, he said to me one day, then you are one.

I established myself in this odd and artificial community early. I played football, a quick ticket to membership; I joined the outlaw crew huddled in the broom closet several times a day for an illicit smoke (to the hallway lookout the closet often looked as if it were about to burst into flames, gusts of smoke pouring from the cracks in the jambs); and I soon led forays into the night after curfew toward Ferry Hall, our sister school a couple of miles down the road, home to a like number of enthusiastic and horny girls.

The Fairies, as we called them, were hard up. We thought of ourselves, on the other hand, as experienced, cool, and detached, each with a sweet and true girlfriend back home, entering a liaison of convenience now, doing the Fairies a favor. Still, for all that, we spent arduous hours sweating through the briars and the brambles in the service of our reckless late-night collisions.

Dorrel Dennis was my own personal Fairie, her eyes, a dark and beckoning narcissistic beam, were like a mirror for me: I could see myself perfectly in her eyes. We necked and petted in the woods nightly for months, but on a weekend pass in the spring she invited me onto the giant canopied bed in the penthouse of the Pick-Georgian Hotel (owned by her grandmother). Afterward she cried in the bathroom while I sat awkwardly on the tub trying to say something consoling—I'm not sad or hurt, she said finally, just overwhelmed; oh, you couldn't possibly understand—but I didn't understand a thing and I was thinking mainly of the boys, of how I would describe this wondrous, triumphant night to Tim or Rick or the guys at school.

During football camp the week before school began, I won a place in the starting lineup—at 145 pounds I was the pulling guard on an unbalanced line, leading the misdirection blocking on every running play, hurling myself into the legs or midsections of huge, immovable defensive linemen. I got the job the old-fashioned way—scratching, clawing, biting, tearing my way. The coach admired my heart. Pound for pound this little guy puts you to shame, he said in a motivational locker room talk one day. He's scrappy. I was proud to be a scrappy player, realizing rather slowly that a scrappy player is a player with neither talent nor ability, possessing only a single screwy qualification: a demented disregard for personal safety. Scrappy rhymes with crappy.

I still wanted days filled with fun, of course, so I developed a couple of tactics to knock even those intimate little seminars with their serious students and formidable masters off the tracks. Señor Caballo, my Spanish master, was a small, sad-eyed Castillian with a beautiful wife, the dark and fine-boned Estella, whose rich black hair was held behind her perfect ears with two elaborate ebony combs and fell suggestively below her delicate waist. We saw Señora Caballo only from a distance, but she was the focus of intense fantasy and desire. Señor Caballo, on the other hand, we saw all too closely, all too often. He was a maestro of the old school, all direct instruction, call and response, drill and kill in the classroom, but he had one weakness. Señor Caballo, I would say just before the start of class, as often as seemed feasible, I read in the paper yesterday that the dictator Franco . . . —and I could go no further.

Franco is no dictator, Guillermo, Señor Caballo would interupt, calling me by my "Spanish name," exploding in passionate defense, gesturing wildly. Franco is a great leader, a fine man, a general, and a president. Caballo offered a sputtering, garbled history of modern Spain from his monarchist, fascist perspective. He would set us straight, we eight future leaders.

But sir, I would interject if his energy flagged at all, wasn't Franco the first in history to bomb civilian populations?

No, no, no, he would cry. Those were military targets. Our problem, Caballo said in a humid, stream-of-consciousness tirade, was that America had no traditions worth defending, that it had adopted an adolescent culture, that America was permissive and without standards or authority or wisdom and, besides, that Communists were in charge of everything here. We listened, pretending interest, glad to be corrected as long as it took us down that happy trail called off-task. When the eruption ran its course, too soon, it was straight back to irregular verbs.

The language masters were all a bit feudal like Caballo—the brooding Prince Peter Orozoff of the czar's extended family who taught Russian; Count Ignazio Fagiz, an admirer of Benito Mussolini, who taught Italian—but most of the masters were young, fresh out of college, wondering what to do with an advanced degree in English or history, likely to move on any year. Some of them brought fresh ideas—Mr. Guy was surely a socialist, although he never even whispered the word in our presence—others had odd passions—Mr.

Crow carved musical instruments in his spare time, Mr. Lance collected butterflies. Mr. Sid and Mr. Worth were gay, but we had no word then to describe it, and so it went intriguingly unspoken.

Sigfried Friend, dean of students, had no new ideas, no interesting passions, and he was never leaving—he was a fixture, and utterly ageless; he'd taught there before World War II, took a long break to serve in Europe, and returned in the 1940s, his hair gone gray, a fantastic scar splitting his face from forehead to neck. He began to cultivate his bushy eyebrows then, and he brushed them so they swept up and out, extending beyond the sides of his head. Over the years the scar had receded, faded toward obscurity, but some days it looked as if it had been oiled, then rubbed or polished for some special occasion, and it stood out fresh and menacing. On those mornings, as Mr. Friend stood frowning at the entrance to the chapel, eyebrows flaring, arms crossed, lips moving silently as he appeared to count us filing in for prayer before seven, the scar was startling all over again.

Mr. Friend was a loner, above and beyond the faculty; he engaged in no society at school, he had no intimates that we could see. His biggest impact was through World Civilization, a famous survey course he had developed over decades covering history, philosophy, and literature. In his classroom I met the Mesopotamians and the Egyptians, Homer and Virgil, Rousseau and Marx. I felt intellectually stirred, challenged, and Kerry urged me to read even more. I adored Rousseau, the romantic wanderer, most of all, and Henry David Thoreau and, eventually, Karl Marx—but only as a philosopher, of course.

"With regard to equality," Jean-Jacques Rousseau had written, "this word must not be understood to mean that degrees of power and wealth should be exactly the same, but rather that with regard to power, it should be incapable of all violence and never exerted except by virtue of status and the laws; and with regard to wealth, no citizen should be so opulent that he can buy another, and none so poor that he is constrained to sell himself." I loved that.

It seemed such a sharp challenge to so much of what I saw at LFA and beyond. Rousseau had in mind a sensible ideal to reach for, not a state of affairs that actually existed. Law for Rousseau should always involve the entire people themselves making the decisions that affected their lives, and so he was arguing against mindless obedience to the status quo. The civil rights activists I glimpsed on TV breaking the Jim Crow laws in the South, were, it seemed to me, following Rousseau's reasoning. The laws they broke were laws enacted by the few, and those laws led to harm to many others. Since the many were not really represented, the lawlessness of the rebels felt, at least to them and surprisingly now to me, too, not criminal but patriotic— much like the revolutionaries at the Boston Tea Party or in Lexington Square. Or like what Henry David Thoreau had argued in militant opposition to slavery and colonial wars, urging his fellow citizens to break unjust laws. Under a government which imprisons any unjustly, the true place for a just man is also a prison, he said, the only house in a slave state in which a free man can abide with honor. And so to jail, singing, went the civil rights demonstrators, and while I couldn't quite imagine going with them, along with Rousseau and Thoreau I could see their point.

Besides making us read wide and fast, Mr. Friend required us to pick someone to read more thoroughly and more slowly. I picked Karl Marx, just because everyone else considered him beneath contempt, choosing the obvious—Plato and Kant and David Hume— and because it was said his children called him the "Old Moor."

I read *The Communist Manifesto* first because it was short. The downtrodden and oppressed have nothing to lose but their chains, shouted the Manifesto. They have a world to win. Marx described the creation of extravagant comfort for a lucky few, and the systematic sacking and brutalizing of many others. It was a system, Marx argued, that did not deliver happiness. Nor a sense of right. Marx wrote with ardor about the laws of history, the inevitability of the capitalist epoch overtaking and then crushing feudalism, and the absolute certainty that capitalism—for all its wondrous might—was itself doomed, destined to be overtaken by a system of sharing the socially produced wealth. Even though they would likely be unrecognizable to one another—each was on a distinct mission—I saw right away that Marx and Mom would agree on one thing: everything will be fine. The leap from Pollyanna to historical determinism wasn't all that wide.

I never made it all the way through *Das Kapital*, densely unreadable and, it seemed to me, unassailable. Marx described capitalism coming into being "dripping from head to foot, from every pore, with blood and dirt." The initial accumulation, he said, was always and everywhere linked to theft and violence, a monopoly of firearms, slavery, savage exploitation, and ruthlessness. Force was the key to amassing property, wealth, and power—nothing more. I wondered if my dad was somehow implicated. Was I?

Kerry pointed out that Marx's ethics were brilliantly expressed in his condemnation of a system built on theft and violence, but Marx also, oddly, seemed to hold capitalism in the highest regard, showing that capitalism has created more massive and colossal productive forces than all preceding generations together, accomplished wonders far surpassing Egyptian pyramids, Roman aqueducts, and Gothic cathedrals, and all in scarcely one hundred years. What confused me was how Marx both kind of loved capitalism and also obviously hated it. Anyway, he summed up a social justice agenda with his socialist ideal—from each according to his ability, to each according to his contribution—and his more distant but imaginable (at least to me) communist goal—from each according to his ability, to each according to his *need*.

There were many, many practical problems to solve. Who would do the dirty work? Who would decide? Can everyone be counted on to act in the common good? What if some people won't or don't? What about the corruption of power? But these problems did not seem insurmountable as I wrote glowingly about the moral argument Marx was making.

It was this last point that drove Mr. Friend to the brink. Our final thesis was to be drawn from all our assigned and independent readings, our seminar discussions, and class notes. We were to write an original, well-researched paper on the proposition that The History of Mankind Is the Relentless Search for Freedom, Mr. Friend's own little variation of Mom and Marx. I drew on Rousseau and Marx, writing a kind of stage theory of economic history—everything was getting better, everything would be just fine—with what I hoped was an eloquent moral argument at its heart. I should have footnoted Mom, but it was already so deeply woven into the fabric of my own being that it felt authentic and original. Man's search for freedom, I wrote, was a rosy path winding its way toward sharing the wealth.

Mr. Friend's angry red pencil disagreed on every page: Idiotic! Wrong! Moronic! One of my classmates, Oscar Mayer III (we called him, of course, Weenie), had written a long, ass-kissing essay in which, among many amazing points, he argued that Benedict Arnold was right and that the Colonies would have fared much better if they'd had the wisdom to remain within the British empire: Friend wrote Brilliant! in his margin. But to me Mr. Friend added what amounted to a short impassioned essay on Marx as a liar and fool, Marx as a ragged man with poor grooming habits who had allowed his family to live in filth. If Marxism is so humane, he scrawled across one page, how do you explain its attraction to every hooligan and bandit in the world? And later, If communism, as you describe it, is so damned noble, why does it exist nowhere, not even in Russia or China? Next to where I had written, It's not difficult, then, to see how America achieved such fabulous wealth: free labor on stolen land, conquest and slavery and an attempted genocide, Mr. Friend inserted the word asshole! and then rubbed it out, leaving a light pink palimpsest. On the bottom of the last page, perhaps out of steam, he left simply an exhausted Unoriginal, Mr. Ayers, and poorly researched. C–.

When he handed it back, he glared a moment, showed his scar, and waggled his eyebrows at me. I got a C for the class, once again, pure gold.

I hated school—everyone walking around in a rut with white smiles pasted on our dead heads. I looked at my fellow students with anguish at first, then disgust. We were mostly conformist bores, I thought, unadventurous in most things, acting out scripts already written, destined for conventional lives of canned happiness just as dull as our parents'.

I remember a heated argument that began at dinner with two of my football buddies and spilled over to the common room, the dorm, and even classes for a couple of days. We're not free, I'd said provocatively, we're just little automatons acting our parts, little slavelike things, except a few of us from here will be running the plantation but still trapped. What do you want to be? I continued. Lawyers for the rich? Architects for the landlords? Look around.

Everyone disagreed.

I quoted Rousseau and Marx, Thoreau and James Baldwin. You're an idiot, one of my buddies said to me. We're the freest people in the world. We can say or do anything we like.

Hopeless, I said. What good is free speech when you, for example, have nothing to say?

But I could, he said.

Idiot, I replied.

Kerry Eisenstein was one of only a tiny handful of scholarship students, and on a bright day in early spring, when a group of us got busted by Mr. Friend in the broom closet, butts ablaze, everyone was suspended for a few days except for Kerry—he was sent packing, back to Des Moines. Thirty-nine of us graduated, but it should have been forty. It was entirely unjust, but I couldn't think of a damn thing to actually do about it. I was pissed off, and I wondered what Marx or Rousseau or Thoreau would have done. I considered running away to Iowa, but where would that leave me? I didn't want any part of school, and I didn't want to be a goy. I drew a Star of David and the word *Jew* on my forearm with a ballpoint pen, recolored it for weeks and kept it hidden under my jacket. In Kerry's honor, and for Marx as well, I invented another identity, part rootless, wandering scholar, part brilliant if ill-tempered Moor—I imagined myself a Jew.

5.

My sister was attending Stanford University, far away, and way beyond my reach, and Katie Blue was at Beloit College and in love with a foreign student—his name was Jacques, and I imagined him worldly, sophisticated, and devastating—not like me at all. I was on the verge of starting over, reinventing, beginning again. But not quite yet. In my casual indifferent way I had applied to only one school, my parents' alma mater, and without much ado, I followed my brother Tim to Ann Arbor, to the University of Michigan.

I tagged along into Tim's fraternity as well, and a few days later went over to the athletic office to see about playing football. I knew less than nothing. The Big Ten powerhouse, it turned out, had no real need for a scrappy 145-pound guard from some tiny prep school no one had ever heard of; the smallest linemen here weighed 250 pounds and attended high schools with big names like Toledo Central, Detroit Metro, and Chicago's Jean Baptiste DuSable. My roommate, a halfback, ran the 100-yard dash in 10 flat, and he weighed 225 pounds. Jesus, I didn't have a chance. I wasn't even qualified to carry the towels.

The fraternity wasn't a good fit either, the Beta house being a lot like the prep school I'd just escaped—a crowd of horny boys all living willingly in a culture of clinging, mindless conventionality— except that here we had easy access to alcohol and no one told us to go to bed or chapel or dinner or, for that matter, to our classes. Most didn't. There was consequently a lot of public drunkenness, a lot of all-night parties with the brothers, a lot of barfing and stinking hang-overs, a lot of forced fun. When John Kennedy was killed there was genuine mourning and real fear in the wider campus, a collective gloom and dread I'd never experienced before descending like a cloud. The brothers, too, were united in their outrage—not at the assassination, but at the administration's hasty cancellation of the football game, an unprecedented measure and a severe deprivation, they all thought.

But still, you could if you chose hoist yourself up, peer over and even leap the thick walls, which I did almost immediately: outside, Ann Arbor was pulsing with energy, vibrating with possibilities. Everything was abuzz and I accelerated happily into its welcoming bosom.

The place was weighty with women. I was like a bee in the honey pot—everything golden, delicious, and sticky. I felt lucky to be in a place so concentrated with such beautiful women, and blessed to be living in a perfect world where new generations of women were being born on every continent and in every country every day of every year. I might die here, I thought, but what a lovely way to go, wallowing with the Ann Arbor women. I fell in love with Cookie Woodford, Janie Moy, and Nora Brown—and that was in the first three days.

I attended lectures: the American Nazi Party leader George Lincoln Rockwell spoke at Hill Auditorium, Malcolm X at the student union, Sargent Shriver, Paul Goodman. I went to the student-run Cinema Guild almost every weekend to see classic and avant-garde films—Bogart and Cagney, Kenneth Anger and George Manupelli. Outside the theater one night a group of girls leaned against trees and tele-phone poles, smoking cigarettes and licking ice-cream cones—one could have been from Singapore, dark-skinned and almond-eyed, one from Hawaii, a third from Finland, pale and transparent with fine blue veins, her lovely eyes like ice—and I met a young painter there named Ruthie Stein who drew me into her community of artists. The tight regimen of prep school shattered with a crack; Ann Arbor was a hot breath of life, and I began to inhale as deeply as I could.

Ruthie Stein was from New York City where she'd attended Music and Art High School, and she seemed to know the museum and gallery scene intimately. Her daily uniform was an oversized paint-splattered T-shirt, blue jeans and sneakers, and a faded leather jacket. She was tiny—under five feet, not a hundred pounds—her uninhibited, frizzy hair framing her small face with a wild light-brown halo. She had deep brown eyes and a little ruby mouth. She painted for several hours every day—I'm no good to life unless I paint, she told me earnestly; I need to do it—and her studio was a chaos of colorful works in progress. When I first saw it, she invited me to make love with her behind an easel and I was moved. It was like touching a butterfly, delicate and vivid, a rainbow fluttering intensely on my skin, and I emerged paint-splattered and happy as well. We were just saying hello in a way that was becoming customary, and we became friends, although we were never really lovers. Ruthie was the most brilliant person I'd ever met, destined, it seemed to me, for greatness.

When I went to work for the student newspaper, one of the senior brothers challenged me in the Beta house hallway: What are you doing there, stupid? Barfly asked. That place is full of nerds and Jews and liberals. Get the fuck out of there.

I didn't feel like a nerd, but the other two. Well, I took his point. I quit the fraternity and, a few months later, quit school altogether. Mom cried on the phone, but Dad thought a little time off was OK if I did something productive and gathered some life lessons to apply later on. Life lessons, I repeated. Right.

That week Ruthie Stein took me to my first picket line at a pizza joint on North Main called Angie's, where Vincent, Angie's husband and manager, had a nasty habit of refusing to seat Black people—For you, take-out only, he would say—and we ringed the entrance, chanting slogans we'd heard on the news from the South and singing freedom songs. One night Barfly showed up and led a gang of four in for a slice. When he saw me, he cursed, pushed me and shoved me to the ground, scraping the skin off one elbow. I never felt happier.

6.

I picked up James Baldwin's "Letter to My Nephew on the One Hundredth Anniversary of the Emancipation" and took the bus to Detroit that winter searching for the community office of the Reverend Gabriel Star, a civil rights man whose number I'd gotten from Ruthie. Baldwin wastes no time indicting the United States: "This is the crime of which I accuse my country and my countrymen, and for which neither I nor time nor history will ever forgive them," he begins, "that they have destroyed and are destroying hundreds of thousands of lives and do not know it and do not want to know it." Baldwin amasses a bill of particulars: "You were born where you were born and faced the future that you faced because you were black and for no other reason. . . . You were born into a society which spelled out with brutal clarity, and in as many ways as possible, that you were a worthless human being." He tells his nephew that "it was intended that you should perish in the ghetto, perish by never being allowed to go beyond the white man's definitions, by never being allowed to spell your proper name." Baldwin argues that even though "the details and symbols of your life have been deliberately constructed to make you believe what white people say about you," that his nephew— along with other Black people—must "remember that what they believe, as well as what they do and cause you to endure, does not testify to your inferiority but to their inhumanity and fear."

Too many white people, Baldwin believes, are without memory, "trapped in a history which they do not understand, and until they understand it, they cannot be released from it." I didn't want to be like the others, just another uptight and fucked-up white man.

When a master stands with a boot on the neck of a slave, Baldwin wrote, the relationship is defined by violence. The slave is the object of violence, the master is the perpetrator of violence, and violence is the essential character and the absolute core of the relationship. No matter what happens—if the slave petitions for freedom, or if the slave breaks the booted foot, or even if the slave cooperates complete-ly—the relationship is already violent through and through. Only when the relationship is ended, only when the slave is freed, will the cause and the nature of the violence be removed. Then the possibility of peace, of nonviolence, and even of equality might become real.

Any socially unnecessary pain is violent in its nature—premature death, incapacitation and ignorance, retardation and distortion. Opposing violence you must fight the substantive core of the matter, Baldwin said. If you truly oppose the violence of hunger, you might understand guns in the hands of the hungry.

Reverend Star was famous locally for linking arms with Reverend King and Andrew Young and Ralph Abernathy, for marching in Montgomery and Birmingham, for bringing the activism of the South back home to Detroit. I hoped he could help me find a con-nection to the movement, and though he'd been rushed on the phone, he had granted me an audience, and here I was.

I felt like a complete jerk waiting in the large entryway while throngs of young people, Black and white, rushed purposefully in and out from the offices in the rear, carrying leaflets or newsletters, exchanging hurried bits of news or instruction. I was mainly invisi-ble, which was fine with me, because whenever I looked up from my book, what I saw seated on the little folding chair was not promising: a well-intentioned college dropout, a well-scrubbed innocent from a tiny prep school. They needed me about as much as Michigan's foot-ball team did. I waited anxiously, quietly reading and waiting. Quietly inoffensive.

James Baldwin's remedy, I read, for the longest continuous human rights crime ever is complex but available—Americans must look unblinkingly at our history, confront our constructed reality, face the tears of the wounded, the consequences of the wickedness, and then we must harness ourselves to a great collective effort toward justice. Baldwin finds hope in an image of "the relatively conscious whites and the relatively conscious blacks, who must, like lovers, insist on, or create, the consciousness of the others in order to end the racial nightmare, and achieve our country." Action and commitment fueled by both rage and love, yes, but nothing until we summon the courage to remember and to look honestly at the world as it is: "It is not permissible that the authors of devastation should also be innocent. It is the innocence which constitutes the crime"; and "We, with love, shall force our brothers to see themselves as they are, to cease fleeing from reality and begin to change it." We must, then, at some point come face to face with reality, and act: "It is not necessary that people be wicked, but only that they be spineless" to bring us all to wrack and ruin.

Ayers! Reverend Star interrupted my reading, barking my name as he poked his head through the door and smiled. I jerked my head out of my book. Come on back here, man. Hey, I forgot you'd called, and then I forgot you were here. He laughed, shook my hand, and led me into his cramped office directing me to sit on a shabby couch. Sorry about the wait, but things get hectic. Eight kids arrested yesterday, looks like a spontaneous sit-in and no one really knows who the fuck they are. Anyway, trying to get a goddamn lawyer in Charleston and raise bail. A little hectic.

Reverend Gabe Star was red-faced and middle-aged—in his late thirties at least or early forties—his hair salt and pepper, tossed and disheveled, his dress careless. His office was crowded with papers and books, the desk unevenly stacked with precarious piles, two telephones perched uneasily on the ones nearest his chair, and a large Royal typewriter peeking out from another. On a far corner, an ignored and partially eaten hamburger of indeterminate age. On the wall next to his desk, an enlarged aerial photo of the March on Washington. And, oh yes, he'd managed to use the words "fuck" and "goddamn" in the first minute of our acquaintance, ingratiating himself, I supposed, to youth.

What's on your mind? he asked, opening his arms in what looked like an invocation or a benediction. I told him that I wanted to go south to find the movement, to participate in the freedom struggle. I told him that I found school, well, not exactly boring, but irrelevant. I told him about James Baldwin's writing and how much it stirred me. There was a movement out there, a thing of real importance, and I needed to find it, I said. I wanted to do something relevant.

When I'd finished Reverend Star waited a moment in silence, looking at me, reflecting, his hands folded now in front of him, his chin resting on the steeple of his first fingers, his brow furrowed and his frown deepening. It's not the best time, he began slowly. Resources are awfully thin right now, and no one is geared up to take volunteers. The following summer would be better, he said, and I should think hard about the wisdom of leaving college so soon. Baldwin, well . . .

I felt myself sinking. But, OK, he said finally. I'll make a couple of calls.

He made three phone calls, two to Atlanta and one to New Orleans. Each time the conversation followed the same line: Hello, Pete, it's Gabe . . . I've got a kid here in my office who wants to come south to volunteer . . . He's well-scrubbed, entirely inexperienced, but I think he's well-intentioned . . . He's *read* about the movement. Sure, OK . . .

He saw me perfectly, I thought, and I felt both entirely transparent and a little like a virgin lamb. In the end Reverend Star gave me the address of a Catholic priest named Peter Paul Streeter. If you get to New Orleans, call Pete, he said. No guarantees. I thanked him and we shook hands.

A week later I hitchhiked to New Orleans—three quick rides to St.

Louis, and then, just outside the city, a long run following the Mississippi River through the Delta in a brand-new Peterbilt truck that a young guy was delivering to Baton Rouge. Where you headed? he asked when he pulled over.

New Orleans, I said.

Hop aboard, friend. My name's Bud, and I'm headin' to the land of Mardi Gras and plentiful pussy myself.

Bud talked a blue streak, popped little green pills every couple of hours, and told a long string of jokes that never let up: What's the difference between a tribe of pygmies and a women's track team? he asked, grinning, rubbing one hand repeatedly through his thick black hair.

I dunno.

One's a cunning bunch of runts, the other's a running bunch of cunts. We shared a brotherly laugh, his a kind of high-pitched snort, and we were comrades of the road.

How do you fuck a fat woman? he asked. Slap her on the thigh and just ride the wave. On and on, rarely stopping, never sleeping.

I'd hoped we could stick to the easy boy-banter of sexual escapades and dirty jokes, but no—in the middle of the night he discovered I'd gone to Michigan, and things got cloudy. You know the Big Ten ain't shit compared to the Southeast Conference, he began. We could kick your ass every which way, but you chickenshits won't even play us. You got so many niggers on your teams, you all don't even know which way's the end zone. He laughed derisively.

I defended the Big Ten dutifully but cautiously, sticking to regional pride. But, once opened, never closed, and Bud was full of "nigger" this and "nigger" that. Every personal misfortune Bud had ever endured and every large calamity he could think of or foretell had "niggers" somewhere near the heart of the matter. See this, he said in one alarming moment, pulling a big pistol from under his seat. This here's a Nigger Neutralizer.

I steered completely clear, and, hours later, when Bud got around to asking me why I was heading to New Orleans, the obvious answer flowed forth like nature from my lips: Mardi Gras, I said gaily. And plentiful pussy.

Father Streeter was a complete bust. The storefront office had closed down, so I called and he invited me to his room at the archdiocese. Things were slow, he said, but if I stuck around, perhaps. . . . Mainly he wanted to talk about books and poetry, film and theater. That was all OK, but not where I was heading. He laughed and smiled a lot, and underlined every point by reaching over to touch my leg. I promised to stay in touch, but I knew I wouldn't, and when I left I felt I'd made a wrong turn. The movement was out there somewhere, I knew, but still elusive, and perhaps farther from me than ever.

I got a cheap room in a fleabag hotel and spent the next few days bumming around the French Quarter. I met a poet from New York and a couple of musicians from Minnesota trying to make it working short gigs in local bars. I hung out for a couple of nights with a short, round waitress with dishwater-blond hair whom I'd met in an oyster bar. But nothing was sparking, nothing was happening for me. I felt adrift, a little rejected, unsure. Restless, I hitchhiked up to Baton Rouge where I'd heard there was plenty of work. Within a week I was signed on as an ordinary seaman working a freighter with a load of midwestern "Food for Peace" wheat bound for Greece. Good-bye, America, I said. And good-bye to the movement, wherever you are.

The past is a foreign country and memory is always in translation— deciphering, paraphrasing, consulting the thesaurus. Memory rewrites rather than transcribes.

Whatever romance might have animated the life of a merchant marine eluded me completely. I'd thought when I signed on that I might write an American novel about a young man at sea, but I didn't have it in me. Not the novel, not the brains, not the will. Anyway, I remember nothing Jack London about that time, nor Jean Genet, Ernest Hemingway, or Jack Kerouac. The North Atlantic in winter was gray and dull, uninspiring and occasionally stormy. It was not the wide world I was seeking; it was not the open road. The swells that rocked us made me woozy and unsteady, and the work was cold and tedious —I was on the eight-to-twelve shift, four hours of cleaning and maintenance in the morning, four hours on icy watch from the bridge or the bow in the evening.

The guys were a motley crew—a few out-of-work artists, actors, and musicians trying to feed their families, several drunks and ne'er-do-wells who couldn't hold a regular job on land, a bunch like Bud who could hardly stop talking about the woes of a world with "niggers" in it.

My bunkmate, Moon Limieux, would greet me each morning with his slow serene drawl: Where ya at there, Bill? he'd say sweetly. Hey, I'd say, and a cherubic smile would crease his shoe-leather face. Moon was compact but powerfully built. He wore a greasy watch cap that never left his head and a precariously dangling Q-tip that never left his right ear. He spent most of the evening shift describing, in his honeyed voice, the details of how he planned to murder all his loved ones: Gotta strangle my mother and then chop her head off, he said, laughing softly, or she'll just keep yak-yak-yakkin' at me; I'm gonna cut my brother's heart out for all the shit he's did to me, and then I'm gonna slice it into little pieces for my dog, George; my wife's gotta get stabbed in her good eye so she'll stop starin' at me all the time. On and on. Moon kept me up much of one night describing how he and several of his confederates fought the National Guard for a day and a half when the government agitated that "nigger" to integrate Ole Miss. Moon was a talker, but I tried not to let him think too fondly of me—his plans for his friends terrified me—and I slept with one good eye open.

Everywhere we stopped—Ceuta, Tangiers—there was a mad dash for a nearby whorehouse and bar where we all acted the fool and pretended to be best friends and comrades for a few hours, buying drinks, spending money. Each of us was armed with a little syphilis-assassination kit—heavy clumsy condoms, tiny alarming needle-nosed tubes of infection-fighting goo to squeeze up our shafts after sex—dispensed by Bones, the third mate who acted as ship's nurse.

In Piraeus, the captain—a shy and quiet drunk who appeared on the bridge only rarely—invited me out for an evening when he heard I would be leaving the crew. He was bald and severely cross-eyed, his thick glasses making his crooked lamps jump right off his red round face toward me as he bought the drinks and sandwiches, flirted with and flattered a madam he had known for years, and picked up the tab as I went upstairs with a small dark-haired girl named Eleni. I was the gleaming American, not so disconnected as I might have liked from the frat boys left behind, nor from every other noisy American abroad.

Later, a sharp disagreement between a Russian and an American seaman over a girl turned into a row that cascaded down the waterfront, sucking sailors from every ship into its maw. There were several bruised and bloodied bodies that day, but nothing too serious; Moon broke his ring finger on another fellow's skull, Sparks lost a tooth, and Bones got a split lip. Heroes all. By the time it was sorted out, I'd discharged from the merchant marines and was bumming my way back toward the States.

In a café in Rome I decided to increase the pace of my wandering. I was sharing a coffee and a *Herald Tribune* with Sofia, a girl I'd met the night before, and the front-page story was about a big American military buildup in a place I'd never heard of. Troops were on their way; more men would be called; the Selective Service was gearing up. The place was Viet Nam. I kissed Sofia good-bye. It was time for me to get home.

7 •

Viet Nam drove me vaguely home, but it stayed comfortably in the background the whole way. It didn't drive me crazy, not yet. I wasn't sure what was next. Who knew? I'd gone south seeking a movement I somehow couldn't find, and then to sea looking for adventure and experiences that also eluded me. I was coming home to Ann Arbor now, but, I thought, if there's nothing here to hold me, perhaps I'll join the army and go see about this war. Life lessons. It seemed a reasonable alternative—I'd read Norman Mailer. Perhaps I'd take in the kind of searing sensation that I could write about.

I'd seen by then only one image of Viet Nam, a photo from the international press. In it young American guys heavy with gear were landing somewhere on a golden beach that stretched for miles toward the distant green mountains—they had splashed ashore smiling and looking purposeful and confident, like the high school football team running through the goalposts onto the field before the big game. It didn't look so bad. They had no idea what awaited them, of what was coming, but then, neither did I.

I called Ruthie Stein first thing. Hey, kid, you're home! she shouted, and we met at the student union to swap stories and make plans. I needed a place to stay, and Ruthie helped me find a little hovel I could afford, an attic room with a small window and a fire escape entrance. There was a couch for my brother Rick, a new freshman stuck in the dorm, and he could stay with me whenever he liked, which was always. I'd registered for classes, but there were more important things to do.

By the end of the week we were settled in, and then Ruthie took us with her to a meeting about Viet Nam. We crowded into a little room in the basement of the union with a half-dozen others—she was on the brand-new antiwar organizing committee.

The faculty senate was considering a teachers' strike to coincide with an imminent international day of protest against the war, and the organizing committee was at this moment discussing whether to invite U.S. State Department officials to campus for a debate.

We can't give these guys a forum, said a tall bearded guy wearing thick glasses and an old army jacket, puffing on a Camel. They'll just confuse matters. He had a large button pinned to his jacket: WE'RE THE PEOPLE OUR PARENTS WARNED US ABOUT.

It's true, said Kelly Marie, a redheaded girl I knew vaguely from the student newspaper whom everyone called Calamari. They aren't looking for the truth, but for a place to spread propaganda, to drum up support.

My instinct says we should invite them, Ruthie said tentatively. After all, they'll be defending the indefensible, and if we're smart, they'll be seen entangled in lies. She argued that the more debate the better, that the antiwar alternative was only strengthened by more light and air and openness. They should be scared of us, she said, but if they're not scared of us, then sure, we should invite them.

I listened intently, blinking and stuttering my way to some kind of new awareness as the room filled with ideas and smoke. The men were mostly uninteresting and forgettable, but every woman had her redeeming feature. Calamari was plain and homely, but she had that red hair and a great laugh. Marianne was skinny but had a lovely ear that cried out to be kissed. Jamie was fat but full of a fighter's energy. A woman and a melon, a poet once said, are not to be known by their outsides.

I had told Rick that I might leave Ann Arbor and enlist, but I hadn't mentioned it to Ruthie or to anyone else. Rick was drawn to pacifism and he'd read much more widely than I had in philosophy, politics, and history. He hated the idea immediately. That's crazy, he'd said. You'll get caught up in something you don't even understand,

and it's not like you can just change your mind and leave. You're not suited to kill anyone, and you don't want to get killed yet, not for this.

Now, in this basement room, the discussion rode on a whole series of pacifist and radical assumptions that would make volunteering for war unthinkable. The ideas were familiar from the civil rights movement—nonviolent resistance, direct action and moral witness, breaking unjust laws—applied in a challenging new context. I would never mention that I'd almost enlisted in the military, and I hoped Rick would just forget all about it. Now I wanted to enlist here. I was opening my eyes, and by seeing the world I became implicated in its problems. It was 1965 and I was twenty years old.

The faculty failed to reach consensus on a strike—too many felt that teachers and intellectuals in particular had a moral obligation to engage ideas, to debate, to never retreat—yet the compromise proved to be unexpectedly brilliant: they would all teach their classes as usual, but the content for that one day of protest would focus exclusively on Viet Nam, its history and culture, its people and its struggle, and, now, the U.S. intervention and something of what this latest chapter might forecast for Viet Nam and for us. This, then, would be a daylong teach-in, leading to a weekend of seminars, speeches, panels, and debates. The faculty had widely divergent views on the substance of the matter, but that turned out to be unimportant. What mattered was opening up a huge new space for discussion, energizing a spirit of inquiry. All of it inevitably, I suppose, provoked a critically activist bent, as participant after participant asked, What do we know now? What are we willing to do about what we now know? I got excited. We were moving, and we were not alone.

A week before the scheduled teach-in, Stan Nadir, a dark and intense graduate student who always wore a black beret with a small porcelain red star pinned on its side, created a small furor in the Fishbowl, a central crossroads on campus. I knew Stan only slightly from meetings—he was a quiet loner, but serious, and no one doubted his commitment, something that counted a lot with us because it was a proxy for morality. He had become mildly famous on campus as the intrepid organizer who spent hours going alone from office to office trying to get faculty members to sign an antiwar petition and then, when successful, trying to get them to donate money so that the petition could be run as a full-page ad in the *New York Times*. In one apocalyptic account, Stan spent half an hour with a sociology professor who finally showed Stan the door saying, in effect, that this was not his area of expertise, and that he hadn't read enough about it, and so he couldn't sign. Stan was back the next day with a large stack of literature, articles, and books which the besieged professor agreed to peruse. The next day, back again, the professor told Stan that it was all very interesting but, again, since he was no expert, he found himself against the war one day and for the war the next. Undeterred, Stan asked if he could come back to collect a signature on one of the days the professor was against the war.

The Fishbowl was the site of all kinds of campus activity every day, its walls typically lined with posters, its passageways dotted with tables where organizations and clubs publicized events and recruited members. On this day, squeezed between the Greek Week Ball and the March of Dimes tables, a recruiter for the U.S. Marines sat in full-dress uniform, tight and sharp. Ruthie and a few other students began passing out leaflets entitled "Fact Sheet on Viet Nam" which they'd prepared for the teach-in but had been deemed by the antiwar organizing committee as urgently needed now. The Fact Sheet was an entirely unadorned, single-spaced, double-sided page, hard to read but comprehensive—"The Declaration of Independence for the Republic of Viet Nam proclaiming liberty from France, begins, 'We hold these truths to be self-evident, that all men are created equal'"; "President Eisenhower declared that a free and fair election in Viet Nam in 1956 would have resulted in an 80% vote for Ho Chi Minh." On and on, all the stuff you could look up if you wanted to, because Ruthie had annotated the Fact Sheet to death. I was struggling to catch up, and this was a godsend, my personal Cliffs Notes on Viet Nam. I didn't know much, but I had the thing mostly memorized by midafternoon.

Some debate sparked up in the Fishbowl that first day, some argument, but it was sporadic and low key. When the marine recruiter arrived early next morning, however, Stan Nadir was already there with tons of literature about Viet Nam, piles of posters, and protest buttons you could buy for a quarter. He had also made a banner out of bed-sheets the night before that he hung strategically high up on the wall over the marine's head:

> **WAR CRIMES ARE ATROCITIES OR OFFENSES AGAINST PERSONS OR PROPERTY INCLUDING MURDER, DEPOR-TATION, WANTON DESTRUCTION OF CITIES, TOWNS, OR VILLAGES. . . . ANY PERSON WHO TOOK A CONSENTING PART IN THESE ACTIVITIES IS A WAR CRIMINAL. . . .**
> **—THE NUREMBERG TRIALS**

Below the blaring quote, in black block letters, Stan had printed six words: THIS MAN IS A WAR CRIMINAL, followed by a thick red arrow arcing toward the marine's head.

Stan's banner electrified the Fishbowl. The marine fumed and thundered and, answering his own call to arms, lunged at the sign. Stan blocked his way. The administration was consulted. The marine insisted on no sign; Stan said no marines. After some discussion and some hand-wringing on the part of the authorities, it was agreed that both would stay: the U.S. Marines had every right to recruit on campus, said the administration, but the students also had the right to protest their presence. The marine glowered; Stan took up a defiant position next to him, arms folded across his chest—they made an intriguing mirror: the strong, the proud, the few. It was a kind of armistice. But not for long.

The Fishbowl filled with students, at first swirling to and from classes, stopping to argue and debate, eventually abandoning school altogether. Groups came en masse to side with the besieged marine only to be confronted by a growing group of antiwar students. People surged in and out all day, spilling onto the Diag and the lawns beyond. I passed out the Fact Sheet at the edges of the Fishbowl with

Rick, each of us happily engaged in little disputes at the edges of the crowd while we kept an admiring eye on Stan at the center of the storm. When Rick overheard a student wearing a Pendleton skirt and cardigan with a gold circle pin at her neck and a sorority pin above her left breast tell her friend not to bother talking to us because, as she said, They're a couple of New York Jews who just repeat what's on that stupid Fact Sheet—we swelled with pride. Do we sound that good? we wondered, amazed.

The debates swam above and around and through us. Viet Nam was becoming for me more than a dot on the map. It was a land with a history and a geography, boundaries and borders like everywhere else, something to look up and locate. In Viet Nam location turned out to be twisty. It included dimensions like hopes and fears, longings and terrors, the personal, the interpreted. The truest map of Viet Nam for Americans would soon rise up as a scribble of psychic scars, a kaleidoscope of crooked footpaths and unbounded horizons. Viet Nam, then, would become a place both out there and a place in here.

Ruthie gave me a book of photographs portraying the daily life of Viet Nam, large color pictures including gray-blue buffalo, heads down, horns splayed out and up, heaving ponderously in the mud with their bellies sagging into the water, small boys with bamboo sticks perched upon their backs; men swinging huge nets across the emerald fields, harvesting crickets for the birds they sold at market; a line of women clad in conical hats against the sun, knee-deep in water, bowing rhythmically to plant the young rice shoots; a crowd of children, black eyes shining in round faces, bursting uproariously into the dirt lane chasing chickens; a river of motorbikes coursing through the old section of Ha Noi, babies perched on handlebars, grandfathers clinging to the rear, everyone going, going. The people leapt off the pages at me, vibrant and alive, some seeming as ancient as dragons, others young as the pale sprouts emerging from the rice paddies, all of them cast in a sentimental light, each the object of my growing romance. I don't know why, but after a while I felt that I knew them each individually. Not true, of course, but they felt hyperreal to me, more than human. And I felt the war escalating, which it really was, being waged in my name personally, by young guys I knew who might have been me. I wanted nothing now except to end the war, to end it now.

Viet Nam was quarantined and no Vietnamese lived in the United States then; anything from Ha Noi was slightly bootleg. Ruthie's book came through Paris, much of Stan's supply of literature, buttons, and books through Vancouver. Stan had taped a copy of quite a different photograph to one of his posters, innocent enough at first, slowly incomprehensible, and suddenly staggering: four American boys kneeling in the sun, bare-chested, smiling broadly, settled in the grass, framed by tropical plants and trees, four Green Beret advisors sent to train the anti-Communist Vietnamese. It was like a familiar snapshot from the yearbook of the swimming team or the soccer squad or the baseball captains—fresh-faced, triumphant kids. One of them looked like Barfly, one like my brother Tim. Hell, one looked like me. But just where the gold cups or cedar plaques ought to have been, just in front, cradled in their hands now, the severed heads of human beings, their dull, unseeing eyes eternally open, their ears cut off, strung into a decorative collar worn around one smiling kid's neck. The head in that kid's lap smiled too, grotesquely, and my head swam. I remembered prep school Marx, the steady unveiling of the inherent barbarism of this system as it turns away from its home base, where the malevolence can assume sometimes respectable forms, to the colonies, where it goes naked. Here were guys like me being turned into monsters; here was an America uncovered, without pretense, bare and open on the ground exposed for every passerby to see. I was dizzy.

The confrontation in the Fishbowl flowed like a swollen river into the teach-in, carrying me along the cascading waters from room to room, hall to hall, bouncing off boulders. In one lecture hall Roger Vanilla, a local anarchist, argued that if you concede that there is an expert class, you've driven a nail into the casket of democracy. Don't follow leaders, he shouted, watch the parking meters.

It's a war of dreams, he continued, and in that struggle everyone is equal and everything is free. He talked tactics, explaining in a heated diatribe that all systems are speculative, based on a presumptive norm, and could, therefore, be destroyed with the serious deployment of our imaginations. The septic system works, he shouted above the crowd, beaming, because they figure the chances are 99.99 percent that no more than a handful of us will flush our toilets at a given moment, and that's exactly what the system can handle. He paused, a big smile slashing across his red face. If we organize everyone in Ann Arbor—or America—to flush at the same instant, we can blow the whole system all to shit. The crowd exploded in raucous embrace of his excited metaphor, but no further action was taken.

8.

We built a bonfire on the Diag and hundreds of us—anarchists and street people, radicals and rockers—stayed up singing and talking. Ron St. Ron appeared in a cloud of smoke and passed around joints the size of Havana cigars. Ron St. Ron wasn't his real name, of course, but like a lot of young people, including his roommate, Roger Vanilla, he was in transition, and for him the process of reinvention included a rechristening. He'd gone from Ron Sinclair to Ron St. Claire, and now this.

First, he said, I feel like saying my name twice, Ron, Ron, and second, I like the sound of it—Ron St. Ron. It reminds me of Bond, James Bond. He paused, took a deep toke, and spoke the rest rapidly in a thin voice at the top of his breath: Plus I want to be a saint someday, but I don't want to wait till I'm dead because there might not be any fucking allowed after you're dead—who knows?—and not only do I like fucking but I think many, many girls might like the idea of fucking a saint. He exhaled loudly, took another hit, and smiled sweetly, his expansive face the color of a delicious apple.

Ron was our local dealer and he did have many saintly qualities. He was exclusively a marijuana man, herb of the gods he believed. Whenever he came by to deliver the goods—a dime bag, perhaps, fished from his fragrant backpack—he insisted on giving a free sample to whoever happened to be home at the time. With great ceremony he would clean and sift, measure and roll, and finally light the swollen thing up and smile benevolently, encouraging evaluative comments and positive vibes as it orbited the room. Ron was a generous soul, it's true—he didn't mind sharing, and the quality of his dope was always prime. He lasted less than a year as an independent in the business; when the sharks moved in, Ron was pushed roughly aside.

I tell you, man, he'd say in those innocent early days, his watery eyes simmering with evangelical fire, if enough people were smoking dope, everybody'd be in a better mood. The big wars would come to an end automatically then, man, but so would all our little squabbles. He believed it.

Marijuana was available everywhere—every party, every gathering, every meeting. We simply called it dope, because it was the only drug in our world, and while we didn't think of it as hard or addictive or dangerous, we knew it was illegal and on the edge and that in some other worlds we were considered demonic dope fiends.

Like coffee or a beer, dope was offered as icebreaker, neighborly gesture, or simply a sign of good manners and proper upbringing. Even the frat parties had dope, but the frat boys were all frivolous and idiotic in our minds now, a bunch of conformist fools going through the motions of hip. Our parties by comparison were completely cool, absolutely righteous. I remember when Studs Terkel's play *Amazing Grace* opened in Ann Arbor we hosted a cast party where, along with the beer and the wine and the chips, dope was passing hand to hand. I offered a fat blazing joint to Studs who said he'd never tried it, but what the hell. A cigar smoker, Studs held the thing between his thumb and first finger, took a puff and then blew it out in a big cloud without inhaling. Hey, he said, holding the fat thing aloft and admiring it like a connoisseur. That's pretty good stuff. Sure—he smiled broadly—I felt something.

Ron St. Ron was a first-order philanthropist in his own mind, an entrepreneurial dharma bum on a spiritual mission of peace and harmony. Just keep passing the weed, man, he'd encourage. Things are definitely looking up. Although the content and the contexts varied wildly, Ron had a firm and unshakable theory toward a better world a'coming, just like Karl Marx and Mom and my English teacher Mr. Friend before him.

The sweet smoke drifted up and mingled with the smell of the bonfire and the embrace of a cool gentle fog, everyone feeling nice and talking low.

I was totally mellow by the time I noticed that Bob Moses was among us, in the center of the large circle, speaking softly, but speaking somehow to all of us. I knew it was Moses, although I'd never seen him before and had had no idea he'd be here tonight. I had seen his pictures often enough—Moses leading a march in Lowndes County, Alabama, Moses registering sharecroppers to vote, Moses being hauled off to jail—and he was already famous as the courageous Black leader of SNCC. In fact it was strange that he was here at all, but those were strange times and I never questioned it. I felt odd standing within arm's length of a living hero, surprised that he was so young and small—like me, average height and build, horn-rimmed eyeglasses, jeans and a denim jacket.

Moses was unassuming in every way, but his words were nonetheless imposing. Justice and peace are twins, he said quietly that night, borne of the same desire, just as war is the twin of racism. To win peace, you've got to fight for justice. He said that his war was not against the Vietnamese people but against a whole system that waged war on the people of Viet Nam and another kind of war against his own people in Mississippi. I was high, it's true, but hearing Moses cemented a connection for me that had been gathering for weeks—I felt suddenly transported as I saw this vague and formless thing start to shape up and materialize, and putting one and two together realized with a jolt that I was at that moment standing in the middle of the elusive movement I'd been seeking.

The State Department did send two young fellows to the teach-in who spoke tidily about the spread of communism and U.S. responsibility to defend the free world against totalitarianism.

If Viet Nam falls, said one, all of Indochina will follow in short order.

Yes, the other chimed in, and then Indonesia, the Philippines, and who knows? We'll be fighting in Hawaii!

They were earnest and perhaps even sincere, but I dismissed them as twerps. I couldn't wait to hear one of us demolish them.

It's a point, Stan countered, that runs entirely the other way. The U.S. conquers whatever it likes—Puerto Rico, Haiti, half of Mexico, and, yes, Hawaii, too—and that's the root of the problem.

One State Department guy offered a simple grunt and a dismissive wave; the other said, You're making this absurd.

When Ruthie Stein challenged them, I felt a surge of pride and power in my blood. If we don't stop this war now, she said, the casualties will include justice and progress here in America.

They were pitiable. I felt ecstatic to be with Stan and Ruthie.

I knew the war was illegal and could hammer that point all night and all day. I felt its dead, dehumanizing grip the moment I saw Stan's photograph, and increasingly so, the more I looked and the more I learned.

I leapt into the discussion then, inflamed, hoping to give the moment its due.

What kind of a system is it that allows the U.S. to seize the destinies of the Vietnamese people?

What kind of a system is it that disenfranchises Black people in the South, leaves millions upon millions impoverished and excluded all over the country, creates faceless and terrible dehumanizing bureaucracies and puts material values before human values—and still calls itself free and still finds itself fit to police the world?

I don't remember much of what I said, but the feeling persists—Ruthie beaming at me and Stan offering a paternal nod, people I knew from campus gatherings but who couldn't possibly know me listening intently, a beautiful woman taking notes. Brilliant! Ruthie told me later, and even though I knew I wasn't—I'd felt wobbly here and there, borrowing shamelessly from Ruthie and Stan and Moses, relying on my desire and will to triumph over my gaps and my faltering speech—I also felt bathed in a kind of clear admiring light. Brilliant in its way.

Paul Potter, president of Students for a Democratic Society (SDS), talked about building an irresistible social movement, something more than a few isolated protests or individual actions, but a powerful popular tide of people willing to transform their lives, challenge the system, and take on the problem of change as vocation and calling. I felt swept along all night by the dream of peace, and the captivating idea of social change as a calling, perhaps as the calling of all callings.

How do you stop a war? Potter asked. If the war has its roots deep in the institutions of American society, how do you stop it?

Do you march and rally? Do you conduct a teach-in?

Is that enough?

Who will hear us?

How can we make the decision makers hear us, insulated as they are, if they cannot hear the screams of a little girl burned by napalm?

His questions reached out at me with the urgency of a slap.

How will you live your life so that it doesn't make a mockery of your values?

That last question set me afire—it rattled in my heart and my head for years to come—and at that moment, I was recruited. The question assumed so much: that we could choose to live purposeful lives, reflective and deliberate, that we could develop and embrace a morality for daily living, that we could choose to act upon whatever was thrown at us, whatever the known world demanded of us.

I joined SDS on the spot, a savory soup, all mixed-up: most of us were students, some were hippies, freaks, and street people, several were intellectuals, others anarchists, cultural rebels, socialists, hard Communists, red-diaper babies, children of the labor elite, sons and daughters of the powerful, beatniks, poets, free thinkers, artists, guttersnipes, rockers, Diggers, Wobblies, and a lot else. We smoked dope (OK, not all of us, but I did), grew our hair long (some guys on their heads and faces more than others, some women on their legs and armpits, but not all), argued hard and hurt each other's feelings and usually hugged and made up. Eventually we would do all sorts of things: some of us organized in poor and working-class neighborhoods; some of us built counter-institutions (schools, clinics, work co-ops) to provide models for a new, more just society inside the decaying husk of the old; some of us built mobilizations against the war; some of us stopped U.S. Marines and CIA recruiters on campus and exposed and opposed the war-related research that we thought was immoral and yet enriching our institutions; some of us fought for open admissions for Black students; some of us, eventually, blasted away at the purveyors of racism, war, and death. Some of us burned out and stumbled away. But in those early days I bounced out of bed most mornings wondering how I could live my life that day so as not to make a mockery of my values, how I might embody justice and enact democracy. I think we were all fueled by a shimmering vision of a democracy that would be participatory, a society free of racism, a planet at peace and full of justice—a state of affairs I thought we would achieve through love, mainly, through goodwill, sacrifice, and applied activism, and soon. It was all romance and righteousness, of course, and it was the dream I lived for.

Life is always a delicate dance of choice and chance, a balance of will and fate. Just when you feel fully in charge of your life, something descends—an accident, cancer—to remind you that in-charge is a delusional condition; and just when you feel life's victim, you might pick yourself up and take control in ways that take your breath away. Each of us is free and fated, fated and free.

I don't think my longing to give myself to a cause would have adapted to any easy or random outlet—becoming a right-wing Christian, for example, just wasn't in me—though I do know something of the pull of the group, the seduction of the ideal, the power of the crowd. But neither do I think that growing up in the cradle of the civil rights movement and in a time of upheaval determined what I would do or who I would become—most people I knew stayed conveniently on the sidelines in another groove. In fact, I didn't understand how they could. Again and again I argued with old friends, guys from prep school, and people I knew on campus that they should join SDS and throw themselves into the movement.

I remember a cousin's wedding outside Detroit and two full days and nights of parties. I tried to recruit the groom and the best man, several distant relatives, one of my aunts, and finally a bridesmaid who, though she didn't sign up, did spend the night with me, a small consolation. By breakfast the second day people gave me a wide berth, and I hung out mostly with my baby brother.

Humanity itself, it seemed to me, was what was at stake. The humanity of people in Viet Nam and around the world, the humanity of Black Americans, and, finally, my own humanity. You could not be a moral person with the means to act, I thought, and stand still. The crisis demanded a choice. To stand still was to choose indifference. Indifference was the opposite of moral. If we didn't speak out and act up, we were traitors. To fail now was fatal, and so there was nothing that could justify inaction. Nothing. In my mind you were allowed only short time-outs—for a little food, for occasional sleep, for abundant sex, for the fundamentals.

I felt now at the epicenter of a resistance so wide and so deep that it would quickly disrupt the cotton wool of consciousness afflicting the country. It had already shaken us lucky ones from the scripted lives we were expected to lead, propelling us in a wide range of unpredictable directions. It was such an outrageous and enormous act of imagination, militant, eclectic, and insurgent—part political, part cultural, part head, and much heart—and once released, imagination has a habit of exploding into exciting and dangerous places. Our watchword was action. Go further, we said. Push the limits. Cross the borders. Go further. I still have my SDS membership card, and it begins: "We are people of this generation . . . looking uneasily at the world we inherit."

I had only glimpsed the terrible wrongdoings and crimes in Viet Nam, the things we needed to stop. I knew the history in fragments, mostly from the Fact Sheet, but some things were certain. Everyone could see that the American war was being fought in a peasant nation 10,000 miles away, the huge disparity in size and power everywhere evident. The U.S. bombed North Viet Nam from the air, but North Viet Nam would never bomb the U.S.; the U.S. bombed the National Liberation Front territory, but the NLF had no air force at all, and couldn't bomb any enemy positions except with tin cans and pineapples; the U.S. fought a mechanized, high-technology war while the Vietnamese fought a guerrilla war. I knew that U.S. soldiers were finding it frustrating and then frightening that they couldn't distinguish friends from enemies, the people they were putatively defending from the people they were supposed to kill. And I heard the language of the war become perverse and revealing: villages were destroyed in order to save them from the Communists; relocation camps called strategic hamlets locked peasants away from the threat of themselves. In time words lost their moorings and floated away, groundless, and doublespeak distorted all meaning. The U.S. destroyed precisely what it said it was there to protect—the land, the villages, and finally the people themselves.

I felt as if my whole generation had turned a corner and walked smack into a violent mugging, a rape in progress: the victim, a total stranger—small, wiry, and ragged with odd, alien clothes, the bearing and whiff of the foreigner; she looked poor, she spoke no English, she held no currency. But—and this was the shock—the attacker was a man we all knew well, an everyday presence, someone we'd admired vaguely without ever actually examining the basis for that admiration.

What should we do?

Stop! we shouted at first in horror and disbelief. Stop it! We saw what was happening close up, and we felt personally responsible. We felt involved.

I'm only . . . you don't understand . . . I'm innocent . . . I'm being pulled into this . . . I'm caught by this awful bitch and it's all her fault . . . the quicksand . . . a quagmire . . .

Stop! we repeated, this time punching him in the head. But he wouldn't stop, and so we reached for the heavier stuff.

The little State Department functionaries had praised President Lyndon B. Johnson's courage and resolve. The president has his fist in the dike, one had said, puffing up a cliché and embellishing the official metaphor. The other added a geopolitical dimension: when President Johnson says, You're not going to have Viet Nam, he must be believed.

The policy people reached deep for religious and sexual metaphors, but LBJ said it best toward the end of his life: I knew from the start that I was bound to be crucified either way I moved, he said. If I left the woman I really loved—the Great Society—in order to get involved in that bitch of a war on the other side of the world, then I would lose everything at home. . . . But if I left that war . . . then I would be seen as a coward and my nation would be seen as an appeaser. I would be seen as an unmanly man.

I thought of him as a tragic figure, but then I remembered all the killing and destruction, all the avoidable pain, the hazards of men and war, and I said, to hell with him.

I felt that my youth was coming to a close that week, and perhaps the youth of the world was ending, too. It's time to grow up, I thought, to look at things as they really are, to examine my conscience, and to get going.

My brother Rick and I met up at the student union for breakfast before the big rally and the planned civil disobedience at the draft board that would climax our first antiwar week, but I couldn't eat. We were going to the demonstration together later, and neither of us had yet decided whether we would sit in and get arrested.

All night Viet Nam had haunted me, dragons and water buffalo swarming through my mind. I woke up early drenched in sweat, my stomach in knots. My own conscience had risen up in the night, chasing me in circles around the room. One minute it demanded that I act forcefully, unequivocally, with courage and certainty, the consequences be damned. But the very next minute it urged caution and scolded me about hurting my parents' feelings. To act would be brave but foolish; to hesitate would be cowardly but wise. The dog of my mind nipped its own tail.

What will you do? Rick asked when we'sat down.

I wasn't sure until I heard him ask it that way.

I'm going to sit in, I said.

Rick said he thought everything would be OK, and I heard an echo of Mom.

It'll be fine, I said.

Rick would bail me out.

Every story of rebellion begins as a story of oppression. And every story of oppression starts with the cries and groans of unjustified suffering, undeserved harm, unnecessary pain—stories of human beings in chains or under the boot.

I woke up one day—hatched out of the hard, white protective shell of my privileged prep school upbringing—to a world in flames. Mass demonstrations in the South, revolution in Latin America, upheaval across Asia, liberation in Africa, roiling tension in our cities, nuclear annihilation and mass murder hanging precariously over our heads. A world of trouble, a world in motion, a going world hurtling toward some distant destination I could not make out. Damaged and self-destructive, but alive with human possibility, filled with energy and contradiction, fantastic and fatal choices to make—my world. I threw my lot in with the rebels and the resistors, the anti-mob, the agnostics and the skeptics. The real damage in the world was not being done by them, but by the docile and obedient, the indifferent or the credulous.

The rally was vibrant and sparkling that day, the autumn air crackling as it embraced me, the spirit of the crowd reaching out to welcome me. Soon I was surrounded by chanting, singing sisters and brothers, and I felt myself a charter member of a just-made society, fresh and crisp, our own beloved community, and lingering doubts were pushed aside. A large banner stretched the length of the library: NOT WITH MY LIFE YOU DON'T, and there were posters and picket signs waving everywhere on the Diag: MAKE LOVE NOT WAR; HELL NO, I WON'T GO; END THE WAR IN VIET NAM—BRING THE TROOPS HOME NOW.

Ruthie spoke through a bullhorn, urging students and faculty and all members of the Ann Arbor community to stand up and be counted as an army of peace. Now is the time to put our bodies on the gears of the war machine, she shouted. To bring it grinding to a halt before it's too late. Yes, our bodies would be the crowbars upon which the machinery would break.

I would stand for peace that day in a way unimaginable a few years before. I would display my opposition to war bravely and defiantly. I would go to jail—the house of a free man, Thoreau had said—and join the ranks of my heroes, Moses and King, Gandhi and Parks. I'd be a nonviolent direct action warrior, in the spirit of the civil rights struggle. I was about to personally disrupt this war, and I tingled all over.

We headed across campus and through town to picket the draft board, the bureaucratic hub for selecting young men for war, a clean and efficient sorting machine for death, we thought, ranking people along all the predictable American dimensions of race and class. Full-time students were then exempt from the draft, and I still had my student deferment, but that felt increasingly irrelevant. The issue was peace and an unjust war. The question was, which side are you on?

Close to a hundred of us entered the office, blocked the doorways, the desks, the phones, and the file cabinets, refusing to leave. I linked hands with people I barely knew, people who would become intimate friends and lifelong comrades, and people I would never see again, but all of us, for this moment at least, filled with a contagious righteousness and a single purpose: END THE WAR. We sang, we chanted, and when we became a little rowdy, a leader from the American Friends would gently remind us of the importance of being dignified in our witness. Then we would sit quietly for a bit, talking among ourselves, but before long Stan would pull out his dangerous guitar

and proud Ruthie would take up the tune, and the singing would
begin. Outside a crowd was growing—supporters, yes, but also a mob
of jocks waiting to kick the shit out of us.

We sang freedom songs and antiwar anthems to ward off our fears
of being puny, and I learned "The Internationale." Two middle-aged
clerks clucked disapprovingly, backed away from the onslaught, and
disappeared out a back door clutching their handbags. We won! I
thought. We hung large signs out the windows to tell what we hoped
was the watching world what we were up to, and we encouraged one
another in the righteousness of our action. When a police captain
announced that the office was now officially closed, and any of us
who stayed would be subject to immediate arrest for trespassing, our
cheers brought the faded green lampshades to rattling life.

Thirty-nine of us held fast.

The police worked methodically, four cops per prostrate protester,
and by the time they'd made their way to me, they were tired and
strained—one offered a muted knee to my kidneys, another held my
upper arm with a pliers-like pinch down several flights of stairs. As
we were carried out and thrown into locked vans that transported us
to the county jail, we were cheered by a few, but jeered by many others in the throbbing, jostling crowd. I was in heaven.

9.

We called our little cell block Strategic Hamlet A, and inside that
county jail we sang freedom songs, loud and often off-key. Strategic
Hamlet A was separated by thick walls from Strategic Hamlet B, the
women's wing, but we could hear their muffled singing, too, and so
we serenaded each other day and night.

In jail I met Tre, formally and formerly Milton Tannenbaum III, an
irreverent anarchist whose dad was an executive at Dow Chemical. He
was Rick's age, taller than anyone else in the tank, and he had to duck
to clear the door. This is killing LBJ, I know it is, he said, poking fun
at our certainty that our sacrifice meant much beyond these gray
concrete walls. He's in agony every hour I'm locked up here. I can feel
his pain.

I liked Tre immediately.

He and I talked about the world, about politics, but soon we were
on to other matters. We agreed that even if complicated and difficult,
it was a beautiful world indeed, particularly because of the beautiful
women who populated and decorated it so splendidly. We were
thankful to be alive in such a world, so many different women, so
much variety. We talked about girls we had been with—a few—and
women we dreamed about being with—a lot more. Each had been
unique in some way, and the future beckoned, warm and wet and
welcoming.

Tre and I and others had an almost chemical affinity, feeling bound
together by our age and our outlook, our great faith in ourselves and

our respect for a future we would create. As our age came into its own, youth made its singular demands. We would act in our own time. We would love in our own way. We would revolt. We would storm the heavens I've learned that nothing keeps young people so united (and in a paradoxical way so safe) as a passionate interest in humanity. There is sweetness in the turmoil, righteousness in the path of revolution.

Ron St. Ron counseled us on how to keep mellow under stress and confinement through proper breath control and posture, but by the second day he was shaking the bars and ranting to be released. We probably wouldn't be here at all except that we had pissed off the judge who couldn't have cared less about our beloved communities or our apparitions of freedom or our inflamed passions, and was inclined to give us time served in exchange for a "no contest" plea. But we marched noisily into his courtroom singing "Oh, Freedom" as he looked at us grumpily, and then each of us insisted on speaking up and speaking out. We were on fire. Judge, Ron said when it was his turn, you know the law, you know this war is unconstitutional. And you know I'm not old enough to vote yet, but I'm old enough to be told to go to kill and die. Now, Judge, you must know that that's wrong! Ouch.

I quoted Shakespeare. Action is eloquence, I said, and the judge cringed, frowned, and gaveled me in for ten days. The graduate students who spoke up got twenty, the professors (both of them) thirty-days, because, the judge explained sourly, the older ones should know better than to act the fool, and they should get extra punishment for leading the younger ones down this treacherous path. We laughed out loud, and then appealed, basing our defense on the illegality of the war and the righteousness of our resistance. After a jury trial and endless delays we were all back in the slammer.

The time in jail changed things for me, and not because it had been particularly brutal or even tough—there were no whipping posts or thumbscrews, no late night beatings. Don't tempt them, Tre would joke as the sleepy turnkeys delivered the food or the mail.

Don't bring out their gestapo side.

Jail was mainly tedious and boring, everyone eventually getting on my nerves. Ron St. Ron to start, at first because he was so ostentatiously calm, then so preachy, and finally because he became a frenzied discharge of pent-up panic. The lack of privacy was wearing, the lack of books, the lack of anything new to say or to hear from anyone. I'd heard it all.

I did spend thirty-six hours in the hole. The hole was an isolation cell with no windows, no beds or chairs, a crack in the concrete in place of a toilet. The ration was strictly white bread and water, a measurable step down from peanut butter or bologna and Kool-Aid, and we were allowed no toilet paper. Seven of us had been sent to the hole—built for one—for starting a fire in our cell using hoarded toilet paper, so toilet paper was banned, as were matches and cigarettes.

Ron had been demonstrating how to make hot chocolate in a metal cup with a candy bar and water over a toilet-paper campfire when he lost control and his little torch flared into a minor conflagration, sending smoke down the hall and becoming a lamp unto our feet and a light unto our path to the hole. None of us was willing to finger Ron—I don't know about the others, but I for one was sorely tempted—so collective punishment was the order of the day. The hole was several degrees more unpleasant, it's true, but there was an abiding sense that this, too, was all a theater of punishment, not the real thing.

My mom had cried on the telephone when I was arrested and my dad had flown out from Chicago to take me to dinner and counsel caution. Don't close too many doors to the future, he said. Don't take too many steps down a one-way street. Measured and moderate-sounding now, his words seemed to me predictably compromising and contemptible at the time.

What are you doing to end the war? I challenged. We may not be doing everything right, but at least we're against the war and we're acting on our beliefs, which puts us light years ahead of Commonwealth Edison.

Edison isn't political, he said. That's not our business. And who's this "we" you keep referring to? he asked pointedly.

We, I repeated emphatically. Me, my friends, and I. Students for a Democratic Society, for example.

I'll tell you one thing, he said, I'd be doubtful about a group calling itself Students for a Democratic Society—this is, after all, a democratic society.

Well, I'm doubtful about a group calling itself Commonwealth Edison, I said. There's nothing common about that wealth.

Our conversations were all like that then, little bombs hurled back and forth across a widening field.

Still, for all that, my time in jail changed me. I had taken a risk, plunged into the unknown, overcome doubts and fears, and put my body on the line. I'd been challenged—and I'd challenged myself—to link my conduct to my consciousness and to summon my courage in the service of an ideal. I'd done it. In my mind I'd gained a credential and earned a certain informal status in the movement: the fellowship of the stockade.

I'd experienced as well a paradox: in the draft board and then in the county jail, surrounded and contained, I felt somehow unshackled. I became used to the peace and complete freedom that only the cage provides. I tingled with freedom, it danced around and through me, and in an odd way I wanted more.

We had refused the world as we found it, and moving beyond dull passivity, launched ourselves as warriors of repair. The drama of living was suddenly unscripted, and we were improvising in a world no longer immutable, no longer finished or fixed. Our imaginations cracked things open, and the intensity was intoxicating. The rules themselves were all up for grabs, life could be anything at all, and we were preparing something new and, we thought, dazzling. That's why in prison a public space was born for me.

In that jail at the moment, freedom appeared as concrete and trembling and real. I carved a red star rising on my left shoulder, my first real tattoo, a bloody and painful inscription gouged with a needle and India ink, my little brand of autonomy and my personal declaration of independence. I wanted to make a claim on my body, to fix my shifting identity. I was already a rebel, and I would now become a freedom fighter.

10.

What do you do on the outside? I'd asked an older guy sitting with me on a steel bench when we were first arrested. This guy had to be thirty-two, thirty-three years old—as old as our professors and teaching assistants, though not familiar from the university, as old as the cops. He was somewhat superior, a bit aloof, the only one of the thirty-nine arrested at the draft board I'd never seen at meetings or demonstrations or rallies before. He might be the snitch Ron had cautioned against in a conspiratorial moment earlier, except that he was if anything too obvious—short hair, trim mustache, plaid shirt, out of nowhere.

Different things, he responded casually. Maybe Ron was right. I write, he said. I invent. I think. I couldn't hold a slave-type job. Murders the mind and kills the spirit, destroys the libido—the three essentials to being a man. Ron was wrong. Right now, the guy went on, I'm volunteering at a new freedom school for young children.

We talked off and on for hours about schools and children, our own experiences in classrooms, and what an education for freedom could look like. His freedom school intrigued me. I had all the advantages of an exclusive and privileged education, yet I had a lot of contempt for it, contempt that ran off in two somewhat contradictory directions. The exclusiveness itself, the privilege, offended my agitated sense of justice. Our masters in prep school had hammered home the message that we favored few should be eternally grateful for the advantages bestowed upon us. Most of my fellow students simply took it for granted. Yes, their faces seemed to say, we are the chosen. And it's true, we read great books, discussed big ideas, imbibed a sense of agency and entitlement. But why should we get that and others something less? Why should thirty-nine get the best, while millions got the mediocre, and millions more the worst? Why all the hierarchical super-competitive games, and mostly why all the pretense of equity when some people get four or five outs to the inning while others get only two? It wasn't fair.

But beyond the injustice of it all, my contempt spilled over into the content of my prep school education. It was irrelevant, disconnected from a vibrant world spinning toward transformation. It was hopelessly dated—who missed Mozart when we had Gillespie and Dylan, for example, or needed Homer when we had Richard Wright and Jack Kerouac? A new world was being built right here, right now. Nothing at face value, nothing received from afar—what counted was experience and more experience. The best education was the education of action, I believed, knowledge of the deed, exactly the education we were soaking up right here in jail.

You reject everything, my dad said to me around that time, and you seem to want to reinvent the wheel. And I said, yes, exactly, the old wheels are all broken and bent, and we have to reinvent everything, especially the wheels.

Memory sails out upon a murky sea—wine-dark, opaque, unfathomable—a little twig cut from a tree and tossed like a toy from crest to trough. We long to construct a streamlined super-submarine of some kind, to pilot a glass-bottomed boat, to read the ocean floor like a book—a mariner's chart of the past on the shelf in easy reach. If only the ocean weren't so deep, we think, the tides so fierce, the sands so shifting—be still.

I was occupied with several love affairs then, the most interesting with the leader of Women Strike for Peace. She was married with children, forty years old when I was twenty, unapologetic about conducting this affair with a kid, and a fearless and joyously generous lover who instructed me on the fine points of female orgasm, evoking the image of a bass fiddle that plays on and on, long after the noisy conductor has packed up his baton and gone home.

When she led a delegation of American activists to meet the Vietnamese in Toronto that year, she invited me to come along, and I was flattered. Our meetings were held in a cheap downtown hotel—eighteen Americans and a dozen Vietnamese from north and south, each beautiful and modest and slim, some skinny, the two oldest absolutely skeletal.

They were friendly but formal, smiling constantly but reserved.

By contrast each of us was noisy and showy, every one of us fat—even the thin ones—and a few of us looking suddenly, disgustingly obese.

I remember clearly a woman named Nguyen Thi Thanh who told me she had seen pictures of Chicago: It is on a vast lake, and the buildings are huge. She laughed. She wore a silver-blue *ao dai*, and spoke so softly you had to bend toward her in order to hear. She had a heart-shaped face and looked twenty-two, but, she told us shyly, she was actually thirty-six. She had left two toddlers in Sai Gon with her parents in 1955 to go north during the "temporary" partition. She was a leader in the National Liberation Front now and lived in the south, but she had never returned to Sai Gon and so had not seen her children in eleven years. At the end of our meetings she gave me a little ring with the number 500 engraved on its face—cut from the five-hundredth American plane shot down in Viet Nam. If she'd asked, I'd have run away with her that moment to Viet Nam, but of course she never did.

America was still telling itself frantic tales of the demon Vietnamese—Asians don't value human life, said the American general in charge—and though we didn't believe any of it by then, it was part of the noisy cultural surround we inhabited, and it helped set the stage for our meeting in Toronto. Here were twelve distinct people who told stories of their lives and their losses with easy dignity and with utter self-confidence. I was enchanted, and then mesmerized. We are fighting for our country, they said, and what right does your government have to determine our future? We make a distinction, they went on, between the American people and the American government, and we know that you are doing all you can to end this aggression. At that point I had to leave the room to cry.

They seemed way, way more than human to me—more intelligent and more compassionate, more courageous and more ethical than anyone I'd ever met. Of course, it was a romantic notion, a romance borne of an excruciating time, a romance that propelled me into a new urgency.

Through the Vietnamese I saw a larger American structure at work. I realized that to some, America was an evil whale swallowing everything it could, and that I was, like Jonah, living inside the belly of the beast, near the heart of the Leviathan.

Now I wanted to be Vietnamese, and I went home with a name for my passion to end the war, and the name was Nguyen Thi Thanh.

I was a full-time peace activist now, and soon a full-time freedom school teacher as well. I walked out of jail and into my first teaching job. The freedom school was a utopian dream called the Children's Community, a handful of preschoolers from all over Ann Arbor housed in a shabby church basement.

I was charmed and captivated the moment I saw it; the promise of the place pushed the slumminess to the background, and all I saw was color and laughter and life. Soon I was volunteering regularly, and before long I was a paid staff member and, at the age of twenty-one, the school's director—youthfulness was all-asset then.

The founding mothers were three gutsy and smart movement women whose young children were nearing school age. Toni had been a teacher herself, and she felt alarmed as her oldest daughter marched off to what she saw as a segregated, regimented, and sometimes cruel kindergarten. They're traumatizing kids there, she said, teaching the most backward values, and I'm not sending her back.

Each of the three had adorable kids, and each was wrapped in a sweet settled beauty and carried a kind of sexual confidence I'd rarely seen before. They flirted easily, joked often, and touched freely. Nancy had blond hair that fell below her waist, an open face and a familiar midwestern sensibleness; Beth, elfish and playful, cursed like a sailor, and in spite of her size, dominated most situations; Toni, dark and angular with long legs, had a wide expressive mouth and sparkling almond-shaped eyes. I fell in love with each of them, and moved into an attic room above Nancy's family and next door to Beth's.

I remember the buzz and hum of my first visit. There were dozens of separate things going on, nothing in lock-step, and it was impossible for me to take in more than impressions. A four-year-old named Tony, tall and handsome with a serious, dignified face, insisted on calling me Bill-Bill, which I discouraged—it reminded me of goofy Ron saying his name twice—but to no avail. There were books and paint and clay, posters of Frederick Douglass and Harriet Tubman on the walls, photos of Andrew Goodman, James Chaney, and Michael Schwerner. Several kids danced near a record-player for a long time, and I remember two who seemed to do little more than run riot through the large room. I loved it.

The kids were sweet, simply because kids are sweet, their wonder and vulnerability always combining to create a kind of special, spontaneous magic. Nothing shocked or even annoyed me—I carried inside of me my shaping experiences as the middle child in a large family; I knew noise and motion and the jumble of a community of kids close up.

Most days were like that first one—pockets of calm, eclectic projects and fleeting efforts in every corner, laughter and tears and a current of wildness that could ignite in a heartbeat, sending a rollicking handful of roughnecks harum-scarum around the room. I believed that most schools tried to break and control kids, enacting some cleaned-up kind of Calvinism, beating the hell out of them for their own good. I embraced wholeheartedly a contrary idea: kids are naturally good and will blossom beautifully if raised in freedom. A little

Rousseau, a little Thoreau. I never figured out how to adequately handle the wildest kids in their fullest eruptions—it didn't fit into my scheme of things, and I didn't know where to turn—so I mostly held on until the storm passed. I figured that love itself would make it all turn out OK in the end.

We organized field trips to everywhere and anywhere: the bakery, the farmers' market, the Ford assembly line, Motown Records, the apple orchard. The Motown trip led to a book-making project based on our favorite singers, complete with song lyrics and autographed photos, creating our own unique primers. The trip to the orchard led to a transformed school next day: now it was a busy little bakery creating apple fritters and apple sauce, apple pies and apple muffins.

Experience, experience, experience. We wanted the kids to think, to be bold and adventurous, and so we pushed one another to be bold and to think ourselves. Trips became a big-letter statement about the centrality of firsthand experience as adventure and investigation and learning. Whenever a kid expressed an interest in anything—the weird, the bizarre, the intriguing, the surprising—off we'd go to have a look. We went to the hospital to visit a mother who worked as a nurse's aide, and to the county jail to visit Tony's uncle. We went to a dairy and followed the milk to market, then to a pork-packing plant to trace the bacon—the man in the bloody apron leading the tour was actually eating ribs. We went to the newborn nursery at the hospital, and then to a funeral home and the county morgue. We didn't know how to stop or where. Experience, experience, we said. Go further.

I recruited Tre to work at the school, and Tre then mobilized a colorful crew of community volunteers. Rasta was a day laborer and out-of-work actor, a huge man and an imposing presence, but solicitous in his dealings with the children and a captivating reader of stories with his booming beautiful voice. Johnny Miller was a bass player who taught us a million folk songs. Grandma Senders was a retired autoworker who came once a week to bake something special. Tim, a retired custodian from the university, and Herb, a retired engineer from Ford, liked to fix things and build stuff, so each carried a large bagful of tools and surprises on the afternoons they visited. Herb might unpack a set of tiny pulleys and levers; Tim would arrange his platform of colored cubes and scales.

Several months later, I asked the founding mothers to say again what qualified me to become the new director, taking over from Toni who was moving to California. Clearly they saw me in ways I didn't see myself, ways I wouldn't even understand for a long time. But I knew that in their assessment of me I was enlarged—they had given me something to grow into.

Look, Beth said, you're twenty-one years old, completely inexperienced, a former merchant marine, ex-con, card-carrying SDS member and college dropout. You're perfect. We laughed, me a bit uneasily, but I felt flattered nonetheless, and happy to be wooed.

Seriously, Nancy added, you should do it because you can carry on the dream of what we're trying to accomplish.

It's always nice to be wooed, and irresistible when the wooers are three beautiful, slightly older women you love.

I said yes.

11.

Whenever I hear the thwack-thwacking of a helicopter overhead or the frantic approach of sirens in the night, I think back to Cleveland, 1966.

I remember a solemn line of troops early one morning marching noisily up Euclid Boulevard in full fantastic battle gear, bayonets fixed, rubber gas masks mutating each soldier into a monster from space, their tall black boots stomping on the pavement, their tin canteens and ammunition belts beating out a syncopated response. I remember a panicky patrol of police advancing toward a flaming building—pop! pop! pop! in rapid bursts—as the hook and ladder trucks idled nervously in reserve. I remember John Davis, a nineteen-year-old from the neighborhood, twitching and clawing at the concrete in the middle of Lakeview Avenue, his left leg bent to an impossible angle, before slumping forward kissing the street absently as blood pooled around his head and ran toward the gutter. And I remember lying facedown on a hard, hot street, gas in my eyes and smoke in my mouth, an M-16 poking into my ribs. It was off the scale, and something came unhinged then.

It was August, the end of a long, hot summer, and, improbably, I was swept up into a big city riot. But the story of any life includes a parade of non sequiturs.

I had come to Cleveland months earlier, recruited to the East Side Community Union to set up an alternative school for young children, on leave from the Children's Community.

The Community Union was part of a joint national strategy of SDS and SNCC (the Student Nonviolent Coordinating Committee), the beginnings of a shift away from attacking the legal barriers to integration largely in the South, now mostly in retreat, toward organizing around de facto segregation and economic injustice everywhere. Our focus was on building a powerful force of poor people in big northern cities—the grassy grass roots, we called them—who could not only change their own lives but could change the world.

Our slogan was "Let the People Decide," and our plan was to live among the poor, to share their travails and their triumphs, then to build action and organization around issues of broad and shared concern: tenant and welfare rights, for example, safety and police brutality, education and schools, racial discrimination. We believed fervently that any legitimate and just change should be led by those who had been pushed down and locked out, and we were certain that struggling in the interest of these forgotten people crushed at the bottom held the key to social transformations that would shake the whole world to its core and ultimately benefit everyone. We saw our political work—to build a mighty interracial movement of the poor—as ethical work. Organizing as righteousness.

There had been a national gathering of community organizers in Ann Arbor the previous winter, and I'd met folks from Newark and Paterson, Chicago and L. A., but the Cleveland group was special to me. For one thing, Paul Potter, the president of SDS and someone I revered, had moved to Cleveland with other movement veterans, including SNCC activists. Also, the Cleveland representatives at the conference were mostly grassroots community folks and not organizers. I was impressed with each of them—welfare mothers, day laborers, cooks and maids and janitors—with their earnestness and determination and clarity, and I supposed that each was more honest, more decent—indeed, like the Vietnamese, more *human*—than other people I knew. And finally, I fell in love with one of the delegates at once.

One night I met with five of them, two from the West Side Community Union centered in the largely Appalachian hillbilly section on the near west side, and three from the East Side Community Union, organizing in the Black neighborhoods on the far east side. Three of the five were welfare mothers with young children at home —Lillian Craig, who was destined to become a national leader as a militant antipoverty warrior and welfare rights activist; Carol King, the president of the East Side Community Union; and Dorothea Hill, who once smitten with the notion of a school like the Children's Community for her own kids became radiant with the dream and began to work me with all she had—and she had a lot. She was easy to love; they all were. But Jackie Morrison, a Black eighteen-year-old and already a movement veteran, was the one who captured my heart that year.

Jackie had grown up on the east side in a beautiful apartment overlooking a park. Her father was a doctor, her mother a teacher, and she and her younger brother were infused with soaring expectations. You're wonderful, you're beautiful, you're extraordinary, their parents had informed them in every way and with every breath, and anyone who thinks less is ignorant or bigoted or wrong. In high school she had played every sport, joined every club, maintained an A average— she was raised for the Ivy League. But at eighteen and not yet out of the house, she'd also organized a high school civil rights club, and now she had a different idea—she would carve herself into a freedom fighter with her own capable hands.

Jackie walked with perfect posture, something beyond what could be taught or learned, and she came into a room the way a flyweight boxer might enter the ring, a tough little guy expecting victory. She wore blue jeans or denim overalls and a crisp pressed white T-shirt every day, her small face framed by big horn-rimmed glasses and a full Afro. Her hair was a political statement, of course, lost on no one. My dad says I look "country," she told me as I walked her home late one hot night. And my girlfriend from high school says I look "ragged." But, hell, this is the natural me. Screw the world.

I think you're the most beautiful woman I've ever seen, I said.

You're the first boy to call me a woman, she said. But clearly, I thought, many had called her beautiful. She took my hand and she felt warm and moist, our hands fitting together perfectly. We stopped talking then, and she kissed me on the mouth. When I touched her face I began to tremble. I was wonder-struck. She whispered something, but I don't know what.

The poverty in our neighborhood hit me at first like a cruel blow. I'd read about poverty in books, seen pictures of poor people everywhere, but I was not poor and so I knew nothing of the smell of hardship, the taste of want, the enveloping feel of need. I saw what it was to be broke, really broke with no backup, and what it was to be hungry, not just ready for lunch. My third-floor walk-up in an anonymous brick building on Lakeview Avenue was one of a long line of shabby buildings that stretched as far as the eye could see. Basic things didn't work—heat for long stretches, electricity, water, and plumbing—and the landlord was around only rarely. Neighbors sat on the stoops in the summer, half-naked children in patched pants made games of pitching stones or chasing mangy stray dogs. Knots of men gathered on corners and in the vacant lot next to our building, smoking, passing a bottle or a skinny joint.

My roommates were Alex Witherspoon and Terry Robbins. Terry, eighteen years old, short with a shock of sandy hair, had the flitting energy of a nervous bird. His attention was unsteady, everywhere at once and at the same time nowhere, and his slight body was wound so tight that the smoldering Camel stuck between his teeth might have been a fuse. Any sissy can quit smoking, he would say, mocking his habit. It takes a real man to face lung cancer. He was in a hurry to experience everything, it seemed, even the inevitable. I watched the restless agitation of his hands as Terry spread his arms and flapped like a penguin running across the ice heading for deep water. Cleveland is too sunny a name for this place, he announced when he arrived. Now that the Jew from Flushing is here, I've got to rechristen you. . . . In the name of the Father, the Son, and the Holy Ghost, I dub thee Clevesburg.

Alex was thirty-three, a veteran of the Korean War and several years of SNCC campaigns in the South. Alex laughed easily, his wide mouth cutting across his narrow dark-brown face, and he joked about everything, especially the everyday dangers of a world with racist crackers in it, but often, when I came home, I'd find him sitting alone in the dark, smoking in silence. Wherever he was in his mind, he'd always smile and come animatedly to life, flipping on lights, talking and joking as he put on the coffee.

Alex was back in Cleveland to be close to his aging mother who lived in the neighborhood. He worked three days a week as a fireman for the city, a real job that paid for his mother's care and still allowed him to be a full-time organizer and activist. We were each paid $2 a week spending money, and our rent and food was covered by the Community Union. Always strapped, we subsisted on small handouts from church groups and labor unions.

Our job, Alex said, is to organize ourselves out of a job, and he meant that though we might be catalysts for change, we could never substitute for indigenous community leadership. We wanted to create organizations of, by, and for the poor people of the east side, and we were deeply critical of professional service-oriented poverty workers—poverty pimps, Alex called them, making money on someone else's misery.

We worked earnestly to become part of our community, listening to what people told us and being as respectful as we knew how to our new neighbors. We wanted to become good citizens of our block first. Don't make a big thing of it, Alex said, but pick up litter on your way to the bus stop.

Soon we knocked on doors, talked around kitchen tables, hung out on stoops, and went to picnics in the park. We were identifiable outsiders, living here by choice. As we went door-to-door we tried to engage people in conversations that might reveal the obstacles they faced in their lives; in naming those barriers, that act itself might enable them to come together with others to struggle, to repair, to overcome. Or so we hoped.

When Alex first knocked on Dorothea Hill's door, she opened it with a big welcoming smile. Oh, you're the civil rights kids from down the block, she said. I've been waiting for you, come on in. They talked into the night about children, welfare, schools, crime, rent, gangs, the problems and the life of the neighborhood—it was the beginning of a beautiful friendship. Later when I asked Mrs. Hill why she told Alex she'd been waiting for us, she laughed and said, "I saw the movement on television for years fighting for justice; as poor as I am, I figured after a while it would have to reach my door."

Dorothea Hill was a natural leader. Perceptive, articulate, respected, she had grown up on the block and was now raising her own children there. Active in her church and PTA, she was a person others looked to for guidance and help. When a child was hit by a car on Lakeview Avenue, it was Mrs. Hill who called a meeting in her living room to press the city to install a stoplight; when a back-to-school welfare allowance was cut, Mrs. Hill organized the protest; when a rat bit a youngster while she slept in her apartment, Dorothea Hill thought up the dramatic tactic of taking dead rats with us downtown to the demonstration and piling them on the front steps of the government offices. Get the rats out of Lakeview and City Hall, Dorothea Hill shouted into a bullhorn, leading the chants.

Mrs. Hill opened meetings with devotions, part prayer, part politics: Thank you Lord for Your many blessings, for Your mercy, and please, Lord, help us out on this demonstration next week. Then we sang several songs—"May the Circle Be Unbroken," "This Little Light of Mine," "Oh, Freedom"—to bring us together as a group, reminding us of our common purpose and making us all feel a little stronger. When she began to set the agenda, Mrs. Hill would always interject her own words of wisdom as introduction: Tonight we'll be talking about welfare rights and the Welfare Workbook we'll be publishing soon. Now remember, just because you're poor and on welfare doesn't mean you're not a citizen, and citizens have rights. Or: Now we'll move on to figuring out about starting that Children's Community school. Our children are poor, true, but that doesn't mean

they don't have fine minds, right Bill? We have to think about how to
stimulate those fine minds.

The first of the month was a celebratory time on our block, everybody with a little money jangling in their pockets. The Community
Union began to host First of the Month potlucks. Mrs. Hill would
often provide the mustard greens and chitlins. Don't eat just any-
body's chitlins, Bill, she would warn me with a sly smile. Now, my
chitlins are a rare delicacy, she said, but you never know what you
might be eating next door.

Slowly the East Side Community Union grew a large, dynamic welfare rights project; a housing and rent strike committee, organizing
building by building demanding fair rents and reasonable upkeep
and repairs; a community health project led by two young doctors; a
storefront office where people could drop in for coffee and conversation; a preschool operating out of a church basement; and a community newsletter. Each activity was an attempt to open a space for
participation, the daily enactment once again of democracy, everything built intentionally with the energy and intelligence of the
people of Lakeview—energy and intelligence largely invisible and
ignored from afar, but, we thought, robust and fierce up close.
Dorothea Hill never missed an opportunity to underline the point:
I'm poor because I haven't got any money. I'm not mentally ill! I'm
not lazy! I'm not stupid!

The immense panorama of waste and cruelty was overwhelming.
Mom sent me a package of chocolate chip cookies and fruit, and it
felt like an anachronistic gift sailing in from another world, a different time. Wanting simply to help, the job would be unending. But I
did want to help. And I thought the Community Union was on to
help of a different type, help that would enable people to help themselves, help that was strengthening and enlarging, help that would
give people the courage to forever resist the casual disregard of their
humanity.

Lofty, true, but down to earth as well. For example, after school
every day for weeks I worked with half a dozen neighbors on a

research project. We bought five pounds of hamburger from the supermarket on our street, and then traveled all over the area on different days buying five pounds of hamburger from every branch store we could find—in other Black communities, the hillbilly neighborhood, working class and wealthy suburbs. We cooked the meat under controlled scientific conditions—in Dorothea's kitchen in her big black cast-iron frying pan over medium heat while we all watched. When we poured off the grease, bingo. The hamburger sold in the Black neighborhoods was twice as fatty as that sold in Shaker Heights; the white burger always leaner than the Black burger. After carefully charting our findings, Dorothea added tomato paste and beans and we all joined in to eat the research results—fat or lean— over fluffy white rice.

When we presented our findings to the city council they didn't believe it, but everyone on the block knew we were right—hamburger tactics ruled.

Mrs. Hill was growing, too, as a leader in the city and then in the state. She led a march of "poverty warriors" from Cleveland to Columbus and spoke at church rallies every night. She was tireless, drawing energy, she said, from God and my children.

Here come the poverty pimps, Alex said, shaking his head in disgust as agents of the government-sponsored poverty programs began to appear. This was the competition, hard to acknowledge as genuine, although several social workers became friends of ours over time. Mainly we thought of them as working to derail the kind of radical transformations we had in mind, dishonest agents of co-optation. They surveyed neighborhood people for a "community needs assessment" using a "scientifically" developed questionnaire that could be quantified to scale and rank. Dorothea Hill was, in their eyes, a vast collection of ills. She had dropped out of high school, become pregnant at nineteen, and was a single mother with three young children, one of whom needed expensive glasses. She had been arrested once as a teenager for shoplifting and had hung out at that time with a group of Lakeview Avenue youngsters who called themselves the Street

Demons. Now she was on welfare, and she occasionally worked cleaning white people's houses while her oldest boy watched the children. She also took cash from the children's father, a long-distance truck driver who sometimes spent the night at her apartment. In other words, Dorothea Hill, by their account, represented the whole litany of behaviors that added up to a tangle of lower-class pathologies: welfare cheat, gang member, criminal, unwed mother, neglectful parent, pregnant teen, high school dropout. Dorothea Hill, they said, represented the culture of poverty, and they were fairly drooling over her.

Lakeview Avenue in Cleveland was a whole world, my world. The men on the corner every morning had names. Eddie Robbins was called Thunderbird, a bottle of cheap wine in his pocket, a friendly greeting each day—What's the word? Thunderbird. What's the price? Forty-four twice. James Thompson was Little Bit, four feet eleven in shoes, an oversized sports jacket bulging with scraps of material, needle and thread, bottle caps, and other found items he used to make dolls he sold to the mothers on the street. Willie Jones was now Ismael Akbar, but he allowed people to call him simply Bar. He was the father of three little girls with their own recent name changes— they were now Mali, Kenya, and Ghana.

The corner men were all street characters, all fixtures on our block, well known, reliable, and oddly reassuring each day. Their parleys were part news bulletins—Big Bob's rig's parked at Dorothea's; he's off to Baltimore later today—part scandal sheet—Louis saw Alice sneaking home at three A.M.—part debate, part Q and A, part bull session, part ongoing dominoes tournament. Soon they allowed me in; I paid for my admission by being the first teacher any of them knew who lived right here on the block with them, and because Akbar, who said that all white people are devils, said that nevertheless I was a good teacher for his girls. I gave myself an hour every morning to stand with the men, drinking coffee from a paper cup.

There was a whole education to be had on the corner: You hear Henry Allen beating up on that gal's been staying with him?

Yeah, it got plenty loud about midnight.

And when she was shrieking there at the end, and he threw her out the window?

Man, I saw her fall, don't know how she lived.

Yeah, and the cops was here in thirty minutes, ambulance took a hour, she could a died.

Black people don't mean a thing to them, man. Whenever you want them, you can't get them for a prayer, but when you don't want them, man, they're *everywhere*.

The buzz was sometimes bitter, sometimes complaining, sometimes boasting, always shot through with a quick line of laughter. The subject of white folks was never far away: Man, Akbar said one day, you see what they doing now? They talking about making kayaking and synchronized swimming Olympic events. Everybody knows Black people don't like the water. Just another racist scheme to keep us from those medals.

Yeah, man, replied Little Bit. You right. Why don't those white people make double Dutch jump rope an Olympic event?

Exactly, and I'll tell you why. Akbar again. Because Mali and Kenya and Ghana'd be up there on that stand, little Black angels giving a black eye to the festival of whiteness.

Yeah, man. Thunderbird now. Or, why not Olympic dominoes? Then you'd see my sweet ass up on that stand, saying, What's the word?

Your sorry ass could not climb the stairs.

Pride, rebellion, laughter.

In the middle of that long, hot summer, something red and violent swept through our neighborhood—to some it was an urban uprising, a rebellion, to others Black anarchy, a ghetto riot. I had an ancient gold Oldsmobile we called the Boat, and I drove a daily shuttle to the hospital with the injured, or to the grocery outside the blockaded area to buy staples to distribute free from our office. Everything was smoke and fire, rumor and incitement.

Stories swept up the street faster than fire: cops on Superior Street beat a woman on her way to church, and on St. Clair a cop shot a boy point-blank and called him "nigger." But on Euclid two cop cars were burned to a crisp, a bank was trashed, and money was blowing in great gusts down the street. True or not, each story was embraced and passed along, each somehow true simply because it was believed.

The strange thing was to live in an atmosphere simultaneously terrifying and deeply energizing. The mood was festive one minute, like a giant community picnic, everyone laughing and sharing and handing things around—although the things being handed around weren't hamburgers but stolen goods, passed through broken windows—and the next minute there was the sound of shots fired from somewhere, or the sight of flames leaping suddenly to life, and we would all turn and scatter. One afternoon I saw thirty or forty people—young and old, men and women, the respectable as well as the neighborhood characters—together pulling to tear a grate off the large plate-glass window of the supermarket. No one urged caution, no one objected. And that night Donald Hall, a kid who worked with the Community Union but would, in a year, join a Black nationalist group and change his name to Jamal Daoud, showed up at our apartment, singed and smoky, and took a shower and left with fresh clothes from Alex.

There was talk of pigs and honkies, yet the action was still in some ways selective, in some sense restrained. When a dozen storefronts were smashed in, it was remarkable that Tony's Pizzeria was untouched—Tony had lived with his family upstairs for years and was well known and well liked, and he was poor like everyone else.

Returning from the hospital one night after curfew, Alex and I were surprised at a checkpoint on Lakeview Avenue, stopped at gunpoint, spread-eagled on the pavement, searched and released. The baby-faced Ohio National Guardsman who, sweating and breathing heavily, searched me, looked wide-eyed and terrified. So was I.

Anger at racial oppression had bubbled beneath the surface calm of the fifties and had burst forth as the civil rights movement, shattering the illusion that America was all right. I thought that the civil rights movement embodied everything that was right about America—its idealism, its urgent yearning for democracy, its belief in simple fairness and the courage and power of ordinary people to shape their lives. It brought home what was profoundly and perhaps fatally wrong about America—lynchings, murders, all manner of inhumanity, American apartheid, the ugly stain on our soul, slavery and its legacy the open wound, festering, infecting the whole body politic. American innocence blew up. Moral concerns became political issues; the search for personal meaning joined a pursuit of public responsibility.

The Cleveland project drew its strength and its focus from the civil rights movement, and it was drawn into its complexities again and again.

When Stokely Carmichael raised the banner of Black Power on a march in Mississippi that summer it roared into our neighborhood full-up. Stokely spoke to hundreds of people at a church down the street a few weeks later—we can't wait for white people to decide whether we're worthy of our freedom, he said. We must *take* our freedom. We can't allow others to do for us. We must *do* for ourselves. We can't accept white standards of beauty or intelligence. We must *rid* ourselves of self-hatred. This much is crystal clear, he said. We're one hundred percent human, and like other humans we need the power to run our own lives. We're Black, and we want power. Black . . . power. Black Power. The church vibrated with the excited chant.

I knew the implications of Stokely's words included the requirement that I get out of the way and that I organize "my own people." It felt both necessary and false, and I was hurt to think I might never have friends like Alex or Jackie again.

I returned to Ann Arbor in the fall. Jackie was off to Tuskeegee, but by now she had changed her name—she was Afeni Shabazz.

The Community Union had been founded shortly after Reverend Bruce Klinger was run over by an earth-mover and killed during a sit-in at a construction site for what would become another segregated Cleveland public school at one end of Lakeview Avenue. It was gone by the time Ahmed Evans and a group of young Black nationalists engaged in a deadly shoot-out with the Cleveland police in an apartment at the other end of Lakeview. In between there was some struggle and much hope; there was even occasional heroism. It was the most loving attempt I would ever see to change so much of what was glaringly, screamingly wrong. And now the riot.

Night after night, day after day, each majestic scene I witnessed was so terrible and so unexpected that no city would ever again stand innocently fixed in my mind. Big buildings and wide streets, cement and steel were no longer permanent. They, too, were fragile and destructible. A torch, a bomb, a strong enough wind, and they, too, would come undone or get knocked down.

But I so loved the unity of those times. I loved Lakeview Avenue, my street—and it *was* my street—and I loved the Community Union. I mostly loved everything I was seeing, and especially all that I was learning.

I thought Stokely made perfect sense. But by that time I also thought I was Black.

12.

In my second year at the Children's Community, Diana Oughton, a graduate student fresh from teaching Mayan youngsters in Guatemala, arrived to volunteer at our school.

The memory I hold still from Diana's first visit was her remarkable calm and quiet, the pleasure she drew from simply being with the children. She smiled and watched and touched a lot, but little more— no dramatic action, no show of importance, no noisy intervention. She didn't read a book aloud, or help with a painting. She walked into the space and was comfortable there. When she was ready to leave at noon, kids swirled around her, asking when she would return. I'll come back, she said, I'm not sure when, but soon.

I walked her outside. They really liked you, I said.

Kids like everybody, she said, laughing. Perhaps if they'd despised me, well, that might be noteworthy, but liking me . . . ? Her voice trailed off.

Well, I went on, undeterred. I liked you, too. You were great with them.

She laughed again. I'll bet you're a lot like them—you like everybody, too.

She said she would come back.

I adored her the moment I saw her, but I knew she was way beyond my reach—too mature, too smart, too experienced. And anyway, everyone adored her, not just me. She knew other worlds and other languages and I knew nothing, she was sophisticated and I was simple, she was untouchable.

It might make sense to tell it from Diana's perspective, or at least from her point of view as I later understood it. She was in Ann Arbor to pursue graduate studies, fresh from Guatemala and a tortured love affair with a young priest that had left her shaken, looking forward to a life of teaching young children. She was a Quaker, and she was excited to find our freedom school bubbling along in the basement of the meeting hall. She wanted to teach while she studied.

She wrote to her sister: I've found a school to work in so I don't go crazy while I'm here, a really amazing place, founded on principles of love and racial justice. The director is years younger than me, but a sweet guy named Bill, filled with those raw American qualities I've missed in some ways—optimism, charm, straightforward friendliness, and ingenuous enthusiasm for just about everything. He's cocky and smart in an American way, naive but gifted. And I'm afraid he's going to be a boy forever—he's got a Peter Pan complex, and no Wendy Girl in sight.

Teaching radiated effortlessly from Diana. There was nothing formal or awkward in it, because it was more an instinct than a plan, more passion than performance. I remember once watching a kid, perhaps four years old, trying to get his mother's attention in a playground while she talked with friends. The kid looked increasingly frantic, and Diana said to me, Who knows? She probably has her reasons, but I hate to see a kid ignored more than I hate to see a kid on a leash.

I could imagine Diana teaching her mother as an infant, teaching her sisters as they grew, teaching the old and the young and the birds in the trees. She taught mostly by example and by illustration, by assimilation perhaps, by noticing or witnessing. Her teaching was often invisible or indirect, muted or enigmatic, its shape and substance apparent only slowly. She taught by breathing in and breathing out.

We were housed then in the Friend's Center where she attended Quaker meeting, and she was intrigued and happy to find us. I don't want to completely lose my connection to kids while I'm studying, she told me. I love what you've started here, and I think I can be of some use to you. She began a couple of mornings a week, but by the end of the year she was coming every day and soon joined the staff—another committed, underpaid core member. She was a natural recruit. She was like us, but beyond us, way ahead of us as a teacher—two years in Guatemala, a year in Philadelphia. And she shared an outlook on life, on the world. Like us she was determined to live a life of meaning and purpose.

Diana was fair with glowing cheekbones, prominent forehead, powerful arms and legs. She was somehow both elegant and simple, her golden hair and classic good looks balanced by a gaze that beamed out with unexpected intensity. Her rolling gait and long strides were willfully unfeminine, and she walked everywhere, always with a pack on her back stuffed with clothes, a sandwich, a book. She had been to the manor born—the oldest of four sisters, she was raised in rural Illinois, her father a kind of gentleman farmer from a previous age. Still, she knew how to can fruit, drive the pickup truck and a motorcycle, sew, cook, hunt pheasants and ducks, worm dogs, make bread from scratch, repair a fence, and a lot else. She knew the right side of a hammer and a saw. And, most important to us, she knew teaching.

Diana's whole story was written on her face, etched with every advantage, accented with privilege. You could easily imagine the rest: a perfect marriage, a comfortable career in banking, say, or the law, two golden children, the clubs, the country home. The script was manifest in her wide open features, the easy inlet of her eyes, all of it exactly as it should be, her lawful claim and birthright. She said she longed to be of use, but that, too, could be adapted. Women should be useful, after all, and women of her class and clan, of her social position, should be service-minded, generous, utilitarian—clubs and charities, then, could be a convenient sanctuary. Except for the urgency of her eyes, and a world in flames, sparks flying everywhere about our heads, singeing us now and then, here and there.

The experience of Guatemala was fresh for her then, and it was apparent in her sandals and her brightly woven shoulder bag, in the Spanish phrases that peppered her speech, and in an unarticulated edge, something deeply sad and mildly impatient. I've seen too much, she'd say when she fell into a mood.

When she filled in an application to teach in Guatemala two years before, she had written in the section on experience: NONE. But that would never again apply. Diana had had an abundance of experience in Guatemala, a torrent, almost more than she could endure. She now sometimes suffered the full flood of her experiences.

Diana was visited by dreams of Guatemala, dreams she called *quetzales*—birds of paradise. I had a scary *quetzal* last night, she might say. I was running on a steep path, when a plane dropped a bomb and the bridge collapsed ahead of me. *Quetzales* could be benign and lovely, but more often were birds of the inferno summoning soldiers in the marketplace, sharp-beaked harbingers of slaughter.

She had worked at first in a convent school in the western highlands near a Mayan town called Chichicastenango. Life there centered around market days when people from the surrounding mountains piled goods high on their backs to sell at the crowded stalls in the town. Most of the white wooden coffins in the market were child-size, she said, for over half the deaths in Guatemala were of children under four. Many of the older children she befriended in the town had swollen bellies and reddish hair from malnutrition.

Diana taught young adults and older people, peasants and weavers, and she worked to embrace the life of Chichi. She played flute when people gathered with their whistles, bells, and drums to make the old music, and she joined in when a trench had to be dug or a fence reset. But mostly she taught and played with the children. I have a picture of her from those days sitting sideways on an adobe wall above a dusty street, a baby in her lap and a crush of kids bunched around her on all sides, a few sailing into the mob while others orbit toward the fringes. The whole thing is an animated, dizzying display of color and motion with Diana still at the center, eyes beaming.

There's so much to admire here, she wrote home. The beauty, of course, and the generousness of people, their genius for survival—I have a neighbor whose house is held together by newspapers, bottles, and string discarded by tourists. Mostly the ability to live life without the coarse desire to own or control. She wrote, too, of measuring her humble efforts against the enormity of a bigger world: I taught Joaquin's mother to read a little Spanish in three months, but 70 percent of the people here are illiterate—87 percent of the Maya, almost 100 percent of rural Indian women cannot read, but not, thank you very much, Joaquin's mother.

The Indians Diana knew worked corpse-sized plots of land for enough corn to stay alive, while a handful of families owned the giant sprawling fincas that swallowed the richest land. It's obvious enough here, she concluded, that for all of our talk, the problem is not the poor but the rich, not poverty but wealth. The problem is us.

Diana's place was small with a dirt floor and a little outhouse. She read by candlelight, carried her water from the well, lived on corn and coffee. She walked the breathtaking mountain paths at all hours to visit students and their families. This land has redefined beauty for me, she wrote. I can see more greens and blues, deeper browns and reds. I'm so happy here. When her father sent her a check to buy a horse for her travels, she returned it asking that he send it to the convent school. They need books more than I need a horse, she wrote. I'm not a better person than any other, and I don't want to live any better.

You'll bankrupt me, he chided her.

No one gets poor from giving, she said. It reminds you that you're human.

Don't worry, I won't forget.

Her father sent some money to the school, and a note to Diana: I've done as you asked, he wrote. But when you say you're not a better person than any other, beware lest that become its own superior stance, with you a new kind of crème de la crème.

Diana knew, of course, that the world is full of poor people, and that the rich are a tiny minority everywhere, but in Guatemala she discovered how deeply the poor despise the rich in spite of their politeness and their deference. It was a complete revelation to her. She became a socialist then, and before she left Guatemala she met secretly with members of the organized guerrilla movement in Guatemala City. She arranged to send supplies and money to them indirectly, and every three months for the next several years she made her appointed drop.

Diana brought books to the Children's Community—children's stories in Spanish and basal readers from her days in Philadelphia. When, in her first month, she read Darlene a picture story with Black characters in it, and Darlene remarked a little breathlessly that she hadn't known that there were books with Black people in them, Diana started a crusade. She bought every book she could find that featured Black characters—this was a renaissance time in publishing African American authors of children's books—and set up her own book-making/publishing area in the school.

We bought a large-print primary typewriter for the kids, and Diana used it to type stories they dictated to her, which they could illustrate themselves, or stories she made up about life in the school featuring photographs of the kids and their adventures. She wrote a whole series about Jingles, our rabbit, that came out in monthly installments for a year. She cut pictures from newspapers and magazines and wrote stories around them. Her favorite was *National Geographic:* Great pictures of kids and moms, she said, but mostly inane text. She used the pictures to spin mysteries and myths.

We had an ethic of sacrifice and anarchy, and any contradictions to that ethic were largely ignored. The Children's Community paid room and board for all core staff, and our pay was twenty dollars a week. Of course, we could afford it. We said that all kids were precious and innately good, and when some parents dropped really difficult kids with tough problems on us, we tended to gloss it all over and see it as a test of our commitment. All we need is love, we said. Pure myth, all this, but we believed it, then, wholeheartedly, and we tried to live it too.

Diana quickly became my mentor in the classroom, repeating the big lessons as I slowly caught on. Look at Cory, she would whisper, and then stand aside, curious and a little awed as Cory experimented tirelessly with the wooden blocks, trying to bridge two pillars he was constructing. Look at Darlene . . . Look at Renee . . . She wanted me to grasp the power of observing, and she wanted me to take seriously the work and effort of the children, to get beyond the heavy emphasis on the actions of the adults, the teachers. Kids know everything, she said. I knew everything as a kid, but who cared?

I was groping toward teaching, and Diana urged me to pay closer attention to our kids, three-dimensional beings, she said, much like ourselves, with hopes, preferences, and unique experiences that must somehow be taken into account. If you keep stretching the context, she said, widening the challenges, offering new tools and possibilities, you have a real chance of becoming effective with kids.

A group of us from the school and the university, movement friends, often met at the Cinema Guild for a film, and then off to the union for coffee and late-night talk. One night we saw *The Battle of Algiers*, a film about the Algerian independence struggle, and felt filled, as we often did then, with a brimming sense of our specialness, the exceptional good luck at being young and awake and eager to take on the waiting world—so much was in such desperate need of repair, after all, and here we were, expectant, intent, hot with the desire to know and to do. To live.

The evening wound down and people began to drift off. Diana finally said it was time for her to go as well, and I offered to walk with her. I had felt a sharp, insistent stab the moment I met her, followed by an uncharacteristic shyness when we were alone together, a clumsiness that went on for months. Now we were side by side, alone.

We headed off down State Street, almost deserted at this hour. Diana was talking as she often did about her time away from America, about how different everything is when you leave and look back. I was listening, and I agreed, of course, but most of my mind was just berating me: Reach out and touch her hand, stupid. Stop and face her. Kiss her. I couldn't. I desperately wanted to make love with her, but I couldn't summon the strength even to take her hand.

She stopped talking and we walked for a while in silence, my head crackling with apprehension. I'll count to five, I thought, and then. No, I'll count to ten. One . . . two . . . three . . . She broke the silence. Back to one.

It went like this all the way to her door. We stood for a moment in silence. One . . . two . . . Want to come up for tea? she offered. Great. I'd been to her small apartment before. It was filled with photos of children, Mayan weavings, earthenware bowls and candlesticks. Above her desk was a framed excerpt of Martin Luther King Jr.'s "Letter from Birmingham City Jail": "I must confess," he wrote, "that I have been gravely disappointed with the white moderate. I have almost reached the regrettable conclusion that the Negro's greatest stumbling block in the stride toward freedom is not the White Citizen's Councilor or the Ku Klux Klanner, but the white moderate who is more devoted to 'order' than to justice, who prefers a negative peace which is the absence of tension to a positive peace which is the presence of justice. . . . We will have to repent in this generation not merely the vitriolic words and actions of the bad people, but for the appalling silence of the good people."

She lit an oil lamp, started the water boiling, as I sat on a small sofa. As soon as she sits down, I told myself, I'll ask. One . . . two . . . I was speechless.

When the tea was ready she brought milk and sugar, poured two cups, took a sip of hers, and settled onto the sofa's arm. More silence—I was all motion and frenzy on the inside, but hopelessly paralyzed outside.

And then her hand inched toward mine, and my mind went convulsive. I wanted to get up and run. She moved closer. She brushed my hand, and then took it confidently into her own, whispering firmly, I want to kiss you now. I was suddenly conscious of breathing, but didn't know where my breath ended and hers began. Please, I replied, somewhere between assent and surrender. I was willing to beg, but she asked nothing, nothing at all.

13.

Viet Nam, never far away, was hypnotic for me, for all of us—in Viet Nam there were no fixed borders or hard lines between the real and the unreal, the visible and the hidden. Things could be both real and unreal, or real in some aspects, unreal in others, and so what drew me in was a contradiction. Countless villages in the countryside were under government control for some purposes, guerrilla control for others. Or one in the day, another at night. It wasn't so simple, and much depended upon your angle of regard. The fantasy of North and South Viet Nam, too, played a large role in policy, strategy, and tactics, but the border was all invention, a fiction. It was real and unreal.

The countryside was booby-trapped from top to bottom—the lush-looking land ready to spring and snatch at any unsuspecting step. The Americans were scared, and why not? They had built an obsessive operation to probe for tunnels and mines, and everywhere they looked, an elaborate network burrowed deeper and further.

Tre tacked a massive map of Viet Nam—maybe three by four feet—to one wall of his bedroom, and every day after reading the *Times* and watching the news we would retire to stand in front of it, trying to make sense of what was going on. Eventually he got colored pushpins and charted what he called the regress of the war—a Pentagon war room, but entirely through-the-looking-glass. We knew more about land reform in the provinces than about the workings of U.S. Steel or General Motors.

There were layers upon layers in Viet Nam, meanings within meanings, wheels within wheels. The newspapers reported that a government patrol had discovered a tunnel entrance near a contested village. Tear gas flushed out two villagers who had fled with the approach of the Americans. The two were roughed up and admitted that three more were down under. Grenades were dropped, and after a pause a little GI called a tunnel rat eased in. He sought evidence, verification, just the facts. At about thirty meters the tunnel ended and that was that, a fact, no others inside, and so the little guy eased back toward the opening. Near the entrance a trap sprang and he was stabbed in the chest and belly with four long bamboo stakes. Another fact, and the tunnel went still deeper, and forever. The three were in there somewhere. And so the drive toward the facts proved impossible to satisfy. The experience was acute, but reality evasive. Your own eyes told lies.

The Americans wanted the jungle path to become a well-lighted expressway complete with surveillance cameras. Of course. They wanted to collapse the tunnels and force the inhabitants out of their burrows into an easily observed complex of high-rise buildings and barbed wire with the quaint name "strategic hamlets." They promoted supervision, reconnaissance. They staked out the entire country, everyone, everywhere.

Seeing a newsreel of a patrol in the Mekong Delta one day I felt as if I were floating above the whole thing, looking down. A big blond American farm kid, heavy with gear, oversized headphones in place, held a long metal rod with a big circular sensing plate at its end and swept it back and forth, back and forth as he stepped cautiously, ponderously, along a country road, searching in vain for the hidden world, while right there beside him streams of children and farmers and women rushed past, barefoot or on bicycles, on their ways to school and work, unafraid, seeing what blinded the outsiders, floating along above the fields with me and with the ghosts. I saw Viet Nam as a 100 percent anti-American guerrilla society. Not quite true, but close enough. Anyway, the Americans in Viet Nam were my problem, I thought, big enough for me.

This reporter spoke unironically about "pacification" and "making the countryside safe," and I couldn't believe he was missing this image. He must be blind, I thought, trapped inside the borders of a made-in-the-U.S.A. metaphor. Trapped in black and white, while around him the pulsing world emerged vivid and intense, deep and in parts gaudy. But the brilliance that many journalists brought home so dramatically was somehow lost on this guy.

The GIs felt themselves to be good guys, nice guys, and now they were besieged. They didn't belong, of course, and increasingly they knew it. They came to help, they thought, but who were their friends? Not the powerful who had sent them on this awful mission, and not the people here. It was total war against everybody, one GI told a reporter. They'd smile at you in the day, and set a trap for you at night. Another added, Hey, an eight-year-old can kill you just as easy as an eighteen-year-old.

The truth we now know is always complicated, layered, evasive, perspectival—it rarely comes to us in a big box, neatly wrapped and clearly labeled. Even then we knew that we lived in a kaleidoscopic world, and that clear conclusions were mainly delusional, a luxury of religious fanatics and fools.

But the government gave my generation an unintended gift—the truth was apparent everywhere in Viet Nam. Official American intentions were evil and her justifications dissembling, her explanations dishonest, her every move false. In the face of that monstrous lie, truth pushed forward, brilliantly on display. The war was wrong. Ending the war was right. How you chose determined so much about who you would become.

Memory is a mortuary, a dead space.

I don't remember—the glib dismissal of the assassin, the alibi of the arrogant, the defense of the overprivileged—a lie of presidential proportions.

Or memory is memorization, habit and routine, the clichés of common sense, ordinary life. Worse, memory can become the black slate monument hiding the bodies, silencing the sounds of longing, the chords of warning.

I don't remember—a cute little phrase, this hiding place of heroes and scoundrels alike, principled response to the witch-hunters and inquisitors or flinching evasion of responsibility to the remaining victims at long last free, confronting their tormentors. Some utter it as conviction, others as opportunism; some in defense of liberty and humanity, others as a convenient cover-up for cowardice, torture, and murder. It's a jagged boundary line, this forgetfulness, between a robust and hearty spirit and abject spiritlessness, between loyalty and betrayal.

One day in Viet Nam "U.S. intelligence gathering" might mean binding the arms of five young peasant men—suspects of subversion in a village—who claimed to know nothing about the resistance, to remember nothing. The Americans roughed them up and herded them onto a troop carrier, their first helicopter ride. Ten thousand feet above the jungle one young man was tossed out, floating and flailing in a long arc to his death, and the other four screamed their confessions to the interrogators above the roar of the motor.

Or intelligence gathering could be fire, electricity, shallow ditches in the red earth, but who can remember such things? It was welts and abrasions and broken fingers. It was boiling water or ice water or water tanks or dripping water. The gauzy curtain couldn't camouflage everything that went on behind it, and the ghosts would not be constrained by a thin cover of intelligence. They wafted above the fields, intruded upon the open world, remembered from the shadows, appeared suddenly out of the mist to offer a correction, an adjustment.

Diana and I moved in together into a tiny little slant-roofed house on Felch Street, on the far side of Ann Arbor in what people called the bad part of town, which meant the Black part of town, shut off from easy access to the giant university by downtown.

She read aloud at night, poetry and stories, essays and prayers. She loved Walt Whitman, and she said that poetry was for her a substitute for prayer—something uplifting. From Otto Rene Castillo, killed with the Guatemalan guerrillas:

My country, let us walk together, you and I;
I will descend into abysses where you send me,
I will drink your bitter cup,
I will be blind so you may have eyes,
I will be voiceless so you may sing,
I have to die so you may live.

From Hannah Arendt: To what extent do we remain obligated to the world even when we have been expelled from it or have withdrawn from it? We humanize the world through incessant and continual discourse; a world without discourse is inhuman in the literal sense.

From Victor Frankl: Life remains potentially meaningful under any conditions, even those which are most miserable. We find the meaning by the attitude we take toward suffering.

It is an immoral world, Diana said. But we create a moral space when we cry out against harm. In the face of everything, good will overcome evil.

Why would it? I said. Why should it?

Because it can, she said.

But that's a kind of naive faith, I said.

Faith, she replied, but not naive. And then, quoting Hebrews: Faith is the substance of things hoped for, the evidence of things not seen.

I want kids, she said early in our relationship.

I know, I said. Anyone who knew you for more than a minute would know you want kids. Kids become you, and besides, those hips. . . .

Shut up, she said. I just want you to see what you're getting into. Kids. Lots of kids. And a reliable father for those kids. And, oh yes, I want long, tangled love affairs every five years.

Of course.

At an SDS convention, a workshop "For Women Only" met intermittently for three days. What's going on? I asked Diana after the first day.

It's exciting, she said. But I can't talk about it much yet. We agreed to wait to include any of the brothers.

I was hurt, with a hint of foreboding. That's silly, I said.

It's not, she shot back. You'll see.

Finally the workshop presented a resolution to the convention, one sister reading the text while her co-writers gathered at the podium:

> **Women, because of their colonial relationship to men, have to fight for their own independence. This fight for our own independence will lead to the growth and development of the revolutionary movement in this country. Only the independent woman can be truly effective in the larger revolutionary struggle.... People who identify with the movement and feel that their own lives are part of the base to bring about radical social change must recognize the necessity for the liberation of women. Our brothers must recognize that because they were brought up in the U.S. they cannot be free of the burden of male chauvinism.**
>
> **1. Therefore we demand that our brothers recognize that they must deal with their own problems of male chauvinism in their own personal, social, and political relationships.**
>
> **2. It is obvious from this convention that full advantage is not taken of the abilities and potential contributions of movement women. We call upon women to demand full participation in all aspects of movement work, from licking stamps to assuming leadership positions.**
>
> **We recognize the difficulty our brothers will have in dealing with male chauvinism and we will assume our full responsibility to resolve the contradiction.   —SDS, July 1967**

Tre and I took it all in, planted in the farthest seats in the highest balcony, our legs draped across the row in front, eating chips, drinking Coke, and smoking cigarettes.

Chicks in charge, I said mockingly. You've got to love it.

You're laughing now, he responded, but watch out—they don't mean men in general, they mean you, brother.

No way, I said. We stayed to watch the pandemonium. It didn't take long. First up, a brother from Boston in opposition:

This resolution elevates a minor contradiction, splitting the working class just when we need maximum unity. . . .

A few catcalls rang out, but the women on stage, purposeful and patient, fought to keep order:

Let the brother speak. Let's have an open discussion of the issue.

But when a brother from Texas, speaking in support, described the sisters in Austin as great typists and office workers, and greater in bed than the unliberated women, all hell broke loose, and the women on the stage let go the reins.

We stumbled from the hot hall into the cooling night air and breathed it all in. What does it mean? Tre said, rolling his eyes upward and imploring heaven with his hands. Where have we gone wrong? We lit a joint.

I'd never given it much thought until then, but if asked, I'd have said that women were equal to men. Actually I'd probably have said that chicks are better than guys in every way, and they should be in charge. Most of my friends were women. The smartest people I knew—women. The hardest-working—same. The most fun, the greatest-looking, the best-smelling—all women. Still, in every relationship I had with every woman, the question of when or whether we would sleep together lurked barely beneath the surface of my mind—I never felt I knew her unless we at least opened the possibility, and I always wanted to open the possibility early. Best of all, we would just give in, make love at least once, and sort it all out afterward.

Free love, Ruthie Stein said to me then, her voice filled with skepticism, it isn't free at all you know. It costs plenty, but only women pay the freight.

What do you mean? I said, surprised.

I mean there's nothing equal between men and women. Nothing.

She said that she was beginning to see that free love only meant that movement men could screw any woman they could get, free of emotional encumbrances, and that there was a lot of emotional dishonesty involved, a lot of distance and desertion and sexual exploitation. She defended her own choice to sleep around, to be a sexual pioneer, she said, but there was always the problem of inequality and the problem of power.

Look, she went on, I love Diana and I love you, but nothing in your relationship is equal. You're the one who speaks all over the place, who travels, who makes the decisions. You're the one who's the director at the school. You still have all the power.

I didn't see it, but when I raised it later with Diana, she enthusiastically agreed with Ruthie.

In its glory days, the adjoining house, with its pointy attic and big porch smiling across its front, had been a stately structure spread atop a little knoll. The shed, our new home to the side, had functioned as servants' quarters and storage. Neither building had withstood the march of civilization. Our small house needed a little of everything, mainly hope. From the oak tree near the front, we leaned severely leftward. The windows were sagging peepers, the door a toothless mouth. The roof, tar and tile, looked as if it might slip off in a breeze.

Tre had found the house, cleaned it out, and tacked burlap on its papery walls. Besides working in the school, Tre was beginning to promote local bands, and his business was run out of an old file cabinet in his bedroom. Everything about the house was teeny: wee windows, a six-foot clearance on the doors, a skinny kitchen dominated by a noisy space heater. Diana squeezed in a double bed, a long desk, a big woven Guatemalan blanket, and stacks of books. She hung a larger-than-life Malcolm X above the desk with the caption: He was ready. Are you? And above our bed, a laughing Che Guevara: At the risk of sounding ridiculous I must tell you that all true revolutionaries are motivated by feelings of love.

Ruthie Stein was a regular visitor, and one of her large paintings dominated the living room. Diana's art of simplicity filled the space: fruit crates for tables, wooden bowls and spoons, big clay dishes and cups. She wore heavy sweaters and boots in the winter, simple lightweight shirts and sandals in the summer. She always carried her raggedy, brilliantly colored woven bag from Chichicastenango.

The movement swept us away completely because it demanded everything of us, and because it offered everything to us—high purpose, real work to do, love, dreams, hope. It told us to be ourselves, and it invited us to reach. It required harmony between thought and action, words and deeds. It said the personal is political; don't let your life make a mockery of your values; wherever injustice raises its head, resist; the revolution is your permanent vocation.

Our agenda was large enough to fill many lifetimes—we wanted to teach the children, feed the hungry, shelter the homeless, fight the power, and end the war. We saw our country as a marauding monster, galloping along leaving behind dead, inert things. We would stop it.

Did you know, Diana said to me one night, that Simone Weil proposed to parachute behind enemy lines in World War II in order to carry out sabotage? To Diana, Weil embodied sacrifice against the inhuman. And here I am, she went on, already behind enemy lines.

We made tortillas from scratch on Sundays in our little sloping kitchen on Felch Street. A week's worth of homemade tomato sauce simmered hot and happy on the stove, a mountain of chopped onions and garlic sizzled in the skillet, fragrant black beans and saffron rice bubbled and seethed in big black pots and set the kitchen steaming. Tre had established the first Ann Arbor food cooperative, and soon huge heavy bags of rice, oats, and all kinds of beans filled our entryway. He was the quartermaster of the counterculture, and Felch Street was a center of a growing collection of oppositional institutions.

We imagined the Children's Community as a tiny tile in a huge mosaic, and ourselves as connected to the poor people's campaign, the civil rights struggle, the movements for peace and justice. We thought of ourselves as lovers and rebels. Our link, we crusading teachers, was to the young, embracing a dream.

14.

Your hair! Christina reeled from the door she'd just opened with a look that brought Edvard Munch vividly to mind. She didn't scream, however, but simply stood tilting away, mouth agape, eyes wide, holding her face in troubled hands. Your hair, she said again, and Diana smiled at her sister and stepped across the threshold, embracing her as her hands fell weakly to her sides.

Well, it's short, isn't it? she said.

Short? It's gone!

Diana kissed Christina softly on each cheek.

Not gone, Bunny, just short.

Dramatically, Christina said, as if hurling an expletive.

And that rhymes with radically. Diana laughed. Now they were both laughing, Christina in a kind of stunned disbelief, and an easy and familiar affection inched forward.

OK. Dramatically, radically, whatever. But your hair, your hair. It was so beautiful before.

You'll get used to it, Angel. And as for beauty . . . Diana laughed again. This is a freedom cut—hassle-free, carefree, convenient for street fighting. A kind of beauty all its own.

Diana had chopped her hair to a boyish length months earlier, and now it was shorter than mine—less raggedy and less disheveled, too—and adorable in a dramatic, radical way. Her attitude about such things was consistent with her habit of packing a toothbrush and Band-Aids everywhere she went—sensible but modest, self-reliant and responsible. Wearing jeans and a work shirt and wire-rimmed glasses she could pass for a particularly pretty boy, a free spirit, an experiment of nature.

We were in Washington, D.C., now for an antiwar demonstration and Christina was giving us her apartment with a view of the Potomac for a few days while she stayed with her boyfriend, the TV newsman Peter Jennings. It was perfect for us—a quasiclandestine base camp, comfortable and elegant but still entirely guilt-free.

Street-Fighting Chic, Christina teased. That could be the name of your boutique—"Special Sale: Denim shirts and shit-kicking boots. Hair chopped off dramatically free with any purchase." You'd be rich.

Great! Diana said. But you'll have to run it, because I don't have a capitalist bone left in my body.

Whenever we saw Christina over the next few days, Diana's lost hair was never far away. Over dinner she told Peter Jennings how beautiful Diana's hair had been, and they were into it again with heat.

It's such a nothing thing, Bunny, you should get over it.

It's not nothing.

Well, you're right. It means something. It means that like a lot of other women I want to be taken seriously for who I am, not because I look a certain way or wear certain pricey pretty things.

I'm taken seriously, Christina objected immediately. I have a brain and ambition and ability. And I'm taken damned seriously. But I can still appreciate looking good and dressing well. One doesn't cancel out the other.

It does though, Diana said. And you can't see it because you haven't rejected it. Cut your hair off one day, Angel, or just give up the beauty parlor, put on jeans and go to work and see what your brains and ability count for.

That's insane, Christina responded. You're saying I have to gross people out and then see how they like me?

I gross you out?

That's not the point. Christina was red, angry, and exasperated. You're acting so superior, like you're the only ones who have any ideas about what's right.

Peter Jennings was smiling in a pinched way. He and I had been happily quiet until now, but then Christina turned to me and added, You're both complete elitists. She meant Diana and me, and she was right, of course—we were unbearably arrogant.

Elitist? Here we were with no money, little income, living in a shack and subsisting on rice and beans and each other. In fact, the tenderloin steak I was working on—and putting on Peter's tab—was the first meat I'd had in over a year. We drove an ancient VW van and had one and a half changes of clothes between us, and right now we were cleverly sponging off the rich—Christina and her worldly boyfriend in this case, who were picking up dinner. Was she blind? Christina, I said piously. The rent on your apartment could pay our salaries combined for a year.

Well, I notice you weren't too good to stay there, she said.

Not at all, I thought. Diana smiled at her sister and looked wounded. We felt righteous and, yes, superior.

Peter and I are for peace, Christina said another time, and Diana challenged her.

You can't say I'm for peace and then not do anything. You have to summon something—strength, courage—and get out there.

You're always so strong, Christina said. I mean it. No one's as strong as you. No one could be.

That's too easy, Diana said. I'm doing what anyone who really knows the war, really sees it and feels it, would do. If you're saying, But I know I'm weak, well, then you know something, you know what your task is—you have to rise up against weakness.

Anyway, I interjected unhelpfully, I'm not so much against the war as I am for a Vietnamese victory. I'm not so much for peace as for a U.S. defeat. I mean, if a lion swallows a lamb and licks its lips, that's peace, right? I'm against that kind of peace.

Christina frowned at me and returned to Diana. It was a family thing.

The demonstration felt at times like a scene from *Ten Days That Shook the World*—tents and armed troops mustering on street

corners, floodlights cutting through tear gas, rumors of battles and
heated exchanges of strategy and tactics, thousands of demonstrators
scaling walls on rope ladders to assault the Pentagon. When we broke
through police lines, troops were redeployed, when we came from the
west, they concentrated in the east. Eventually we reached a stale-
mate—thousands of us had seized a large plaza at the Pentagon itself,
and troops with fixed bayonets held us flat, right there. We were nose
to nose all night.

We sang and chanted, feeling jubilant to have gotten this close. I
peed on the Pentagon. I burned my draft card a foot from the line of
troops, threw the ash on the ground and spit on it. No one moved
in to arrest me, and anyway I carried a duplicate card, a spare for
emergencies.

Diana took a different tack. She had a provocative sign that said,
GIRLS SAY YES TO GUYS WHO SAY NO. Her dream was to organize the
soldiers to refuse to fight, and eventually that dream came true. She
spent hours going down the line of troops, looking each in the eye,
telling him a bit about herself, and begging him to put down his gun.
Others did the same as officers walked behind their troops repeating,
Hold the line, Hold the line.

When in the middle of the night a roar erupted from a section of
the crowd a hundred yards away, and just as quickly a flying rumor
rumbled into our midst that two soldiers had dropped their weapons
and joined us, I thought the revolution was imminent.

People floated into the movement now for a thousand reasons:
resistance to the war and the draft, certainly, to the gathering torment, and in opposition as well to segregation and racism, the
lengthening American nightmare. People joined for love, too, because
liberation was in the air and the idea of freedom was in full flood,
breaking banks and borders, cascading into new channels and forks
and surprising possibilities as it rolled along. Everything was on the
agenda now: justice and peace, education and culture and spirituality,
work, sexuality, gender, art. The old gods failed and the old truths left
the world, and we asked: How shall I live? What is this thing called

living? I wanted to become a new man and to dance or to march—or both—with others toward a brighter future, an expanding sense of humanity.

The revolt felt both strange and natural, and we threw ourselves into it, more or less consciously, for something we dreamed might be better. We dragged along, each of us, the old and dominant ideas of our culture and our times, and yet something bright and new would surely come through love and resistance. The movement was creating history, I thought, and it was a heady place to live, suspended between worlds, everything possible, nothing guaranteed.

15.

*Memory is a marvel, quick as a monkey and just as silly. And it's all
we've got—we live by distorted memory rather than verifiable truth.
Memory is feeling, not fact, ghosts and fears that haunt us, floating
desires and falsifying dreams more powerful and more compelling than
hard reality will ever be.*

*I remember marches and protests, chants and songs turning into
shouts and screams, church basements and community meetings and
then secret cells.*

*"We Shall Overcome" and "Blowin' in the Wind" gave way to "Street
Fighting Man" and, come on baby, "Light My Fire." Bring the Troops
Home Now! became Bring the War Home! Love in our hearts lit fires in
the streets.*

*I remember civil disobedience, tear gas and dogs, billy clubs and shat-
tered bones, and then explosions of death.*

*I remember the poster of Malcolm X in our kitchen: By Any Means
Necessary! he instructed, and we took it in and chanted it lightly, fists
pumping, a message of escalating resistance as everything heated up
around us, but what we meant was that the consequences should be
harsh for the masters of war, the architects of death. We didn't know at
all what it would take until it began to take a piece of us, and then we
had a small sharp glimmer of what could come, but no memory, and
soon it was too late.*

Nineteen sixty-eight began with staccato bursts and gunfire from all sides, the rat-tat-tat of everyday events tattooing the air. I was twenty-three. It was the year of wonder and miracle.

In January, Benjamin Spock, baby doctor to our generation, was arrested and charged with federal conspiracy to help young men resist the draft.

Khe Sanh, once a modest American military observation outpost in the central highlands of Viet Nam, was beefed up with thousands of GIs, and U.S. airpower soon turned the area into the most heavily bombed target in the history of warfare.

On January 30, the Tet Offensive exploded across South Viet Nam, punctuated by uprisings in thirty-six provincial capitals including Hue. In Sai Gon, U.S. forces battled to retake their own embassy, briefly under Viet Cong control. I was riveted to our little black and white television as CIA operatives in business suits crouched behind walls, rose and fired machine guns—rat-tat-tat—into their own windows, and then ducked back down again. I thought, this is here, this is now.

When South Viet Nam's wiry chief of national police, Nguyen Ngoc Loan, bareheaded, strode purposefully up to a skinny unnamed boy of maybe twenty—torn shirt, hands cuffed behind his back, face misshapen from a recent smacking around in interrogation—and without a word or a pause raised his sinewy arm and popped a round from a silver pistol into the boy's temple, even those of us with no illusions gasped. The whole thing was captured on throbbing newsreel tape—the young man pulling his face away, eyes forced shut, like holding his breath before going off the high dive, falling to the street as a steady stream of blood pulsed rhythmically from a neat hole onto the pavement, and—BAM!—into every TV in America.

In March, a presidential commission announced in a long-awaited report concerning last year's urban uprisings—including the deadly flare-up I'd lived through in Cleveland—that "Our nation is moving toward two societies, one Black and one white, separate and unequal." Moving toward? I thought, remembering the fire and the fury. Where have they been?

In Orangeburg, South Carolina, police fired on student protesters whose demonstrations had grown in anger and intensity. Thirty-four Black students were injured, and five were murdered.

On the Ides of March, American casualties surpassed those of the Korean War. Keeping with the cynical fiction, Vietnamese casualties were always reported meticulously in a daily body count and these were always in the zillions; U.S. casualties were always vaguely "light" or "moderate" and we would soon win the war. There was an official and oft-repeated light at the end of the tunnel.

Senator Eugene McCarthy launched a "Children's Crusade" against LBJ and nearly won the New Hampshire primary. Robert Kennedy quickly entered the presidential race then, and although we didn't know it yet, on the day he announced his candidacy, U.S. troops rampaged through the hamlet of My Lai, slaughtering women and children and throwing their bodies into a ditch, later reporting to headquarters that they had killed 128 Viet Cong troops. Those 128 were added to the official body count. Rat-tat-tat.

And then without warning, LBJ went on live national television to announce that he was suspending the bombing of North Viet Nam and added, seemingly out of nowhere: "I shall not seek, and will not accept, the nomination of my party for another term as your president. . . ." I almost fell over. I didn't know how to feel. Relieved? Victorious? Cynical? Vindicated? Happy?

I thought of LBJ just four years before, running for president and painting the Republican candidate Barry Goldwater as the loose cannon not to be trusted with his itchy finger on the big bomb—Goldwater's answer to the persistent charge of right-wing nuttiness had been that extremism in defense of liberty is no vice—and promising that we were not about to send American boys ten thousand miles away to do what Asian boys ought to be doing for themselves. I'd rallied for Johnson, marched in his campaign, and two years later was leading the chants: Hey, hey LBJ, how many kids did you kill today? It drove him nuts and maybe now it even drove him from office. He looked sad and spent that night, but I felt not an ounce of sympathy.

A spontaneous celebration broke out, then, and people poured from their houses to dance in the streets and sing at the tops of their voices "I Believe the War Is Over." There was a sense of unreality, none of us quite believing we'd at last reached the end. It was the eve of April Fool's Day, anyway, and Ron St. Ron said it was more than likely just a big joke. But for this night I wanted nothing more than to revel and rejoice.

We weren't happy long.

On April 4 on a motel balcony in Memphis, as his body slumped and a crowd of comrades rushed to his side, looking up and toward the path of that fateful bullet, pointing in desperation and disbelief, Martin Luther King Jr. was assassinated, that certain dream once again deferred.

Dark smoke smudged American skylines as 125 cities exploded simultaneously in response. Fifty-five thousand troops were called out to quell the riots, and by week's end twenty thousand people had been arrested, forty-six killed. Mayor Daley, quivering and stumbling with rage, famously ordered Chicago cops to shoot to kill all arsonists, to shoot to maim all looters. To me the rising smoke indicted the country, and the spontaneous rebellions were a small part of the dues for broken promises and dashed dreams.

At Columbia University students were agitated by the trustees' plan to build a new gym in Harlem—a massive temple to jocks where only the golden youth of the Ivy League would splash in privileged splendor in their Olympic-size pool—and then incensed when they unearthed clear and graphic evidence that their citadel of freedom and intellectual inquiry had become a whore to war with lucrative research contracts flowing from the ivyed walls straight to the Pentagon. Buildings were seized, and it took a thousand New York City cops to clear the campus. One hundred and twenty charges of police brutality were filed.

The whole world was spinning wildly now, and the escalating upheaval sent an urgent jolt of energy through me. In Paris, 367 were injured in rioting as a worker-student strike toppled the government, while in Czechoslovakia Soviet troops overran the country, ending the nonviolent resistance of "Prague Spring." University protests were huge, police responses violent in Bonn and Frankfurt, Rome and Zagreb, Tokyo and Turin.

Mexico City convulsed as police and army troops fired on student demonstrators on the eve of the Olympic Games—ten thousand rallied in Tlateloco Square, and five hundred were killed. The Mexican government admitted to thirty-two. U.S. athletes set world records in the long jump, the 100, 200, and 400 meters, and the 4 × 400 relays, but on the victory stand Tommie Smith and John Carlos bowed their heads and raised their fists in a Black Power salute as the national war anthem groaned over the stadium. The U.S. Olympic Committee stripped them of their medals and sent them home. When Tommie Smith spoke in Oakland he looked triumphant, not disgraced, and the crowd serenaded him with freedom songs. It would be a glorious day indeed when "We Shall Overcome" replaced "The Star-Spangled Banner,"
and I thought it likely it would happen in a year or two, three at the outside.

In Atlantic City, Ruthie Stein and a small group of other feminists burned bras to protest the Miss America pageant. Women are not meat, they chanted.

Robert Kennedy was shot in L.A., and I watched the image on TV over and over, the repeating chaos stretching for days and weeks. Robert Kennedy dying again and again, just like his brother.

When JFK was killed, Malcolm X said it was a case of the chickens coming home to roost, the mighty U.S. so vehement to have its way everywhere, exporting murder and assassination, scorching the earth and then forced to face itself.

Everything seemed urgent now, everything was accelerating—the pace, to be sure, but also the stakes, the sense of consequences. Madmen were at the controls, several compartments were already in flames, and our future existence hung in the balance. It fell to us— and we were just kids—to save the world. Don't trust anyone over thirty, we said to one another in solidarity and in warning, the slogan of a conspiracy so deep and so wide that no one outside of it could quite imagine its furthest dimension. Stay young. Stay beautiful. Youth will make the revolution. But ours was becoming an exacting idealism, and I hurled myself forward, racing toward the edges, stumbling over things trying just to keep step.

Day to day the air itself glowed and shimmered, intoxicated me, seared my lungs, crackled, exploded, and made me high. I'd been beaten and hurt and arrested and jailed. Undeterred I became euphoric, feeling every day blessed to be alive and aware at this most excellent moment. I was on a freedom high, and all I needed to feed my habit was one more hit of the action. I couldn't remember a world without war or a day without resistance. The war and the idea of freedom defined me, propelled me out of bed every morning, powered my hopes and my fears, troubled my sleep, and, for better and for worse, consumed me. I would, I was sure, be a casualty or a hero of war, or both.

I felt myself hanging on a hinge in history, suspended in midair, one hand gripping familiar ground—our intimate existence, our awakening into a moving world, our growing awareness of the corruption and evil woven into the fabric of our favored little nests—the other hand stretching toward a distant highland barely visible through the cottony clouds. We were, all of us, on a hinge: utopian dreams and wild visions beckoned from the distant shore, and yet, as everyone but us seemed to know, hinges swing both ways.

"Where have you gone, Joe DiMaggio?" sang Simon and Garfunkel, the nation turning lonely eyes to him. There were no American heroes left for us, even as *Apollo 8* circled the moon. We were bent on revolution right here on earth, right here in America.

Ho Chi Minh, Viet Nam's venerable and legendary leader, once a battle-hardened jungle fighter and guerrilla commander, now the first president of his nation, issued a New Year's greeting to the antiwar movement. I send you, my friends, my best wishes for the New Year 1968, he wrote. No Vietnamese has ever come to make trouble in the United States, he continued. Yet, half a million troops have been sent to South Viet Nam who are daily massacring Vietnamese people and burning and demolishing Vietnamese towns and villages. In North Viet Nam, thousands of U.S. planes have dropped over 800,000 pounds of bombs, destroying schools, churches, hospitals, dikes, and densely populated areas. The U.S. government has caused hundreds of thousands of U.S. youths to die or be wounded in vain on Viet Nam battlefields. Each year the U.S. government spends tens of billions of dollars, the fruit of the American people's sweat and toils, to wage war on Viet Nam. Friends, he said, in struggling hard to make the U.S. government stop its aggression in Viet Nam, you are defending justice and, at the same time, you are giving us support. We shall win, Ho concluded, and so will you. Thank you for your support of the Vietnamese people.

I loved that New Year's letter.

With his wizened face and reed-thin body, his laughing eyes and wispy whiskers, he was Uncle Ho in Viet Nam, and he had become like an adopted grandfather to me—I thought of him as saintly but very tough. Ho had said in *The Saturday Evening Post* in 1962, "I think the Americans greatly underestimate the determination of the Vietnamese people"—and in his humble, understated way, he summed the whole thing up. Ho Chi Minh was warrior and sage, fighter and poet—the loving activist, the human face of resistance. I knew several of his prison poems by heart.

> *Neither high nor very far,*
> *Neither emperor nor king,*
> *You are only a little milestone,*
> *Which stands at the edge of the highway.*
> *To people passing by*
> *You point the right direction,*
> *And stop them from getting lost.*
> *You tell them of the distance*
> *For which they still must journey.*
> *Your service is not a small one*
> *And people will always remember you.*

The milestone, to me, was Viet Nam itself. I copied out that poem and carried it around in my front pocket for years.

By 1968 I had taught in the Children's Community for three years, participated in training a first generation of Head Start teachers, helped to organize a community union in a poor neighborhood, and picketed, marched, mobilized, knocked on thousands of doors peddling the notion of freedom and the possibility of peace. I'd been arrested a dozen times, and knew how to fight in the streets with my head up, bobbing and weaving. Disorderly conduct, resisting arrest, simple assault, mob action—the charges became predictable along with the consequences: time served, charges dismissed, $200 fine, whatever. A couple of times smart and dedicated lawyers tried to get a judge to consider the war as a context that justified a nonviolent direct act of civil disobedience. The response was always the same: This is not a case about the government, the president, foreign policy, whatever; this is a case of trespassing, destroying property, disorderly conduct, and the like. Sometimes I got hurt—I sprained an ankle leaping a wall and was immediately set upon by two pursuing cops, cut my arm smashing a window and went to the emergency room, burned my left hand and broke my right ring finger rescuing a flaming Viet Cong flag from some counterdemonstrating frat boy during a swirling onslaught near the Vietnamese Embassy in Washington. My consolation was that my ring finger broke on his nose, which also broke.

I'd had a whole range of jobs by then, from short-order cook to air conditioner installer, been to the hospital six times, and gotten two tattoos. My particular inner longing came alive, linked to a huge outer quest, my youthful and personal vibrations aligned in some magical way with magnificent social shocks and eruptions. I was filled with energy, intensity, and engagement. And still nothing prepared me for what was coming.

All spring and summer the impending demonstrations in Chicago grew in significance, the Democratic National Convention looming before us finally as the great white whale we imagined we had to harpoon, even if, in that desperate act, we were ourselves dragged under and drowned. School was out and Diana and I worked full-time that summer organizing against the war and mobilizing for the Chicago action. We were mariners on a collision course with destiny.

Mayor Richard Daley played a perfect Moby Dick for us—white and fleshy, he reeked with the stench of evil. After King was assassinated and Daley's cops buckled before the ensuing fury, he had called out the National Guard and troops and tanks rolled down Madison Avenue, up Austin Boulevard. Daley issued his famous "shoot to kill/shoot to maim" orders then. Thousands of people were rounded up wholesale and, it turned out later, illegally jailed. Mayor Daley had said repeatedly that "there are no ghettos in Chicago" even as compounds that looked like detention camps were steadily erected in Black neighborhoods and the lakefront was sacrificed to the highrise rich. All through the summer Daley urged demonstrators to stay home, intimating the possibility of blood in the streets. In my favorite Daley malapropism he had proclaimed indignantly to a group of delighted scribes, "The police are not here to create disorder, the police are here to preserve disorder." No kidding. We girded our loins and sharpened our spears, preparing for the monster.

Our Captain Ahab was Tom Hayden, former president of SDS, now leader of the National Mobilization to End the War, the coalition leading the convention protest. Tom was using the Mobe to build a militant confrontation under the broadest, most responsible, and well-resourced banner he could get; the Mobe was using Tom to gain credibility with youth and with the civil rights movement. Each had something at stake as they stepped willingly forward in awkward embrace. It wasn't a marriage, after all, only a quick affair, shacking up for the summer, risky but hot.

When Tom came to Ann Arbor in July we organized a rally where he spoke about the war, the international situation, and our responsibility to be in Chicago at this precise time. Tom was a brilliant speaker—articulate, charismatic, knowledgeable, and often understated but with eyes ablaze. He said that this year would be remembered as a turning point in world history, and that our choices now would have implications for the lives of people everywhere for generations to come. You simply must come to Chicago, he concluded, to participate or to witness. This is the moment when we can stand up unequivocally for peace and justice, this is the place where we can end the madness and bring the monster down.

His last words could of course be taken many different ways. Seen through one lens, the madness was the war in Viet Nam, and the monster was the politics and policy of that war. Through another, the madness was an aggressive and acquisitive foreign policy, and the monster the military-industrial complex. And through a third lens, our lens, the madness was the export of war and fascism into the third world, racism and white supremacy at home, the inert, impoverished culture of greed and alienation: The monster would be capitalism itself, the system of imperialism. Perhaps Tom chose his words carefully, and he hoped to capture, enlist, and embolden any impulse toward resistance.

After the rally a group gathered at our house to further consider strategy and tactics. Tom had asked me to collect a few experienced and trustworthy militants—people like Tre, Ruthie, and Diana who were veterans of the struggle, people willing to up the stakes and pay the price for resistance—and he got right to the point: Chicago will be many things simultaneously, he said. Large marches, street theater, a cultural festival—and everything matters, each piece plays a part. His voice took on an edge, somewhere between fanatical and giddy, as he described bold plans and playful pranks. But you folks—veterans of the movement and the streets—have a pivotal role to play in all of this, he continued, the color in his face deepening, his eyes once again blazing. He looked intently from person to person. He was the same articulate and thoughtful speaker as before, but these were words for only a few. This demonstration has the potential like nothing we've done before to expose the face of the enemy, to strip him naked, to force him to reveal himself as violent, brutal, totalitarian, and evil. It will be difficult—and dangerous—taunting the monster, stabbing him in his most exposed and vulnerable places, but it's got to be done. He paused. And you're the ones to do it.

Tom envisioned the convention meeting behind barbed wire, encircled by troops, besieged on all sides by a massive storm of out-raged citizens. He imagined conflict and contradiction erupting with-in enemy ranks as they were forced to overreach in their zeal for order. Finally, he thought we might provoke the convention to implode, to collapse in upon itself while the whole spectacle—the vision of a dying social order—was recorded and beamed out to a waiting world. We can reduce this demon to a pitiful, helpless giant, Tom said. And then we can move to finish him off. I imagined Tom repeating this scene at every port of call.

Late into the night we shared plans and talked tactics. We would divide into affinity groups, small cells operating for a specific area of operation semiautonomously, each responsible as well for the fighting spirit and safety of its own. My affinity group included Diana, of course, Ruthie Stein, and Tre. But we recruited others: David, tall, bearded, slightly stooped, the oldest at twenty-eight, a Ph.D. in poli-tical philosophy, holding a post-doc at the university and completing a small book based on his thick dissertation; Andy, a college dropout at nineteen, a karate master, founder of a guerrilla theater group—the Women's International Terrorist Conspiracy from Hell (WITCH)—and veteran of a dozen arrests and violent confrontations at the University of Texas; and Daniel, a part-time auto mechanic and Andy's longtime lover, dishwater-blond hair curling down the length of his back, a pouch of the best weed always happily secured in his vest pocket. Dan and Andy were inseparable, and over time were known to all by a single name: Dandy. In early August, Terry Robbins from Cleveland joined our affinity group. Let's go kick some ass, he hollered, and on to Chicago. We were ready.

The war, which should have been slowing down by now, seemed only to spin further out of control, following its own deadly logic.

The Americans in Viet Nam called the rural areas "Indian

Country," an incomprehensible and inhuman place of hostility and barbarity, and wherever they went they scattered pigs and chickens, burned homes, knocked down fences and walls, drove people from hiding places and killed them, like the Indian wars of old. The military command designated whole areas free-fire zones, enemy strongholds where non-VC residents had been urged by leaflet to flee. Everyone who stayed was then considered the enemy. The most infamous was "Pinkville" to the military, Son My to the Vietnamese, My Lai forever in history. Americans had had a terrible time in the area, sustained many losses, been beaten up again and again. In March 1968, a search-and-destroy mission entered the village, throwing hand grenades into homes, burning them to the ground, and then rounded up women and children in groups and murdered them. Five hundred and sixty-seven Vietnamese died that day in that one village. "There weren't any friendlies in the village," an officer said by way of explanation. "What's a civilian?" asked another.

By 1967 every military target in North Viet Nam had been damaged or destroyed—look it up—and still resistance was high, the morale of the Vietnamese people unshaken. The only tactics left were to flatten Ha Noi, to destroy the dike system, or to drop nuclear bombs. As one Vietnamese official said to an American journalist at the time, If your government would like to try those last tactics, well, then, go ahead. And when you are done, then we will win. No one on the U.S. side understood that kind of resolve.

Every afternoon the press was officially briefed in Sai Gon in what came to be known as the "5 O'Clock Follies," a mishmash of hypocrisy, half-truths, and outright lies. Since Viet Nam was a war of attrition—there were no battle lines, no decisive areas to conquer and hold—the measure of success became the body counts carefully enumerated by army bureaucrats at the end of each day. Little specks on the deck, cloth and flesh, colorless. It became too much.

We'll bomb them into the Stone Age, an unhinged American politician had intoned, echoing a gung-ho, shoot-from-the-hip general, head of the Joint Chiefs of Staff, actually, each describing an

American policy rarely spoken so plainly. Boom. Boom. Boom. Poor Viet Nam.

Almost four times the destructive power unleashed by the U.S. in all of World War II was falling on this ancient land the size of Florida snaking its way down the southeast edge of Asia. How could we understand it? How could we take it in? Most important, what should we do about it? Bombs away.

There is a certain eloquence to bombs, a poetry and a pattern from a safe distance. The rhythm of B-52s dropping bombs over Viet Nam, a deceptive calm at 40,000 feet as the doors ease open and millennial eggs are delivered on the green canopy below, the relentless thud of indiscriminate destruction and death without pause on the ground. Nothing subtle or syncopated. Not a happy rhythm.

Three million Vietnamese lives were extinguished. Dig up Florida and throw it into the ocean. Annihilate Chicago or London or Bonn. Three million—each with a mother and a father, a distinct name, a mind and a body and a spirit, someone who knew him well or cared for her or counted on her for something or was annoyed or burdened or irritated by him; each knew something of joy or sadness or beauty or pain. Each was ripped out of this world, a little red dampness staining the earth, drying up, fading, and gone. Bodies torn apart, blown away, smudged out, lost forever. Their names obliterated.

Each now seemed to me a personal responsibility, America's gory and extravagant legacy. We might try to learn those names, if we had the courage, and to speak them each morning as we awoke and each evening before bed. And those most responsible, the reckless who brought this all about and who lived in privileged pleasure, free from violence or want or need or sanction of any kind, should spend, I felt, every moment of the rest of their lives reciting the names of those they killed, the names of human beings butchered for this pathetic adventure. Or, Tre suggested, they should crawl on all fours the length of Viet Nam, going home to home with their apologies. Henry Kissinger, Robert McNamara, McGeorge and William Bundy, Dean Rusk, William Westmoreland. Bombs away.

A certain twisted American genius was embodied in its bombs. There were in Viet Nam, for example, "clean bombs" that sucked the oxygen out of a huge area, killing everyone in reach but leaving the physical infrastructure neat and intact and usable for the onrushing conquerors. Clean. There were "seismic bombs" that weighed 15,000 pounds and shook the earth violently for several minutes within a five-mile radius, knocking things down, a man-made earthquake. Not clean, but seismic. There was a whole new lexicon to learn: cluster bombs, fragmentation bombs, carpet bombs, napalm bombs, phosphorous bombs with their delicate spidery fingers stretching in all directions. And then there were the gaudy results—forests burned and blackened; ancient dikes toppled, floods cascading across the land as far as the eye can see; the body of a slim peasant boy, his torso pocked with tiny razor cuts from knees to shoulders, a thousand little rivulets of blood sucking his life out of him; the eleven-year-old girl running naked down the road, jellied gasoline clinging to her, incinerating her back. We stared into the chamber of death, the theater of extinction, and we refused to turn away.

We were appalled that—at this late date—anyone could claim innocence, but, incredibly, many did. We would wake them up. One day we passed out thousands of leaflets advertising a demonstration on the Diag in which we would burn a dog to death with napalm in protest of the war. When hundreds of students showed up to stop us, we had no dog and no napalm, only another leaflet, this one with pictures of charred and injured Vietnamese, and a headline that announced: The Opposite of Moral Is Indifferent.

Bomb them into the Stone Age, Terry repeated quietly to himself, folding the newspaper and laying it aside, a thin, bitter smile sneaking up on his face. It really is their policy, those bastards, he said more loudly, fixing his gaze dramatically first on me, then on Diana, the three of us huddled over coffee at the kitchen table. Bomb them into the Stone Age, he practically shouted, his voice betraying a hint of glee. He took a gulp, shifted his body slightly toward me.

Why not? We're taking slingshots to Chicago and they've got guns and bayonets? Are we nuts? Where are our guns and bayonets?

I looked at him, amused and a little awed. Terry was part actor, part clown, our wordsmith and intellectual and sometimes single-minded narcissist. He was a lonely, charming, driven, trembling mass of contradictions. Who wasn't? Sure Terry's a son of a bitch, I'd said more than once, but he's our son of a bitch. And I loved him.

Why not? The question hung for a moment more. That should be our policy as well—bomb them into the Stone Age. He was smiling now, amused with himself, with his outrageousness, his singular audacity, and the symmetry of his brainstorm. He felt himself an angry young poet of the revolution, and his wild mind had hit an imaginative high—we would give back to them exactly what they had offered to the world. Perfect. If the Stone Age in Ha Noi, then the Stone Age in Washington; whither goeth Viet Nam, there goeth America. Even though it was only a little metaphor, Terry felt himself a cat triumphant, and he showed sharp little teeth.

Diana, six years his senior, offered a patronizing smile. Well, no, she said, baiting him a bit. That's a dreadful idea.

How can you say that, he howled, wounded. It's brilliant.

You're brilliant, of course you are. But you're being silly. We don't even know how to use guns, there would be no chance in a battle of bombs.

Exactly! Terry was crowing again, happy to be brilliant. Exactly! But these are brutish times, and we'd better learn, and fast. Bombs away.

Well, then, she pressed on, how many innocents killed or hurt would be acceptable?

That question, too, hung like a murky cloud.

I'm not sure, he said. Then, after a long pause, But I think there's got to be a place in this revolution for a man of principled violence.

You know you can catch the very disease you're fighting, Terry—you want to stop war, you become warlike. You want to fight inhumanity, and you become inhumane. It's contagion through combat, and then what's the point?

As I write this late on a hot July night, I see a deranged young man—half naked with a large black plastic bag slung across one shoulder—rushing down Broadway with a purposeful look on his face shouting about his appointments, his schedule, and his responsibilities. The street is piled high with garbage, and he stops at every promising mound to tear through it in search of something to be carried off. He seems a perfect metaphor for me.

16.

When the Democratic Party convened in Chicago to nominate a candidate to oppose Richard Nixon and succeed LBJ, two Americas faced each other across a smoldering field. The exuberant, turbulent uproar that shook the city, we hoped, would send shock waves across the land and into the distant world.

The theater that became Chicago, 1968, played on a thousand stages, each filled with its own drama, its own feeling, action, and life. Together, from the thousand stages, came a joyful noise, a thunderous hubbub arching toward the heavens, the riotous clamor of hope unleashed. Or, at least that's how it felt to me.

We arrived on the evening of the large rally in Lincoln Park, settled our belongings into the church basement which would be our home for a week, and hurried to the park. From the hill overlooking the great lawn it was as if two armies had mobilized: above, a disciplined force in blue helmets and straight lines, a massive, efficient, technological thing, armed to the teeth with steel and gas. Below, in brightly colored tents and lean-tos, sharing food and drink, semi-naked and longhaired, with clouds of marijuana smoke and strains of protest songs rising from their midst, were the rebel troops, armed merrily with their imaginations. I lingered, looking down into the swarm of people, each one distinct and flickering, dull or bright, sparkling or smooth, but together a raging blaze. I watched calmly for a moment, quietly from above, before the inevitable plunge.

Mayor Daley, pale-faced and blubbery, had decided on preemptive strikes, a strategy of disruption at every turn, seizing the initiative and hoping to disorganize and demoralize the demonstraters, setting them on the defensive. Daley would run us out of town before we could reach the Amphitheater, before we could nominate Pigasus the Pig for president and release him, greased and squealing, into the Loop, or drop acid into the water supply, or mobilize ourselves. Of course, sowing disorder in the jumble of Lincoln Park that day was child's play—our banner was chaos, our operating assumption anarchy. Had they left us entirely alone, we would have been disorderly and a bit unglued dancing in the demonstrations to a hundred different drummers. But they imagined us more organized and threatening than we ever were, and for once our imaginations were eye-to-eye, running on a parallel track, for we wanted desperately to believe the account of the enemy's paranoid wing—the vast conspiracy, the actual threat, the government on the brink of being overthrown. Who knows? It matched our highest hopes, our deepest dreams, but were we ever, even for a moment, as tight and directed and threatening as all that? Oddly, their extreme metaphors and the violent police assaults through the park combined to bring us intensely together in the field and forge a fierce fighting identity that dissolved within days, but for one week rose ominously as a formidable and terrible thing.

The police, like angry cattle, their nostrils flaring, stampeded through the clouds of tear gas into Lincoln Park that night, swinging nightsticks with wild abandon, cracking heads—BAM! BAM!—leaving people bleeding in the grass, or grabbing those who resisted, piling them like logs into paddy wagons. We smeared on the Vaseline and answered with rocks and bottles, obscenities and chants. People were driven from the park into the streets of Old Town, coughing and running, while some of us regrouped to fight back. Terry grabbed a gas canister tumbling along the pavement and hurled it back toward the advancing line of blue. Dan and Andy—Dandy—hand-in-hand, danced near the cops hurling rocks and invectives, and then retreated into the crowd. I fired twelve or fifteen rounds from my slingshot—I saw one marble hit a cop in the arm, another strike the hood of a squad car and bounce away wildly—before I broke and ran with the others.

Even though we'd been routed, everyone felt triumphant. We had fought like madmen and been beaten down, but we had also upped the stakes, we thought. We exhaled energy, and next day the jubilee in the park became more extensive and more festive. Someone built a bonfire and people sang and danced, smoked weed and made love not war. Workshops sprang up everywhere: Non-Violent Direct Action, Revolutionary Parenting, Guerrilla Theater, Love-Making Possibilities from the Kama Sutra, Recipes from the Anarchists' Cookbook. On a long open-air table were all the books and pamphlets you'd ever want to read: *The Crime of Obedience, The Immorality of Marriage, Free Land/Free Love, Poetry for the People, Proceedings from the War Crimes Tribunal.* A large sign proclaimed, TAKE WHAT YOU WANT, LEAVE WHAT YOU CAN.

Some people practiced a disciplined form of dance-march with locked arms designed to break police lines, imported, it was said, from Tokyo, while others baked bread and cooked brown rice in twenty-gallon pots to distribute to the crowd. A speaker harangued a rapt crowd on the theme of free love, and I thought, of course, how could love not be free? I was as high as I'd ever been, excited by the festival behind the barricades. Here there was free food and free love, no cops and no capitalism, sanitary squads and itinerant teachers, open doors and infinite possibilities. People acted in ways that seemed suddenly so natural and so easy—with audacity and spontaneity and self-sacrifice, with energy and experimentation and joy, camaraderie and fellow feeling. Perhaps we could always be this way. Perhaps the shambles of the park was in fact the birthplace of a brighter world, the beginnings of the new man and the new woman we longed to be, guided by nothing but boundless love. Why not? In wreckage and celebration I felt, again, reborn.

We pushed the limits, changed the norms. And, as always, there was a buzz in the background: You're hurting your own cause. I agree with your goals, but not your tactics. Of course you're right, but the rest of the world isn't ready yet. You'd be more effective if you slowed down. It's all a problem of communication, really. On and on and on, I'd heard it all before.

When I dated a Black girl in college, my roommate said it was OK with him but the world would never accept it. When I burned my draft card, Dad agreed with my goals but not my tactics. When I was arrested at the draft board, many of my closest friends admired my courage but told me it was hurting the antiwar cause. They blended together now as one big disingenuous whine.

It was a time of transgression, and I was of a generation guided by the precept, Break as many rules as you can. The system was death; defiance and insubordination was life itself. Go further, we said. Shock, offend, outrage, overstep, disturb. Know no limits. Lose control. Events cascaded on, new limits replaced old ones, standards were reassessed.

When the cops waded through the park the next time, they were led by a line of squad cars, and motorcycles covered their flanks. The fight back was strictly strike and retreat, ranging over a wide field, hand to hand, for almost an hour. Tre circled around one side, moving fast, and surprised a slow-moving motorcyclist from the blind side, sending the cop sprawling to the ground, his machine gyrating to a short but dizzy crash a few feet beyond. Half a dozen policemen pounced on Tre at once, whaling away as he covered his face and head as well as he could. We ran toward him, but too late; we were beaten back as he was hauled off, bloody and subdued. Eventually, we were overwhelmed, and the air became thick with smoke and rage.

Perhaps this is when rage got started in the movement, this very night. I'm not sure, but before this, every meeting, every rally, every demonstration was filled with singing, and afterward the singing stopped. When we opened our mouths now, we could only scream. Idealism was there, but in abeyance. The apocalypse approached.

Like the seekers skipping hopefully along the yellow brick road toward Oz, our little accidental affinity group had longed mostly for the basics: a heart, a brain, the nerve, and ultimately, a home. We also wanted weed, free love, and rock 'n' roll. We were confronted with all kinds of obstacles, plagued by witches and flying monkeys, but still we skipped hopefully on, twisting and turning.

We wanted to bear witness, to put our bodies on the gears of the death machine, to stop a war and bring justice home. We wanted to intensify the action whenever possible. We would each wear a red headband and carry a small backpack with Vaseline and gloves and goggles to protect us from the anticipated tear gas, a first-aid kit, a hammer to break windows, marbles to scatter in front of any potential police cavalry charge, a bottle of water, and a sling-shot or homemade blackjack fashioned out of a length of hose with a four-ounce sinker jammed into one end and trussed up in electrical tape, strictly for self-protection. I also had an ample supply of cherry bombs and a lighter just in case they could be useful. We weren't in Kansas anymore.

Ruthie Stein called in bogus bomb threats to the Days Inn where the Michigan delegation was eating its liver. At night she and Diana dressed up in high heels and makeup. You look just like a convention hooker, I told Ruthie, and she scowled at me and toned down the lipstick—and walked right through the Hilton security. They wrote *STOP WAR* in lipstick on the elevator mirrors, and near the penthouse Diana scrawled *MURDERER*.

The Yippies were in Chicago, uniting the cultural forces of the movement under the banner of dope and a militant good time. They preferred the tactics of people's theater, making a mess, pointing to the farce. They nominated Pigasus the Pig for president with the campaign slogans: "Let's have an honest-to-god pig in the White House," and "Today's pig is tomorrow's bacon." At the press conference downtown Pigasus squealed and shit on the podium. The cops didn't get the joke and quickly hauled the nominating group off to jail. Pigasus was put into protective custody after the cops pursued her running greased through the Loop.

Many older radicals and peace-marchers came with the Mobilization for Peace. A civil rights caravan paraded majestically in mule-drawn wagons down Michigan Avenue. We carried the flag of the National Liberation Front wearing durable but loose-fitting clothes, knapsacks, and our red headbands. We argued that to be opposed to the U.S. and also opposed to the NLF means you want everyone to lose—only one side invaded, and only one side is fighting for their land, we said.

We pasted big newspapers on walls all over town filled with up-to-the-minute information about the demonstrations, about meetings, rallies, news about movement centers, and news about the cheap fix going down inside the convention hall. The *Street Wall Journal*, published in the typeface of the *Wall Street Journal*, and with the slogan "All the News That's Writ to Fit," addressed a letter to Eugene McCarthy's Children's Crusade:

> **Brothers and sisters—You are engaged in a vital search to change today's society, a battle we've been waging for eight years now as a national student organization. The major decisions have been made long before this convention began, and so we reject your candidate, not because he's yours, but precisely because he's not. He can make statements and become a figurehead, but those who really hold power are largely invisible. There is a system—call it imperialism—that must itself be challenged. Our experience has been one of frustration in attempting to effect change. Where do we turn? Finding liberating solutions by joining forces with other oppressed people we can do it. We share a common future. Join US!**

In Chicago close to a thousand people were busted and hundreds more beaten and hurt. One young man was killed by the Chicago cops, Dan Johnson, seventeen, a Lakota Indian from South Dakota. No one knows for sure if he'd come to Chicago for the demonstration or just come to Chicago.

Around the world, Chicago represented the inability of the U.S. government to rally even its own people to its side. The U.S. was poi-

soned by power. It could export its evil but it was incapable of positive peace or organizing its wealth and technology for liberty, dignity,
equality, general prosperity. All week we chanted, The Whole World Is
Watching!

Tom Hayden was right: the convention began to implode. The
police were rioting in the streets and violence, as American as cherry
pie, was unmasking before the waiting world. The besieged convention erupted with finger-pointing and vain attempts to present a
united front. When Senator Abraham Ribicoff denounced the gestapo
tactics of the Chicago police from the podium, Mayor Daley, his face
a catastrophe of crimson, his jowls trembling in white fury, cried out
from the floor, Fuck you, you Jew son of a bitch . . . go home! And
that, too, was beamed with lip-reading commentary to an astonished
world.

Tre was released and we patched him up, but we were arrested
together a day later. We had conceived a little street theater for the
delegates on Michigan Avenue, an in-your-face piece of agitprop. In
the spring Diana, Tre, and I had disrupted war games organized by
the U.S. Army in Ohio by scaling a fence and sneaking across a field
to occupy a mock Vietnamese village, defending it with our bodies.
Although I'm sure some would have loved just to let the artillery rip,
the press was on hand recording our dialogue of the deed, and we
were carried off before the village was flattened. Now we would
reverse the flow: we would be Viet Cong guerrillas attacking an
American outpost, the audience of convention-goers would play the
unhappy Americans, besieged. It seemed so natural.

We moved stealthily toward them, rushing from tree to lamppost
to parked car, hiding, bobbing up now, moving on in mock attack.
Police ears pricked up at first, noses sniffed the air, eyes suddenly
alert; they stiffened, came to attention, weapons poised, searching the
gloom. We approached. We hid. We approached again. At fifty feet a
cry went up from their commander and a heavy charge shot toward
us, a phalanx of blue, billy clubs swinging wildly, cutting the air. I
wheeled away, rebounding toward the lake. But as I left the bright

lights of Michigan Avenue behind, heading toward the bridge and freedom, I was gripped suddenly with fear, then naked panic. Police lights loomed on the far side, and I knew if they got me on the dark-side, alone, suspended on that overpass, they'd as soon drop me to a violent death on the Illinois Central tracks below as breathe. I was fucked.

Spinning again, I sailed back toward the light and into the waiting arms of three pink pigs in bright blue uniforms, one with prickly whiskers, another with rippling fat from jowl to hoof, all three glistening and welcoming as they broke my fall with their padded embrace on that hot and fiery night, carried me gently off the stage, and then beat the shit out of me in the soft green grass of Grant Park. It was sheer joy and wild relief to be there cherishing every lovely blow, bleeding a bit, but neither broken nor murdered on the IC tracks below.

I was charged with disorderly conduct, mob action, resisting arrest, endangering public safety, and "possession of a deadly sap," my modest homemade blackjack.

17.

The serpent of rage was loosed in the wide world, and it sank its passionate fangs deep into our inflamed hearts, power and corruption lying in the tall grass side by side along the pathway of wrath.

Uncontrollable rage—fierce frenzy of fire and lava, blowing off the mountaintop, coursing headlong, in an onslaught of unstoppable chaos—choking rivers, overwhelming the living things in its disastrous path, consuming to exhaustion.

Purifying fury, white-hot and cutting laserlike through illusion, burning a fine, straight tunnel to the very soul of things. Illuminating anger, passionate and perceptive, eliminating all distraction and doubt, our bright shining pinpoint of lucid, absolute certainty at last.

Malignant memory, cruel, taunting, deceiving—it twists and turns, flatters and begs, often torments. But everything gets garbled in the end, everything burns to ash, and I can't remember the half of it.

This string around my finger? That's a little fuse. These are the feverish, blazing days of rage.

The following summer Diana and I returned to Chicago for a week for the annual SDS meeting. This was our convention, not theirs, and it was held on the other side of the tracks in the barnlike Chicago Coliseum. It had been a tumultuous year for the student movement since the demonstrations at the Democratic Convention, marked by over five hundred campus revolts. Black student organizations sprang up everywhere, and the Black Panther Party multiplied. Organizers and agitators swept across the country. Larger and more experienced, facing, we thought, issues of massive consequence, we gathered our forces to debate our future.

Militants and radicals of every stripe filled the convention hall with noise and color and heat. Inside there was intense and sharp discussion starting the first day, while outside the Red Squad unit of the Chicago Police Department, familiar shadows and adversaries, smashed the windows in our parked cars across the street, flattened our tires, and stood menacingly nearby as we emerged for lunch.

The Red Squad was a special group of guys, J. Edgar Hoover's shock troops, each particularly groomed to be paranoid, sadistic, brutal, vicious, and law-breaking, each one armed to the teeth, weighted down with weaponry—clubs, saps, chemicals, gases, firearms—and always traveling in a pack. They were as well, although this was harder to see at the time, Korean War vets, 1950s-style anti-communists, big galumps totally unprepared for us. Certainly we had a hand in creating them, in our imaginations and then on the streets themselves.

Gee, one of them said to me as I passed him. Look at that, what a mess. Who coulda done that? I been here most of the morning, and I ain't seen a thing. He smirked. 'Course you could call the cops, but they're all just a bunch of pigs. So why don't you try calling a hippie—that's the ticket. His comrades squeaked in derisive delight.

We were captivated by the autobiographies of revolutionaries, encouraged by stories of lives lived in struggle, and so we rummaged through them from time to time for inspiration and even guidance. For reasons that entirely elude me now, we had fixed at that moment on *My Life*, a didactic account of the Russian revolution by Nadezhda Krupskaya, Lenin's comrade and widow, and on a passage that we held aloft in defense of our growing obsession with our political line:

> **Every word, every sentence had been motivated and weighed and hotly debated. . . . Many practical workers regarded these**

disputes to be of a purely abstract nature, and did not think it mattered whether a "more-or-less" proviso was left standing in the program or not. Vladimir Illiych and I were once reminded of a simile used by Leo Tolstoi. He was going along and saw from afar a man squatting and waving his arms about in a ridiculous way; a madman, he thought, but when he drew nearer, he saw it to be a man sharpening a knife on a kerb. The same thing happens in theoretical disputes. From the outside it seems a sheer waste of time, but when you go into the matter more deeply you see that it is a momentous issue.

Momentous or puny, we were into the matter deeply, conversing, meeting around the clock, drafting and redrafting, shouting down opponents as we shook our Little Red Books in the air, waving our arms like madmen. Sharpening our knives on the kerb.

The big line debate in the hall that summer was over the role of the national liberation movements in the world struggle, or what Marxists called the National Question. We read Castro and Guevara, Lenin and Mao, Cabral and Nkruma, but on any point of ideology we turned most often to Ho Chi Minh:

> After World War One, I made my living in Paris, at one time as an employee at a photographer's, at another as a painter of "Chinese antiques" (turned out by a French shop). I often distributed leaflets denouncing the crimes committed by the French colonialists in Viet Nam.
>
> The reason for my joining the French Socialist Party was because those "ladies and gentlemen"—so I called my comrades in those days—had shown their sympathy with me, with the struggle of the oppressed peoples. . . .
>
> Heated discussions were then taking place in the cells of the Socialist Party, about whether one should remain in the Second International, found a "Second-and-a-Half" International, or join Lenin's Third International? I attended the meetings regu-

larly . . . and attentively listened to the speakers. Why should the discussions be so heated. . . ? Why squabble? And what about the First International? What had become of it?

What I wanted most to know—and what was not debated in the meetings—was: which International sided with the peoples in the colonial countries.

I raised this question—the most important for me—at a meeting. Some comrades answered: it was the Third, not the Second International.

Formerly, during the cell meetings, I had only listened to the discussions. I had a vague feeling that what each speaker was saying had some logic in it, and I was not able to make out who were right and who were wrong. But from then on, I also plunged into the debates and participated with fervour in the discussions. . . . My only argument was: "If you do not condemn colonialism, if you do not side with the colonial peoples, what kind of revolution are you then waging?"

Our group in SDS, now calling itself the Revolutionary Youth Movement, siding with Ho, believed that support for self-determination of oppressed nations was a matter of principle. Capitalism had grown into a worldwide system, we said, an octopus of conquest abroad but relying heavily on racism at home. Racism, we argued, was a tool to divide the working class, but it was much more than that—it had become the glue that held the whole thing together, providing privileges and material benefits like better jobs and longer life to white people, mystifying many and winning their allegiance. These were like crumbs from the banquet table, a grand illusion in the sense that they were such a small payment for such a gigantic swindle, and yet white skin privilege was also a real and effective bribe against consciousness and struggle. In any case, we thought that the oppressed nations at home and away were leading the fight against the whole system through national liberation struggles, and that revolutionary consciousness could only develop if we led a movement that successfully rejected privilege and mounted a mighty attack on racism.

We were a few hundred crowded into the old Coliseum for our convention; we were mostly students, mostly white and young, and yet our ambitions stretched around the globe. Could we understand the aspirations of people ten thousand miles away? Could we understand the lives of Black people at home, or of poor and working people? Of course we're tiny, I thought, because white people are mostly brainwashed. We lucky few will wake them up. I could imagine the tall towers in downtown Chicago shaking.

The opposing line held that all nationalism was inherently reactionary, and that racism was a matter of prejudice mainly. It felt like a wide, wide divide. So we argued and fought, chanted and waved our Little Red Books like madmen.

And we fought it out hand-to-hand on the SDS convention floor, our lines like the clanging of steel on armor flashing across the room, each polemic demanding a stable identity, a WE or an US in capital letters. The convention split, and a piece of SDS regrouped around a dense and difficult tract with a title borrowed from Bob Dylan's "Subterranean Homesick Blues"—"You don't need a weatherman to know which way the wind blows." Whether we heard it on the news or not, no matter if it had any official recognition, the world was in flames, we knew, and our turgid manifesto proclaimed it loudly.

To all but those fully initiated into the sectarian battles of the day, the Weatherman paper was incomprehensible in large parts—a close reading of the lengthy, overwritten, single-spaced piece, it was said, could drive you blind or leave you gasping for air. But the thesis was simple: the world was on fire; masses of people throughout Africa and Asia and Latin America were standing up everywhere to demand independence and democracy and national liberation, leading a struggle that could transform the world into a more just, a more peaceful place; the worldwide anti-imperialist struggle had a counterpart inside the borders of the U.S.—the Black liberation movement; and the responsibility of mother country radicals here in the heartland of imperialism was to aid and abet the world struggle. That was our line.

The revolution was at hand, the question of power in the air, and, along with the question of power, the question of armed struggle. We wondered how to develop an armed unit, a brigade or a legion or a division, how to build a force of clandestine militants with an advanced fighting capacity. We meant to learn to fight through fighting, moving from small to large, developing skill and experience, growing in strength and power though the practice of revolution. We set about to found an American Red Army.

Our courage and purposefulness is a marvel from here. We took ourselves so seriously—OK, a little too seriously, we were too earnest by half and way too insistent—but we felt, personally and specifically, the full weight of the catastrophe unfolding before us. The world was in flames, as I've said, little Viet Nam bearing the brunt and racism at home paralleling most of the horrors visited upon the third world. Human existence itself seemed in grave doubt as, armed to the teeth with nuclear weapons and the masters of war at the controls, the world raced at warp speed toward oblivion. The dreadful and inescapable fact was that it was up to us to rescue everyone. We imagined that the survival of humanity depended on the kids alone. And, from the edges, we were entirely inflexible, maybe even a bit goofy.

We wanted to break from the habitual and the mediocre, to step into history as subjects and not objects. We would combat the culture of compromise, rise up and act decisively on what the known demanded—we could think of no basis on which to defend inaction, and so our watchword was simple: Action! Action! Action! We were kids in combat, with little to lose.

Because we were so single-minded and serious, everything we did had to find a justification, a place in our political line. But because we were so young, much of what we did was wildly unruly and disruptive. The personal is political, we said, and we meant that nothing was beyond examination and analysis, everything was part of a grand experiment in liberation. The trick was to translate our chaotic behavior into our increasingly leaden narration. Nowhere was that work more taxing or more eruptive than in the collision of politics and sex.

We experimented feverishly because we were kids, and because our instincts were anarchistic, vigorous, and unrestrained. One night after a fierce and bloody demonstration in Washington, a hundred of us created a moaning sexual pageant in a loft off Dupont Circle, flaunting and parading our outrageous exuberance. So that no one could miss the point, we ran a large cartoon strip in our newspaper sketched by a comrade. In one frame a zillion bodies cuddled under a giant Viet Cong flag, resting up after the street battle—and remember, kids, said the caption, when you're smashing the state be sure to keep a song in your hearts and a smile on your lips.

Another night Diana and Rachel and Terry and I bedded down together, our sleeping bags and pillows scattered across the living room floor. In the mayhem we searched out every possibility and I woke up with Terry in my arms, Rachel and Diana curled up across the way. We were, we said, an army of lovers.

You can smash monogamy all day long, Jennifer said on another occasion, but that doesn't mean I'm going to fuck you.

Smashing monogamy took a lot of energy—it was part of the political line to renounce all the habits and cultural constraints of the past, to make ourselves into selfless tools of struggle. We were an anti-Puritan police force—you were supposed to fuck, no matter what.

Anyway, Jennifer continued. I'm for smashing polygamy as well as monogamy; I'm against all the gimmes. And no, I'm not going to fuck you.

If this is liberation, Diana said to me one day, then why don't I feel free? I had returned from a trip of several days and I'd not even called to check in. Sometimes, she continued, I feel like getting you to slow down and pay attention here is like getting a pig to fly.

I didn't respond.

Oh, God, she said. There's that look again.

What look? I said.

That look. The look you finish off an argument with. The "I'm Bill" look.

Sex was, of course, our own personal invention, our own generational discovery. Whatever had gone before to propagate the species bore no resemblance we could see to what we were discovering, the creative and consuming fires we unleashed. No, nothing we had heard or read or saw—neither health education classes nor stern instruction from our fathers (mothers were entirely out of the sex picture), no peeks at pornography—prepared us for this. We did the fool wherever we could—with whomever we met—with inexhaustible energy, finding each other by some sizzling sense or scent, some tingling airborne vibration. No one before had ever rubbed each other so vigorously, we thought, with such propulsive purpose and inventive abandon, in such gloriously ecstatic poses.

So you enjoy fucking each other? asked Abby Stern skeptically, as she came into the room bearing a fresh pot of coffee, taking a deep drag on her ubiquitous Camel, blowing smoke high into the air across the table. That's revolutionary? Abby was ageless, the mother of one of our comrades, her life of activism etched across her animated face, her bulldozing personality on constant display. We assembled in her spare but welcoming apartment to meet, to plan, and she rarely missed the opportunity to give us some unsolicited but almost always wise and welcomed political instruction. She said "fucking" this way: "fo-KING," and the pronunciation plus the incongruity of this correct and classic working-class lady hurling our crude constructions in our faces got our attention. Let me tell you what we did in the thirties. According to her account, they were as cheerful and enthusiastic as we ourselves. The difference? You confuse youth and fun with politics, and you're so goddamn *public*.

Still we found ourselves there, on the sexual front—as in the political and cultural and social wars—tireless freedom fighters, filled with optimism and energy. We imagined the possibilities, cast our lives as more than predetermined sets of conclusions, once and forever. We assumed an outlaw stance, embraced a subversive sexual style, and resisted civic instruction in sexual propriety, blazing utopian trails shimmering with mystery and romance, dripping with desire, swollen with excess. Our lovemaking filled the crackling skies. Or so we imagined.

The sex police and the culture gestapo, liberals, our elders, and the rest of the left, as could be expected, charged us with bad citizenship—uncivilized, boorish, pleasure-seeking nuts. Guilty, guilty, guilty.

Still, Ruthie Stein increasingly pointed out, gender inequality was everywhere—encoded into laws, enacted in the economy and the culture, and always apparent to her in relationships within the movement. There's no poison worse than power, she said, and male power is entirely intact—you say you want a liberated future, but you're prisoners of the past. She organized meetings—for sisters only—and women began to search out a common voice.

Look at this! Terry whooped with glee. Look at this kid! He was holding aloft a black-and-white photo hot off the AP wire; in it a young boy cradling a big brick in his tiny hands—crooked, gap-toothed smile, hair standing in clumps across his head, Alfred E. Newman ears—stared mischievously into the camera. Terry read the caption aloud twice to shrieks of laughter: Marion Delgado displays a piece of rock he used to derail a freight train in Italy. There were no injuries in the accident, but rail service was disrupted for hours, and damage to freight and rolling stock was extensive.

Marion Delgado! Terry shouted, pumping his fist in the air. Live like him! Everyone rocked with laughter.

Marion Delgado became our antihero mascot and icon, his face appearing on T-shirts, buttons, and in obscure corners of our leaflets and newspapers, identifiable only to the knowing. On phone call after phone call we began to routinely identify ourselves to one another as "Marion Delgado"—in one twenty-four-hour period the FBI logged 124 calls initiated by Marion Delgado from 57 separate bugged phones. Marion Delgado was everywhere. Live like him!

Terry pulled out his small, stained notebook, sinister little notes and diagrams scribbled everywhere. A year ago he had a sketchbook filled with plans for a Revolutionary Carnival—the Haunted House featured pop-up Nixon dummies, the roller coaster zoomed along strafing the Pentagon, and the prizes included *The Quotations of Chairman Mao*, a Che Guevara beret, and a coupon to have your face painted in the likeness of Patrick Henry or Nat Turner, John Brown or Harriet Tubman.

Look here, he said now, smiling, drawing me closer, as he flipped to a blank page and began diagramming furiously with a charcoal pencil. Snap! Crackle! Pop! Something new for breakfast, he said.

Sometimes he was a little professor, slightly off-kilter. He knew a few facts about everything, and sometimes he was like a tape you couldn't turn off. He inhabited an anarchic solitude—disconnected, smart, obsessive.

I figured this out this morning, he said, based on some earlier designs. He continued, outlining a bottle, roughing in the bottom two-thirds with diagonal lines, blocking out the remaining third with horizontals. This is the gasoline, of course, he gestured to the larger portion of a standard Molotov cocktail. And this smaller part is typically motor oil. He paused, pencil poised, eyeing his work. Here's the twist. His pencil descended sharply, broke the drama, added a heavy hail of angry dots. We thicken the whole goddamn thing with detergent, it turns sticky, becomes flammable paste, and guess what? What? Napalm!

His idea was elegantly simple, the embodiment of a slogan we'd all embraced, BRING THE WAR HOME. It was a metaphor, of course. Why should we struggle and demonstrate and get our heads bloodied and risk our lives to bring the troops home, I had shouted into a bullhorn at a rally on the Michigan State campus months earlier, if the result is that those same troops are then sent on their murderous missions to Santo Domingo or Guatemala or Bolivia or right here in the cities of America?

Right on! Right on!

We have a responsibility as mother country radicals to attack this monster at its heart and at its head, to disarm it and disable it, I had said, and people pumped fists into the night sky, black and consoling and infinite, covering the whole wide world. Our leaflets spelled it out: When we move with the people of the world, against the interests of the rulers, we can expect the pigs to come down on us. So we're building a fighting force to struggle on the side of the Vietnamese, the Blacks, the oppressed people everywhere. There's a war we cannot resist. It is a war that we must fight. We must open up another front against U.S. imperialism by waging a thousand struggles in the schools, the streets, the army, and on the job, and in CHICAGO. . . .

I spoke and people chanted and pumped their fists, a kind of call-and-response theater. It filled me with an intoxicating sense of strength every time I did it.

Metaphors matter: for human beings metaphors are causal—we function on the metaphors we ourselves fashion. We imagine a world, we create a reality, we bracket a piece of experience, and it becomes acute, hyperreal, dazzling, revealing, enabling, and also blinding, perhaps deadly. Metaphors set us in motion. Metaphors matter.

LBJ and then Richard Nixon painted Ho Chi Minh—Old Ho they called him contemptuously—with horns, imagined that communism had a superhuman capacity to trick and deceive, and made a model of the world as flat as a card table with a long line of dominoes snaking across it. If one domino fell in their scary nightmare the chain reaction would be a cascading, noisy, and devastating collapse—at the end of the line, America. The card table sat in the White House situation room. They would keep each and every domino upright and erect.

Our metaphors were constructed on other barricades—the metaphor of world revolution, for example, imperialism in decline, of the U.S. as an ultimately doomed and helpless but temporarily deeply destructive giant. Picture an oversized, somewhat dim-witted monster, greedy and capricious, its eyes put out by fiery stakes and now flailing in a blind rage, smashing its way through villages and over mountains, murderous and wild, wrecking without plan or purpose. Nobody is hurting me, shouted the enraged Cyclops as he hurled boulders into the sea toward Odysseus. That was our metaphor, as we sailed away with our stakes smoldering.

Their metaphor demanded action, and tactics that sounded

absolutely insane outside themselves: we have to destroy that village in order to save it. Of course, our metaphor allowed wide leeway, too, in bringing the giant down. Terry saw a house of mirrors—if they demarcated free-fire zones in Viet Nam, we would map out free-fire zones in the U.S.; when they bombed Ha Noi, we might just figure out how to bomb Washington; search and destroy might be played both ways.

For Terry, metaphor was beyond decoration—it was an actual place to live, a shape to color in, a figure to become. I want to be a tool of the struggle, he said, and he meant that he badly wanted to be of use. Many of us were drawn to take the pose of a saw, a rasp, a crowbar, a hammer—bending ourselves toward a function of revolution, squeezing out any nagging doubts or questions.

Terry studied *The Blaster's Handbook*, a publication of the Explosives Department of E. I. du Pont Corporation, his cranky notebook lying open on the ratty sofa, each inflamed sketch coiled tight, busy with detail, poised to detonate on the page—pressure-trigger device, nipple time bomb, magnifying glass bomb, cigarette fuse, alarm clock time bomb, homemade grenade, walking booby trap, Bangalore torpedo, book trap, pressure-release gate trap, loose floorboard trap, whistle and pipe traps. He had created an annotated encyclopedia of street weapons—sticks, batons, billies, saps, garrottes, brass knuckles, beer-can hand weapons, hat pins, knives of every possible modification and description. There were detailed drawings of bridges—slab bridge, T-beam bridge, concrete cantilever bridge, truss bridge, suspension bridge—with wild X's indicating the pattern of placements that would drop every goddamned thing into the water or the ravine below, and architectural sketches of the skeletons of numerous buildings, with the requisite accompanying fury of X's designed to doom the thing, reduce it to chaos. There were maps of highways with notes on sabotage and destruction.

Page after page was piled with calculated steps for making high explosives with all-but-indecipherable formulae; the formula for nitroglycerin, the formula for mercury fulminate, for dynamite, for chloride of azode, for ammonium nitrate, for black powder. A list of household equivalents to chemical ingredients stretched across two tightly packed pages: acetic acid = vinegar, carbon carbonate = chalk, graphite = pencil lead, sulfuric acid = battery acid, sodium carbonate = washing soda.

The pigs need a strong dose of their own medicine, Terry said grimly, shoved down their throats. He paused, smiled briefly, and exploded with a sudden laugh: Ha! And up their asses, too. A napalm enema for Nixon.

Terry was merely making a point, of course, the excessive rhetoric of revolution—two parts intellectual exercise, one part armor-piercing humor. There was no need to argue, to contradict—the spirit of the moment was to name the contradiction plainly, to extend the logic sharply, and then to reduce the whole situation to the ridiculous—our huge aspirations set against our very real limits.

Everyone caught the spirit and laughed along, but Diana couldn't resist her habit of correcting Terry. It's a corrupting thought, you know, she said when the laughter faded, the idea that they deserve the worst of what they do. It's so easy to become everything we hate. Their phallocracy toppled by our machismo.

Come on, Terry chided. If we could get a big brass enema tube large enough, wouldn't you stick it right up the asshole of the Pentagon? We all laughed again. Something the size of the Washington Monument, say, but hollow, lowered in by massive transport copters. Diana smiled too.

Later Terry and I walked alone among the warehouses near the river. Our reason for being was slipping—confronting the problem of liberty, enlarging the fight for humanity. I'd rather go to hell than stand still, Terry said. He saw himself sometimes doomed, but he rushed on with his trigger-happy arguments and his little sketches of bombs. Reload, he said. On with it.

I don't know where it will end, he added quietly. But I'm sure of one thing—the crisis is real, and there's no American exception. Leadership would absolutely be military leadership, figuring out how to successfully wield the weapons of a guerrilla war. I don't know how yet, but I want to learn, he said. And I want you to learn, too. Come on, Billy. Don't leave me now.

I knew I wouldn't. I couldn't. Bombs away.

18.

That summer was steamy. In the collectives, hot and dank, our ragged groups of militants mustered up and prepared for war. Diana and I were in Detroit, surrounded by seasoned comrades—Ruthie, of course, and Fiona, bilingual in Italian, her Afro-American father a militant for two decades in the United Auto Workers, her immigrant mother a devout Catholic, taking a bus each morning to St. Francis to say mass for her wayward daughter; David, who had abandoned his dense little book on politics for the greater glory of making a revolution; the still inseparable Dan and Andy, powder and shot, hammer and sickle, ball and chain; and small, intense Rachel, acid-tongued daughter of a lifelong Communist functionary who looked with undisguised contempt at her entanglements, at her tactics, at her petit-bourgeois so-called comrades—longhaired, drug-addicted individualists, her father had called us, who would never recognize the working class even if it came marching up Grand River Boulevard toward them with red banners flying—but most of all at her incorrect political line, sending her a steady stream of polemics refuting with scientific certainty her ultra-left sectarianism and her deluded adventurism.

Tre had stayed back in Ann Arbor, working with a group of anarchist artists and cultural revolutionaries, fed up, although he never said so outright, with what he saw as our increasingly self-righteous pose within the movement, and especially with our newfound appetite for sharpening the political line. Fuck your political line, he'd say, laughing. A fishing line might feed someone, a line of poetry might fire an imagination here and there, but a political line? Useless. It sounded too much like everyone in neat little rows to Tre, menacing toy soldiers set in motion by the bad kid on the block, all uniform and marching mindlessly. You have the haunted look of a half-mad prisoner, he told me once, kneeling in a cell of your own creation—without light or air you'll be completely gone by winter. He thought a battle line might be worthwhile, or a line of fire. But fuck your political line. Diana and I laughed along, but we thought he needed to get more serious.

Diana recruited a dozen local kids and students from nearby colleges: Carolyn Roulet was an aspiring poet and high school senior; Lytton Carter a freshman at Michigan; Jerry Priestly the leader of the SDS chapter at Detroit University; and Jennifer Chang a junior at Wayne State. From this modest beginning, we thought, we happy few could forge a people's army. When Fidel landed on the Granma, he was considered a goofy crank, Rachel said. But who's laughing now?

The Granma was becoming our icon and inspiration, a terrible defeat at the time, but the disaster from which the Cuban revolution triumphed. Fidel was reported to have surveyed the catastrophe and remarked, "The days of the dictatorship are numbered." I didn't doubt it then, but have often wondered since how many thousands of others uttered similar quotable lines only to be obliterated and erased from history the next day or the day after that.

But never mind. Conditions were intensifying, the wide world beckoned, and we swung our metaphoric machetes purposefully, cutting our way to a base area in what we imagined were the liberated mountains of Detroit.

Our small street-fighting collectives hunkered down in dingy Spartan apartments or scabby tenements in the desperate parts of town. We threw mattresses and sleeping bags on the floors and moved in. Only Ruthie carved out a personal space—a back room where she stretched canvas and painted furiously. I had no firm idea, really, of what a collective was, even though I was part of the national leadership collective and a leader in the Detroit collective. It was our political line, after all, a necessary part of the struggle against individualism, the effort to build a fighting force, and it was likely correct. We were in no company save our own.

Each day began before dawn in the gray light near the field house of grimy Jackson Park. Jerry had a black belt in karate, and he guided the troops in push-ups, sit-ups, and jumping jacks before leading us on a one-mile run through the park. Then it was time for the real work: punching drills, parrying moves, side-kicks, front-kicks, backkicks, and combinations, each move accompanied by a high, sharp shout to focus strength and intimidate the enemy. Right punch—Whoop!—parry, side-kick—Whoop!—back-kick, parry, left punch—Whoop! Repeat. Again. Again. Repeat. Whoop! Whoop!

We were, no doubt, a spectacle—ragtag intellectual activists on display. I remember a bum early in summer raising his tired eyes in our direction, shaking his head slowly before going back to sleep. David always finished the mile run in a slow, limping walk well behind the others, and Daniel's coordination left him ever a beat behind Jerry's commands. Too much weed, I thought. Several mornings two elderly Black women who looked like sisters, hand in hand wearing housedresses on their morning walks, passed us, always smiling politely, looking amused. Each of us would be much more comfortable, I knew, with a book in hand, leaning, perhaps, against a broad shady tree. But here we were every morning, all through the summer, steeling ourselves for struggle, remaking ourselves as revolutionaries. What we lacked in physical prowess, we hoped, would be compensated for by our iron will.

We ate simply in the collectives: oatmeal and strong coffee to begin, later, rice and beans with broccoli or carrots. Cheese was an occasional delicacy, meat mostly a distant memory. Dope and alcohol became off-limits, but more and more of us were popping bennies. Our uniform was simple, too: blue jeans and white T-shirts, perhaps a colored vest with pockets to carry street supplies, heavy boots. By seven we were on our way to the factory gates or to the community colleges or schools to leaflet against the war, to build momentum for our militant national action—the "Days of Rage" to be held in Chicago in the fall. We mustered after breakfast for assignments: one day Dandy and I would head off to the Hamtramk stamping plant, Diana and David and Fiona to GM, Rachel and a small group to Ford; another day Jerry would lead a group to the Chrysler gates and David would announce without a wink of irony, "Carolyn and I are going downtown to organize ticket sellers on the Detroit ferry." We passed out thousands of leaflets every day, and every night we painted slogans on highway overpasses: BRING THE WAR HOME! VICTORY TO THE VIETNAMESE! VIET NAM WILL WIN! We were busy, busy, busy every waking moment.

I remember one morning on a crowded bus downtown, there were two girls twenty feet apart holding the commuter poles, each peering into a book. One looked Jewish, her long black frizzy hair pulled back with red barrettes, her almond face split by a lovely narrow hooking nose I longed to kiss, and I called her Esther; the other, perhaps Haitian, perhaps named Jeanette, her small round face framed by a short Afro and gold hoop earrings, her perfectly round breasts and bottom hypnotizing as we bumped along. The silver poles ran floor to ceiling, perhaps two inches in diameter, and Jeanette's hand moved subtly up and down, while Esther's held firm and tight. Each was reading *The Age of Innocence*, and I imagined introducing them, pointing out the coincidence, and the three of us getting off together and laughing arm-in-arm, then stumbling to Esther's cold water flat where we made love in every pose and posture for three days, one day devoted to each of us, and then, not to be greedy or irresponsible, right back to work. It never happened.

On weekends we issued outrageous challenges to ourselves—one Saturday, chanting antiwar slogans, thirteen of us marched the length of a beach frequented by young autoworkers, engaged in spirited discussion, and were encouraged when a group invited us to join them for barbecue in spite of our unfurled Viet Cong flag; on Labor Day we passed out leaflets at a Hell's Angels rally in a city park and swelled with pride to escape without a major ass-kicking. We could never have admitted it then—the cops were all pigs, our sworn enemy, the bikers and autoworkers our natural allies, the working-class youth—but police in the park made us feel a little safer; those Hell's Angels were unpredictable, after all, and really scary. "They took us damned seriously," David insisted earnestly, against all evidence.

The collectives engaged in bizarre competitions, contests to prove our worth, our revolutionary zeal: we heard that a women's group in Pittsburgh entered a big city high school, seized the office, and spoke for half an hour over the P. A. before they were arrested, and another captured the public address system at a stock car race, so we took over a movie theater and lectured the crowd until the police arrived. The Boston collective had smashed up the offices of the "counterinsurgency" Harvard Center for International Affairs, and the Cleveland group had marched into the amphitheater of the international Davis Cup tennis matches, so we burned an effigy of Henry Ford III in a parking lot he could see from his window. When that got little response, we burned a car and then ran as fast as we could.

We borrowed a line from LeRoi Jones in which a subway mugger cries out, "Up against the wall, motherfucker, we come for what's ours," and we practiced an up-against-the-wall-motherfucker politics of running confrontation. Whenever the police arrived, we fought like hell to provide an example to others and when, inevitably, they overpowered us and hauled us off to jail, we rested up for a couple days in the relative calm of the slammer, and then, right back to work. Our logic went something like this: working-class youth can never be won to a movement that is soft and overly cerebral; even though we are soft and cerebral, we're working on it and trying to prove our courage and seriousness; when they see us raising the question of power and contending for control, they will join us in droves.

It was, as a friend said to me, the intensity itself that no outsider could ever fully grasp. People who have never been in a hundred-mile-an-hour gale think that it's a thirty-three-mile-an-hour breeze times three. They link it to something normal and within their experience, something they already know, and then they multiply. For them it's familiar, but stronger. No, you explain, that's entirely untrue. A thirty-three-mile-an-hour wind is stiff, but it can pass over and around you and leave you standing. You can still breathe, still hear, still make some sense of the known world. A hundred-mile-an-hour wind sucks your breath out as it howls through your emptied head; a hundred-mile-an-hour wind is unrestrained, and it reorders the world. It smashes things up: trees are shattered, doors ripped from their hinges, shorelines rearranged. Afterward, the people who've only felt a thirty-three-mile-an-hour wind think you're exaggerating with stories of the hundred-mile-an-hour wind, embellishing and colorizing. But we were in a hundred-mile-an-hour wind, and we knew the difference.

All through the summer we worked and fought and practiced, and when we got time for a breather late at night, we criticized ourselves for not doing enough. The hundred-mile-an-hour wind wouldn't let up. We jogged. We marched. We drilled. More criticism. Organize, fight, practice, criticize. Criticism and self-criticism. We built a spirit and a commitment, we told ourselves, that was sky-high.

It was fanatical obedience, we militant nonconformists suddenly tripping over one another to be exactly alike, following the sticky rules of congealed idealism. I cannot reproduce the stifling atmosphere that overpowered us. Events came together with the gentleness of an impending train wreck, and there was the sad sensation of waiting for impact.

Most exits were closing, but I found a way out occasionally. I watched a baseball game alone in a bar, or I snuck off for an afternoon movie. One day Rachel and I, returning from a day's work, stopped for coffee and ice cream, a clear (if regular) deviation on both our parts, and talked a while about our hopes and fears and dreams; we shared a few favorite poems with each other before coming home to the collective. It had felt to me like a hot, sudsy bath after a week trudging through rugged uncharted mountains.

Criticism/self-criticism became a regular practice in the collectives, but it was harder and harder to manage because any particular honest sense of self was disappearing, and the collective assumed the stance of an eagerly policing superego. We had read about how the Chinese revolutionaries ended even the most brutal and excessive criticism sessions saying, Thank you for your encouragement—and before long a ritual, a purifying ceremony involving confession, sacrifice, rebirth, and gratitude, took hold of us. At the GM plant this morning, Jennifer said one night, I wimped out when a guy grabbed my leaflets and called me a bitch. . . . I should have punched his lights out. We backed down on the beach, Daniel said another time. We didn't raise the question of white supremacy sharply, and so we lost an opportunity to put those guys up against the wall and create the kind of tension that might have opened their minds. Every action, every word, every thought was subjected to rigorous scrutiny.

A focus on failures, gaps, inadequacies, and perceived mistakes in the work devolved rapidly into an exclusive interest in backward tendencies within ourselves, the small but grave obstacles to becoming revolutionaries. I was frightened, or I was doubtful, or I had a defeatist attitude—these rose in prominence and crowded out lesser concerns. We had to be stronger, we told ourselves, more selfless, uncompromising. We had to combat liberalism with a revolutionary political line, oppose idealistic foolishness and sentimentalism with hard materialist reality. We had to stomp out anything that might cloud our steely-eyed judgment in combat. We had to toughen up, and quick.

Attachments were suspect, particular affections nothing but the dead hand of the romantic past. One night Rachel warmed up by pointing out to the group my obvious sexism—not because I had slept with several comrades, no, that was a good thing, smashing monogamy, severing any unique or private ties that might distract (a political line with a large helping of male self-service at its center). I had, rather, failed, she said, to position more women in the front ranks of a recent confrontation, an obvious error. I thanked her, and she moved on to deeper matters, revealing our secret coffee and ice-cream break from earlier in the week. I had been buoyant and deeply grateful to her for those few moments. But now came an unexpected cold shower: You read from Brecht, she accused, and it was true, and then she quoted the few lovely lines slowly, her voice oozing contempt: "Indeed we live in the dark ages," Brecht wrote, "a guileless word is an absurdity, a smooth forehead betokens a hard heart." While some might have thought Brecht doctrinaire, where we were headed even Brecht would be banished: "You who shall emerge from the flood in which we are sinking, think, when you speak of our weaknesses, also of the dark time that brought them forth." Clearly I was not as resolute as I let on. Fucking poems, she concluded, and I felt, of course, that she was right. I had slipped. I had deviated, and not for the first time. I thanked her for her encouragement, and knew that I would get even the next day, or the next.

Art and politics, joy and struggle, love and engagement—this had been the rule of our logic. Now we would excise the art. We began to speak mostly in proverbs from Che or Ho. Soon all we heard in the collectives was an echo.

We talked politics in the morning, politics in the daytime, politics throughout the night. For one thing, it kept the inevitable fear and confusion temporarily at bay, but it also was, at bottom, what really drove us.

The basic story line for us—a story I accepted instinctively and intuitively without knowing a lot—was that Viet Nam was fundamentally united fighting an aggressive invader from the West, that the Vietnamese allied with the West were puppets artificially installed, and that Viet Nam would ultimately win. So much undeserved suffering, and so much pain, but an astonishing resistance, too, a powerful lesson for the rest of the world. And so it was unspeakable disaster and profound blessing, both. Viet Nam will win! Viet Nam will win! A chant and a poster, a slash of graffiti on every underpass: Viet Nam will win!

This war was, like all others, politics by other means. For the U.S.

generals this maxim reduced easily to something else: because we
Americans are so decent and democratic, because we are always the
charming good guys in the white hats with the straight teeth, and
because ours is the best country in the world, our wars must be
always and forever winning. These generals said, "We could have won
that war if we had only . . ." But here they were wrong. Nothing
could have defeated Viet Nam—the depth of the resistance, the unity,
the determination was altogether too much. Take the most barbaric
possibility: nuclear bombs over Ha Noi. Devastation, yes, and lasting
horror. But the unleashing of a howling political storm, too, one that
might well have torn the U.S. government itself from its tentative
moorings, overwhelmed it, and turned the world upside down.

I threw myself into this story without caution, without regard for
safety. I had been a scrappy pulling guard in high school, after all, and
I was a happy militant for Viet Nam. Viet Nam will win! Like falling
in love, it was a story bristling with promise. Disbelief was entirely
suspended.

There were corollaries for us, the young American radicals: End the
War! And then: Bring the War Home! And then: Create Chaos in the
Mother Country!

Oddly, Viet Nam will win! as a story, and Bring the war home! as
strategy and tactical impulse, provided the best available framework
for action at that moment, even though it was probably impossible to
pursue without becoming in some sense its victim. This, too, was
pushed to the background.

The world is in flames, we thought, the people of the world rising
against the octopus of imperialism and cutting off its tentacles one by
one. It was a compelling image, apocalyptic: Cuba, one, Korea, two,
Guinea-Bissau, Mozambique, Angola, Algeria, Ghana, and Viet Nam,
of course, number eight, where the monster had overextended itself
once and for all. National liberation movements active in Chile,
Panama, Argentina, Guatemala, the Philippines, Jamaica, South
Africa, Mexico—dos, tres, muchos Viet Nams—had heated up and the
world's aggressive policemen were pinned down in Southeast Asia. A

pitiful, helpless giant. Driven back to its own borders, the contradictions seemed to be boiling before us. The Black struggle at home was the domestic equivalent of national liberation abroad. Our job is to drive a stake into the heart of the monster, we insisted, opening up a front behind enemy lines and fighting, then, side by side with Black people and with the people of the world. It was an exhilarating and exhausting politics. The city was full of fervor and fire, and we intended to stoke it with anything at hand, even our own bodies.

I embraced the line, the broad strokes of our politics, but the political line was increasingly harsh to manage. Every change of line, no matter how small, required a change of direction, no matter how slight, and with the gate swinging open and shut rapidly, several times a day, it was so easy to become unhinged.

19.

Diana spent part of the summer with Bernardine, Teddy Gold, and dozens of other Americans in Cuba meeting with a delegation of Vietnamese to exchange views on strategies and tactics for ending the war. When they returned to North America on a sugar boat bound for St. John's, Newfoundland, I drove up to meet them with CW.

Most of us had come to our understanding of the world from our involvement in the civil rights and peace movements—ideology, we thought, lent a necessary seriousness of purpose to our efforts—CW, by contrast, found the movement through his involvement with a tight little leftist sect he'd joined as a teenager. When part of the movement turned forcefully toward a political line, CW's two-year head start provided leverage, his skills already honed. He knew how to win debates inside those dark and suffocating halls, and he had mysterious friends he could call on who knew Marx and Lenin and Mao, chapter and verse.

The ascendency of ideology among us foretold the end of what had been a genuinely new left, a left that refused received ideas and based itself, instead, on the wisdom of experience. Until now the way out of disagreements was practice—if some of us believed that knocking on doors in working-class neighborhoods and engaging people in discussions about the war was effective, then that's what we did; if others of us thought a large mobilization in Washington was the way to go, then that was our assignment. Or we could do both, and/or a hundred other things in between. The key was to act on what our knowledge demanded of us, to experiment, and then to sum it all up in order to move forward, to link our conduct to our consciousness. Our ideas would all be the fruit of our own labor, our lived experience.

Ideology became an appealing alternative in so many ways. Practice was uncertain and inexact; ideology cloaked itself in confidence. Practice was slow and ideology a smooth and efficient shortcut. Mostly, ideology was serious—people with ideology meant business. I didn't know yet how domesticating and cruel and stupid ideology could become, or the inevitable dependency it would foster in all of us.

There was a danger now from inside, from ourselves. We were becoming prisoners of our schemes, intoxicated on theory.

The triumph of an ideology divorced from practice brought along a new reign of intellectual terror—the rule of the ideologue—and CW was its chief among us. Whatever power he had, the rest of us had handed to him. We were desperate to end the war, lurching to find a decisively effective weapon. And he knew that his big brain was perilous. I remember once when he was winning some obscure argument and Bernardine said to him, Just because you can always win, doesn't mean you're always right. He paused and turned to look at her, his face momentarily troubled. He looked as if he might cry. You're right, he said softly, and that sometimes terrifies me.

CW and Bernardine had been dating before she went to Cuba, but the contrast was bizarre. She seemed to me so passionate, warm, and three-dimensional, so hardworking and selfless, almost sacrificial, a person to admire and follow. He was demanding, manipulative, and cruel, someone to be feared. There was something seductive and compelling about him, about his intensity and the intellectual gymnastics, but I didn't love him. In fact, I came secretly to loathe him, but I never said so. And since increasingly a particularly harsh ideology ruled, CW could be both feared and followed, his role as Great Political Thinker guaranteeing his survival. He was too important to be busted, he thought, too essential to be beaten up with the mob. It was enough that he think deep and talk tough—he was guaranteed to be off the scene when things got messy. His every gesture encouraged abdication of the right to think, and his suicidal tendencies were all displaced.

Our drive to Newfoundland was a late-night affair, uneventful, me driving, CW sleeping mostly and offering intermittent lectures when he awoke. We wandered the gray St. John's waterfront together in a morning fog, row after nondescript row of trampers and steamers, until we found the little sugar boat from Cuba, impossible to miss in this drab company because its smokestack was painted in the likeness of a bright, exuberant Cuban flag and right in the center a huge fist grasping a machete signifying the mobilization to harvest ten million tons of sugar. It was unexpected and entirely beautiful to me.

The look on Diana's face told me I shouldn't have come. She kissed me stiffly on the cheek and held back. You shouldn't have come, she said looking away, but I'd already figured that out.

Diana was having a love affair with the third mate, it turned out, and these last days were important to her. But this didn't really explain it because we had both had lovers, and though my presence might be a little awkward, and frankly nothing much was awkward to us anymore, it would not be entirely disruptive. I felt a sudden stab of jealousy, and just as quickly pushed it away. I could imagine how she often felt. We were supposed to be hard, not fragile, but I wasn't, and I knew Diana wasn't, either.

The small group of Americans on the boat had had a charged experience in their meetings with the Vietnamese—many felt they had come to a new understanding of how to galvanize the popular opposition even while developing a measured clandestine operation. They had then built a purposeful and precious community on the boat, she told me. I could think and breathe for the first time in months. We really worked together and cared for each other. She had been in the center of things there, the translator for the Americans to the Cubans, the Cubans to the Americans, the bridge between languages and peoples, she thought, but also a force holding everything together. She wanted to hold on to that focus for another day or two, to use the last days together to talk and plan in peace.

CW quickly pulled together a meeting in the mess hall, a low-ceilinged, L-shaped space with bolted-down tables cramped together, just like the boat I'd shipped out on except that here the walls were decorated with framed photographs of Fidel and Che, Marx, Lenin, and Ho Chi Minh. Bernardine described the weeks in Cuba, the inspiration of the Vietnamese, the spirit of the group, as CW looked on with a patronizing expression of feigned concentration and mild amusement. When she finished he asked if anyone else would like to add to the report, and a few comrades spoke up with an anecdote or a memory, but you could feel what was coming. Bernardine said, finally, that she was convinced that we could be as militant as necessary, and maintain a positive and hopeful stand toward the mass struggle.

Then CW took the floor. He congratulated the group on its work, but, he explained, much had changed in the time they were gone and much had eluded them in Cuba. Conditions had intensified, repression was peaking, militant resistance was breaking out all over. All of this was what we'd been telling ourselves all summer, and I agreed. We all did.

There's no time now for sentimental journeys or Caribbean romance, he said pointedly. The revolution is at hand, and we've got to be serious. The vacation is over.

In retrospect, that was perhaps the last chance we had to reconsider and to pull back from the cliff edge we were walking. Diana would tell me later that the Vietnamese were only mildly interested in our willingness to die for their cause and much more animated about how we planned to reach our Republican parents, something that didn't interest us at all. Soon we would escalate again, then divide angrily into parallel groups, give up on hope and one another, burrow off in different cities to see what would become of us. Soon enough some of us would die for these decisions. But that weekend we spent hours in the mess hall of a Cuban sugar boat in St. John's,

Newfoundland, sharpening our political line, while down below, in Woodstock, New York, a youthful multitude gathered in open fields to celebrate with Jimi Hendrix and Santana and Richie Havens the coming of the age of Aquarius. I missed it.

Terry paused, cupped his hands around the igniting match, and hunched against the bitter Chicago wind to light up another Camel. It could have been a bomb, but it wasn't, not yet. There it is, he said conspiratorily, arching his eyebrows, the top of his head poking through the sulfurous cloud, gesturing toward the end of the block. There's the pig.

His eye filled with the looming figure—rigid cap pointing skyward, big broad coat frozen open over sturdy breeches, durable bronze boots sunk stubbornly into the cement below—arm outstretched, palm upward, mustachioed face drawn into a look of authoritarian sternness, his entire cast body crying out HALT! CEASE! STOP OR I'LL SHOOT!

And etched into the concrete base, this simple sentence, *In The Name Of The People Of Illinois, I Command You To Disperse.*

The statue was an ironic icon from an earlier era, a monument to a historic upheaval centered in the heart of Chicago. On May 1, 1886, Albert Parsons had led a march of eighty-thousand workers up Michigan Avenue as part of the long campaign to win the eight-hour working day as a sensible and just standard for industry and agriculture everywhere. As a tribute, May Day is celebrated to this day as labor's official holiday in almost every country of the world, but not, of course, in the U.S. On May 3, Chicago police fired into a crowd of workers protesting wage cuts and a lockout at the McCormick Reaper plant on Blue Island Avenue. Two workers were murdered: A demonstration was organized for May 4 at the city's Haymarket, at Randolph Street and Des Plaines Avenue.

As the protest neared an end, rain began falling, and the crowd dwindled. Mayor Carter Harrison, who observed the protest until almost 10 PM, told the police brass to send their men home because the demonstration had been peaceful and it was all but over. The last speaker was concluding when a force of 176 Chicago cops entered the square in a line and waded into the crowd swinging nightsticks—a long tradition still observed. In the name of the people of Illinois, I command you to disperse! shouted a lieutenant just before a bomb was thrown into the ranks of the police, killing one officer immediately. The police opened fire, shooting wildly into the dark, killing at least four protesters and wounding many more—seven policemen died later, several from police gunfire.

No one was ever charged or captured or convicted for the act itself, but authorities indicted eight labor leaders and conducted a show trial. There was no evidence that any of the eight were involved in the bombing, and in fact several weren't even present; the state attorney's closing argument essentially charged them with something freely admitted, proudly embraced—their socialist and anarchist views: They are no more guilty than the thousands who follow them. . . . Gentlemen of the jury, convict these men, make examples of them, hang them and you save our institutions, our society.

Seven were sentenced to die. One of them, August Spies, told the judge, If you think that by hanging us you can stamp out the labor movement, then hang us. Here you will tread upon a spark, but here, and there, and behind you, and in front of you, and everywhere the flames will blaze up. It is a subterranean fire. You cannot put it out. The ground is on fire upon which you stand. And as the hangman sprung the door, Parsons shouted, Let the voice of the people be heard! And then he was gone. Shortly afterward the city fathers erected this garish police statue that Terry and I were now casing, this tribute to police power and tyranny.

Terry knew the story by heart. Fight, fight, he said. What else is there to do? We rushed into danger out of solidarity, out of a need for battle, and, yes, out of despair. The voice of the people, he said now, his own voice low, is demanding justice. We would become that subterranean fire about to blaze up. August Spies and Albert Parsons would smile on us from their graves, and rest just a wee bit easier. It's our turn, Terry said, turning to me, and I'm going to knock that fucker over. Let's go. Bombs away.

The sweltering summer gave way to a penetrating chill. The air ached and the fragile leaves flamed orange and gold, exploded into red, and were gone. The Cubs were in the pennant race, but we hardly noticed. There was much that eluded us then.

The bag was small and neat, but a world of fire and fury beckoned.

Are you sure that can knock it down? I asked.

Knock it down, break its legs, hurl it across the freeway, and break most of the windows on this block. Terry cradled the dark little thing in the cloak of his arm.

Terry, I said. This is too good—it's us against the pigs, a medieval contest of good and evil, but this guy is made of bronze and he won't even fight back. It's pure theater. Anyone with even a single progressive bone will stand up and cheer, and anyone with a sense of humor will fall down laughing. The only improvement I can think of would be if I drove past at high noon on a motorcycle with you riding on the back, and we knocked it over with a jousting lance. Sir Talk-a lot and Sir Lance-a-little. Terry didn't smile.

On October 5, 1969, a dynamite bomb toppled the police statue at Haymarket Square, the exact site where we would gather for the culminating action of the Days of Rage. Mayor Daley said it was an attack on all the citizens of Chicago, called for law and order, and appealed to the youth: Let the younger generation know that the policeman is their friend. The Patrolmen's Association called it war—We now feel it is kill or be killed, said their leader—and we were deeply flattered.

Oh, come on, Terry responded, looking glum. That was child's play. Symbolic bullshit. He looked tired and he gave a futile shrug. We need a real reply. John Brown hurt them; Nat Turner hurt them. If we're going to do this, take the risks and all, shit, we've got to hurt them. Don't you see?

John Brown was hanged. Nat Turner, too. I agreed.

On May 4, 1970, the Patrolmen's Association re-erected the repaired statue in a somber ceremony. So on October 5, 1970, we knocked it over again. Soon bombing bronze monuments in elaborate poses of conquest became a specialty, and all over America, heroes decked out in sword and shield became our targets. We'll rebuild the statue, declared an incensed Mayor Daley, and they did. It is now standing in the atrium of the Chicago Police Academy on Jackson and Loomis. It has a full-time armed guard and is entirely inaccessible to the public, but I imagine still vulnerable from the air, and perhaps the sewers.

20.

All summer we had jacked ourselves up and spurred ourselves on, whipping ourselves into a kind of frenzy of reinvention, remaking ourselves into street fighters and persuading ourselves against all evidence that the working-class youth were with us, that our uncompromising militancy was winning them over, and that Chicago would be the wild, unruly embodiment of a Revolutionary Youth Movement. It will be a huge action, I declared to doubters and slackers throughout the whole summer. Thousands upon thousands will be on hand, and the whole wide world will see what a radical fighting force in the mother country can look like. I don't remember any hesitation: we would fight in the streets, the kids would come and join us, and we would march arm-in-arm in the service of world revolution. Without a doubt.

Terry was skeptical, arguing to move away from any public display at all. Away from any open action, tilting tentatively toward the hidden world, toward an invisible movement of leaderless resistance, secret cells, and autonomous guerrillas swimming silently in the sea of the people, he said, emerging only to engage the enemy, and only in our own time and on our own terms. And then return right back to the magical element of our watery survival.

The bigger the mess the better, many of us said then. Blood to the horse's brow, Terry wrote in large black letters on a subway wall, and woe to those who cannot swim.

What does it mean? I asked, the biblical-sounding reference beyond me.

I borrowed it from the Panthers, he said. It means a vengeful river of blood will wash through this place, and soon. And it will be way deep, full of wrath, and all the way up to the head of a horse. Terry was sounding more Old Testament every day.

Terry had given up sleep by now, fortified instead with methamphetamines, little green pills he popped constantly. Speed provided the satisfying sense of being incredibly streamlined, buoyant, and brilliant, and unquestionably on track, all of it combined with twenty-four hour staying power—that much more time to be dazzling. Everything old is bad, he said. And everything new is good. He began to see himself in dreams living and dead. He saw airplanes in the sky. One night he woke me up at 3 AM and showed me his design to burn the First National Bank building in downtown Chicago—all fifty-seven floors of it, several floors leased by Commonwealth Edison—to the ground, and, simultaneously how to torch the Christmas trees in Rockefeller Center and the Mall in Washington. Exhausted, I called him an idiot. We shouted insults at each other for a moment and woke up everyone in the apartment, and then he punched me and I knocked him down. Jeff Jones jumped in to break it up. We were tense and brittle and charging onward.

We had planned to rally with thousands of working-class kids from the base cities and the militants from our collectives at seven thirty in Lincoln Park on that first night of the Days of Rage, but it didn't work out like that. By eight, when I slipped in from the north, no more than a couple hundred people were milling idly around a small fire. I'd passed I don't remember how many cops held just out of sight, fully armed and poised to strike—we weren't only outnumbered and outgunned, we might just be out of our minds. My stomach sank. Where were all the revolutionary youth? I felt like running away, slipping into the darkness and disappearing, but I knew I couldn't or wouldn't. Our objective was to make it all the way downtown, to assault the Federal Building full force with a tough and multiplying youth army, to smash the windows and batter the walls, to once more enact our outrage and rehearse our resistance. There's no turning back now, I said to myself, and I tried to remember the Granma.

This, then, was the hard core stripped bare, the collective members from Michigan, Ohio, Colorado, Maryland. But it slowly became, for all its deflated weirdness, an exciting sight for me—a small, determined group suited up for battle, everyone wearing an odd motorcycle or army-surplus helmet, many with goggles and gas masks, heavy boots and gloves, pants and shirts taped securely at ankles and wrists.

I remember that some looked like warriors, some more like clowns. David appeared to be going out to collect Halloween candy in oversized orange coveralls, motorcycle boots, and a World War I helmet several sizes too small perched on his bespectacled egg-shaped head. Terry looked like a rogue Cub Scout bent on mischief.

Stashed out of sight in backpacks and under jackets, most of us carried an arsenal of unanticipated street weapons: steel pipes and slingshots, chains, clubs, mace, and rolls of pennies to add weight to a punch. No one had a gun, but no one would be helplessly assaulted tonight either, I thought. We would up the stakes again, and again we'd pay a price. How high? High, I guessed, but I had no real idea as I waded into the group and we greeted one another with desperate hugs. I found Diana quickly, and soon our entire affinity group was fully assembled—Terry, Diana, Rachel, Ruthie, David, Fiona, and me. We would fight side by side, protect one another from harm, and try our best to break every window in our righteous path.

Before long our bonfire was full up, feeding on large pieces of splintered park benches we'd randomly smashed up for fuel. The cool air crackled, the mist receded some, and then the crowd roared and I remember looking west to see a contingent of chanting fighters break fiercely through the fog and wheel into the park—maybe a hundred or a hundred and fifty strong, but maybe, just maybe, in their determination, a thousand or even ten thousand. Ho, Ho, Ho Chi Minh, the Viet Cong Are Gonna Win. What a sight—this lovely little guerrilla army in tight, disciplined formation, two abreast, approaching and then surrounding the bonfire quickly, purposefully, and pivoting smartly to face us, leading chants punctuated with war whoops and ear-piercing whistles. The collective energy surged, the tension turned thick.

My blood became hot, my forehead ice cold, sparks leaping from my skin. I'm not kidding—I looked at the backs of my hands then and little blue and white electric currents danced wildly across them. When I turned to show Diana, holding my hands aloft, she glanced past them and stared instead at my face. What happened? she asked, sounding mystified. How the hell did that happen?

What?

Look at your glasses.

I pulled them off and sure enough, each lens was a little starburst of tiny cracks and fissures spidering out from the center. I hadn't been hit or bumped, I hadn't felt a thing beyond the weird electric light show—but my glasses were shattered. Shit, I said, puzzled, but also a little delighted and then dazzled. This is so, so strange.

The chanting escalated, sending sparks into the night sky, and the theater of revolution filled the park. We shouted and buoyed each other up, clinging to the lifeboat of our hope and each other. Terry circled away to greet late-arriving comrades, and I held tight. Somewhere I knew that a killer wave was gathering in the gloom beyond, and I secretly hoped someone—not me—would show up on a rescue ship and pull us all to safety. But it seemed doubtful, impossible. And soon I didn't care.

The feverish revelry was at a peak when Bernardine Dohrn appeared on a slight rise to the left of the fire and the troops exploded into a chanting frenzy. HO, HO, HO CHI MINH, THE NLF IS GOING TO WIN! She was wearing a black leather jacket over a black turtleneck, her trademark short skirt and high stylish black boots, an eye-liner pencil peeking from her breast pocket. Her blazing eyes were allied with her elegance. She had earned her role as the voice and the leader of the militants through practice, but she was also a stunning and seductive symbol of the Revolutionary Woman—J. Edgar Hoover had dubbed her "La Pasionaria of the Lunatic Left"— and as she stood in that frenzied park late that night, her dark hair whipped by the wind, her brilliant eyes flashing in answer to the fire, I would have followed her anywhere.

She raised one hand and the park was suddenly, eerily quiet: Brothers and sisters, she shouted into the emptiness. It's time for mother country radicals to take our place in the worldwide struggle. It's time to BRING THE WAR HOME! A roar erupted and the chanting began anew. She could write legal briefs or law review articles, handle a crowd, or brave a police assault. She could concoct fantastic plans, and she was a captivating speaker. Tonight is the anniversary of Che's murder, she said. But Che's death has not killed the revolution. Cheers and whistles filled the air. Che lives! *Venceremos!* HO, HO, HO CHI MINH! The refrain reverberated through the park, echoing, beguiling, and finally hypnotic for some.

When the chanting slowed, Tom Hayden, on trial in federal court with seven others on conspiracy charges for leading the demonstrations at the Democratic Convention a year earlier, emerged from the crowd. When his trial had begun in late September a group of us had disrupted the proceedings, and now Hayden was bearing an echo of solidarity to us: I bring greetings from the Chicago Eight, he said. We love you! We are with you!

Ho, Ho, Ho Chi Minh, we sang in answer, and Hayden added, Anything that intensifies our resistance to this war is in the service of humanity. The Weathermen are setting the terms for all of us now. Tear this monster down! Tom was caught up in the spirit of the moment, and shedding his careful demeanor from court, became the old inciter. Our chants escalated again and swirled like fireworks into the air. As improbable as it all was, I felt giddy and newly emboldened. We were about to leap arm-in-arm into the inferno of the unknown, and I remember trembling with giddiness and holding on to Diana.

The night was darker and deeper, the air colder, when Jeffrey Jones, heavily costumed with wig and helmet and paste-on beard but easily recognizable to the comrades, leapt to the front and, evoking our little monster icon, the ten-year-old boy who had derailed a train that year in Italy with a chunk of concrete, shouted, I am Marion Delga do! A great roar engulfed him. We're heading down to derail the train of injustice! Tonight, this city is ours!

A little path opened and Jones began to head south in a hard run, and three comrades linked arms in neat synchronization to his left, three to his right. We fell into quick formation behind, lines of eight to twelve people materializing like magic out of the mist. My group was intact, front row. Hundreds of us left the park that way, at a sprint, without any resistance at all—the cops had prepared for last year's battle, huddled to the north ready to contain us when we defied the curfew, but instead we stormed south into the city, into the world beyond, rocking them back on their heels. We were in full attack.

We shrieked and screamed as we ran, ululating in imitation of the fighters of *The Battle of Algiers*. I saw us become what I thought was a real battalion in a guerrilla army, and it felt for that moment like more than theater, more than metaphor. I felt the warrior rising up inside me—audacity and courage, righteousness, of course, and more audacity.

As we plunged out of the park onto North Avenue and Clark Street, David and Rachel hauled chunks of brick and pavement from pockets and packs and hurled a barrage at the huge inviting windows of the first building on the block, a big and gleaming bank.

The glass shattered and a vibration exploded through us. It was Pavlov's bell. As in the collectives months ago, the competition was on, each act inspiring another. The bigger the mess the better was the incentive zinging in my brain. The crowd thundered down Clark, every windowpane a target, every bit of glass in every business crashing joyously in our wake. With our pace now a dead run, some of us turned to car windows, hotel windows, the windows of the luxury high-rise apartments we streamed past. I swung my billy club into the windshield of a Cadillac and then a Mercedes.

The streets became sparkling and treacherous with the jagged remains of our rampage, and we had to dance lightly in our heavy boots to avoid diving into the crystal chaos. I kept watching for a comrade to go down, knowing the result would be something like death by a thousand cuts, but no one did. On we charged, slip-sliding away.

We heard sirens now, but saw no barricades, no massed police presence, and we were moving fast. Suddenly a single cop car appeared half a block ahead, lights flashing, and someone yelled authoritatively, Stay in formation! Stay in formation! I don't think it was me; maybe it was David. We swarmed over and around that car, smashing windows, slashing tires, trashing lights and fenders—it seemed the only conceivable thing to do. I leapt from the trunk to the roof to the cheers of friends, jumped up and down several times until it caved in slightly, and then slid off easily and kept moving, glancing back to see a broken shell with two cops hunkered down in the front seat; one's eyes opened and staring in vacant disbelief, the other's locked on me with what felt like murderous intention. In a second I was beyond reach.

Then a real barricade materialized just ahead, serious with several cars and hundreds of cops. Several affinity groups split onto side streets and kept moving. We veered east two blocks, and then south again, smashing everything in reach. Another barricade, another sharp turn and a rapid readjustment, on and on, stampeding through the night on the Gold Coast toward the heart of the city.

At this point our battalion was breaking apart, one large group heading onto Lake Shore Drive, another pushing down State Street, and several small units looping out in all directions. I felt oddly like a kite cut from its string, and I began to float above the crowd, to hover just out of harm's way. For a moment, from where I hung, an odd calm enveloped me as if I were watching all this on a screen.

I saw a horse shy from the crowd and back slowly into a store window which gave way with a crash. I saw a cop car run straight into a crowd of comrades at high speed, scattering bodies in all directions. I saw a cop pull a shotgun from his trunk and blow both barrels as screaming filled the air. I saw a whole group of bystanders caught unaware in our outrageous ferocious narrative: a young man leaned precariously from an apartment window and wearing a New Year's Eve hat threw confetti into the multitude, laughing and blowing air kisses, and a big man shaped like a shark with no neck wearing a gray suit, standing square in front of a large Lincoln, swung a crowbar methodically as the mob approached, split, and swam quickly past him.

At State and Division our small group fought through a police barricade of cars and traffic barrels, but we took terrific casualties. David got smashed in the side of the head by a police club and the sound of his jaw breaking was distinct and sickening. His head snapped and blood and teeth spewed from him as he went down. Then two cops dove on top of him, punching with both fists. I swung my club wildly but got nowhere. I spun and saw Ruthie being choked with a billy club. We were breaking apart and Diana was nowhere to be seen. What should I do? There was no time to stop, to consider the options. I pushed on, through the worst of it, and I was running fast. I was the speedy pulling guard in football again, leading the play. I heard gunshots and the sounds of clubs and combat, and I was all alone but I kept running. Should I go back? Am I right to run? I ran and I ran.

Tear gas seized the air as wailing sirens crisscrossed the city streets. I dove into stairwells and alleyways when I saw a car ahead or heard a siren approaching from behind; I hid in bushes and behind trees as I twisted and turned in escape. My feet were a spinning blur, and I hardly touched the ground. I saw fire in the firmament, and vengeance in the faces of my pursuers. And on I ran.

We were, of course, no match for them, and once we were split apart we were easy targets—the cops completely kicked our asses wherever they found us, left some of us for dead, bleeding in the streets, and hauled others into the city's deep and dingy evil backdoor lockups where we would be subjected to something close to torture. I was scared but still exhilarated, swept along in the darkness, hunched over, gliding with a cosmic energy coursing through me, something large and mysterious powering my fateful rush. Soon the flashing lights and the whining alarms were all in the distance, echoing only in my head, but on I sped until I was completely swallowed by the huge and buoyant night.

When I finally slowed enough to look up, I was disoriented, lost in a maze of warehouses and loading docks, cracked and crumbling concrete, deserted streets. Where was I? Behind me the city was ablaze, the country choking on evil. I knew Chicago up and down, inside and out, but I'd never seen this before. I was somewhere west of the Loop I knew, and still a little north. I could smell the river. I wandered on for a few moments, hoping to get my bearings, but I never did. Heaven was brilliant, the moon glowing in the dark cold air, the stars trembling in the wide sky. Where was Diana? I made a little wish then, a wish for survival. A wish that I'd inherited from my mom for all occasions: I wished that everything would turn out fine.

Just then I was startled as a phantom hurried past me mumbling, more shade than human, but a flesh and blood man nonetheless. He appeared out of nowhere, a watch cap pulled down over his ears, an oversized filthy trench coat flapping around his scrawny frame. Yo baby, yo baby, yo baby, he muttered over and over, glancing at me vaguely. C'mon, man, let's go. C'mon, man. He never shut up, and for some reason I fell in step mindlessly. I didn't, after all, have a better idea. We cruised together down the block into an alley that opened onto a dirt path leading through some scrubby brush near the river. The path ended at a broken iron staircase, and I followed Mumbles as he plunged underground, his heavy unlaced boots rebounding noisily on each step. C'mon, man. C'mon.

At bottom we climbed over and around a graveyard of wrecked and abandoned cars, skirted a well-lit section of road, and plunged finally into a chaos of heavy cardboard packing crates and lean-tos. Once inside, the tangled outlines of this fugitive city became plain, rows of improvised shelters, haphazard sleeping quarters, piles of mattresses and old clothes here and there, little campfires dotting the landscape, each the center of a huddle of hobos or wanderers or the recently homeless. Mumbles led me deep into the city and parked at a large fire with maybe a dozen ragged spirits basking in the warmth. Yo, Brother Red, Mumbles called to an imposing man with a small felt fedora cocked atop his large head and a heavy woolen blanket tossed across his shoulders. Look here, Brother Red, I found another one.

Brother Red laughed warmly and stepped out to greet me. Yes, yes, yes, he chuckled as he sized me up and took my hand, I believe you did. I felt tiny and white and suddenly exhausted in his presence, the stench of tear gas clinging to my clothes, the warmth of the fugitive fire pulling me in. He paused a moment, and then said to me, But is it true? Are you one of them?

One of who?

One of them revolutionary brothers, he said. One of them—what do you call 'em?—Weathermen.

I guessed I was, and Brother Red embraced me, laughing. Brother, brother, brother. Brother Red pulled up a crate for me and made introductions all around.

Brother Red was a large block of a man with an open reddish face and round, watery eyes. He had a halo of long frizzy gray hair, the circle made complete by an exploding full beard. He was a storyteller and a critic, and he loved to talk. Yes, friend, those Chicago cops getting just what they deserve, just chickens coming home to roost. They haven't had the time to come and roust us for days now, and for that alone I salute you. The brothers passed a bottle of wine my way. I pulled three candy bars from my pack and shared them around the circle.

What does he mean, another one? I asked.

Brother Red laughed again. Well, son, he said, this here jungle is just about the end of the line—it's the lost and the lonely here, folks that's on the loose and on the run. Yep, we get them all, outcasts and outlaws, irregulars and illegitimates, and tonight two of your brothers-in-arms beat you here by half an hour—oh, and both of those brothers are actually sisters.

Mumbles led me down the line to a packing crate, and pushed a cloth aside, ducked and entered. Inside Diana bent over a bloody young woman stretched out and sleeping on an old mattress. Oh my God, I said. Diana looked up, her face tight, exhausted, and strained, but without a hint of surprise to see me there.

When I kissed her I felt a large lump on the side of her head and I could see that she had been crying. She told me that she'd been with the group on Lake Shore Drive when the melee there broke out, that she'd fought in close formation with several others, and that as the fighters retreated slowly toward a construction site locked in combat, the cops had suddenly disengaged and vanished. In a flash a shotgun cut through their midst. Most broke and ran, but at least three went down, a guy from the New York collective and this one bleeding on the mattress. They had escaped arrest somehow.

She's a local high school kid, Diana said. She's got buckshot in her left side. She's going to be OK, but what a mess.

For myself I wondered at that moment if I could ever live a normal life, a nonfugitive life, after all this, after all that I'd been through. It seemed impossible that there was a life beyond the river, beyond the mountain of broken brick. I wondered if I would ever eat a hot dog at Wrigley Field again. If I really choose this warrior life, if I go on and refuse to pull back to normalcy, will I ever have another chance? How much will I suffer? This bizarre and violent time, this ritual of combat, this surreal setting combined with ferocious demons vomited into the dark-eyed night, pursuing me now with anonymous, deadly hatred. I was sure of only one thing: whatever happened next, I was choosing with eyes wide open, and while I might be wrong or foolish, limited and inadequate, mine would not be the suffering of the hapless victim. I might get crushed, but I would never complain and I would never bring suit. Life's tough. Get a helmet.

Diana and I held each other and talked through the night. Brother Red looked in on us twice, once bringing water, and once news that the radio was reporting twenty-eight cops injured and over a hundred comrades locked up. He could hardly contain his glee, and what looked like pride in his watery eyes. Twenty-eight, he repeated with emphasis and a deep chuckle. God-*damn*.

At dawn, Brother Red told us we looked to him like angels now, glorified and risen up. You've been severely tested, he said, in a preacherly voice, and found worthy. I was growing up.

He led the three of us to the border of his fugitive city, where he introduced us to Brother Chick, who would chauffeur us in his beat-up taxi to our next destination. On the house. Chick smiled. Their generosity was embarrassing, and we insisted on offering Brother Red some repayment for his kindness and his hospitality. It has been a privilege and a pleasure for me to be a small part of this, he said formally, bowing slightly. I am deeply honored.

I never found out what became of Brother Red or that high school kid after that night. Never saw either one again.

We found one another—those of us still standing—the next day at a designated safe house on the South Side. The radio reports said that twenty-eight cops had been injured, but that seemed high to us. The reports put our arrests near a hundred, and we knew, because we were there, that each arrest was in fact a collision of pain and blood and ripped skin and chipped teeth or broken bone: broken arms and legs, fractured skulls and jaws, concussions, lacerations, burns, and abrasions. Once in custody it got worse—systematic beatings, breaking people's glasses in their faces, mace at close range, stompings, and gauntlets to run. We also knew that at least eight of us had been shot—the report said two, one seriously, and that those who did the shooting were unidentified. I wasn't complaining—no whining now—but it was at least eight, and each was shot by the cops. I had floated above and I had seen it all. What did we expect? What would we do now?

We would show up for every planned demonstration in the coming days, our numbers diminished, but our spirits getting harder and higher. Were we crazy? Seventy women, including Diana and Bernardine, busted in Grant Park at the All Women's Demonstration one day; a hundred and twenty-three comrades busted the next. Bloodied and wobbly, wounded and hurt, we staggered to the assigned launch each and every day. Like a bad penny. And each and every day we fought until we were taken down. We became what we'd promised, a fighting force in the streets of America.

Events continued to overwhelm us—all we lived for was activity integrated into history. We were interchangeable now, and none of us felt we had any right to a personal existence at all.

Our rhetoric and our posture, our actions and our threats had tended to isolate us, and now this. When we gathered at the charred and damaged base of the Haymarket police statue for our final march to the federal building, we were surrounded by infuriated cops. It's Gandhian violence, Abbie Hoffman would say later. Tell them where you'll be and when, and then hope for "bomby weather."

I remembered the postmortem at the defeat of the Paris Commune. A handful had lifted the banner of revolution and been crushed to bits by the reaction. Those who survived were marched to the graveyard and shot. The left cluck-clucked about it endlessly, while Marx responded that their resistance may have been futile, but to their eternal credit they had stormed the heavens.

Don't you see? Terry said to me later. Can't you understand what's about to happen? I'll be dead pretty soon—I know it. His voice softened, but his eyes blazed in the dim room. I'm living now for all the time I'll miss, he continued. When I go down, I mean for it to stand for something, something no one can forget. Something big. I want to storm the heavens, and when I go down I want it to be in a fiery blaze of glory.

He looked so terribly happy when he said that.

The police harassment crescendoed. Our apartments were regularly ransacked, our cars vandalized, our comings and goings monitored and recorded. We learned not to travel alone after I was picked up walking from the subway to our apartment and taken on a two-hour tour of back alleys and deserted streets in the back seat of a cop car. I emerged with a bloody nose and two black eyes; I'd pissed on myself. We began to vary our meeting and sleeping patterns after the pigs broke down the door of a fifth-floor walk-up after midnight, terrorized three comrades, and hung Terry upside down by his ankles out the window. It was all bad, of course, but we knew, too, that even here we were enjoying the privilege of our skin. We were being pursued and beaten, true, but our Black Panther comrades were being targeted and assassinated. Twenty-seven Black Panther members were gunned down by the police, and we knew many of them. Michael Soto was killed in the Henry Horner Homes, and his brother John was murdered only days after returning from Viet Nam. We attended the funerals and grieved with the families.

The Chicago Black Panthers were led by Bobby Rush and Chairman Fred Hampton, formerly the charismatic leader of an NAACP youth chapter. Fred had a round face and ready smile, clear, penetrating eyes, and a short beard. He loved talking, swapping stories on anything from sports to politics. We saw Fred every day—our offices were several blocks apart on Madison Avenue, and we owned a huge German printing press that the author Anna Louise Strong had sent us from her home in China, and which the Panthers used to print their newspapers and their posters.

Fred was famous for his bravado, his charm, his improvisational tactics. One hot summer day he seized a Good Humor truck—I imagine the hapless driver walking down the street wondering, Why me?—and distributed everything free to the kids in the poorest Black neighborhood on the West Side. He built a kind of Robin Hood reputation and he talked in a kind of stream of slogans: I'm high on the people, he would say smiling broadly. I love the people, and I'm going to die for the people—ain't going to die in an airplane, ain't going to die in a car crash. I'm going to die for the people, because I love the people.

In early December the phone rang before six. Fred's been murdered, Jeff said, and I leapt to my feet.

What happened?

Turn on the news, he said. Fred and Mark Clark have been gunned down by the pigs. Get over here as soon as you can.

The news described a bloody shoot-out initiated by the Panthers. The official story was that various law enforcement agencies led by State's Attorney Edward Hanrahan surrounded Hampton's apartment at four thirty in the morning with a warrant to search for illegal weapons. Two Panthers were killed, four were wounded, and several arrested, led out in chains to waiting paddy wagons. Only later would we learn that over ninety shots were fired into the apartment, none out, and that Fred had been slipped sleep-inducing drugs by a police informant who later killed himself. But we didn't buy the official story, even for a minute. Fred was a threat, a true grass-roots revolutionary leader. He was twenty-one years old.

Fred's funeral was simultaneously a political rally, a show of force, and a community in mourning. What do we say? I asked Jeff before we got there. Just say you're sorry and look fucked up, he said.

The line to view the body stretched for three blocks, and it swelled with young and old, Black and white, street people and professionals. People wept openly, chanted angrily, sang and cheered. Fred was wearing his black leather jacket and beret, and by the time I reached the front of the line his casket was heavy with movement buttons and pictures and memorabilia. I pulled the ring that Nguyen Thi Thanh had given me off my finger and put it in Fred's hands before I moved on.

We were ready now, our dress rehearsal behind us, to plunge headlong into the whirlpool of violence. The space of what we wouldn't do narrowed, but we didn't know yet by how much. We doubted that many of us would survive, hoping that history would at least judge us freedom fighters, but knowing that terrorist was tattooed over every inch of us, a footprint with every step we took. In a minute we would be called upon to sort it all out.

Part II 1970–1975

21.

March 1970.

I can only imagine what it was like to see such a thing from a middle distance. The strangest thing, I suppose, from there.

I picture the street coming alive, awakening from the fury of winter, stirred from the chilly spring night by cold glimmers of sunlight angling through the city. The first fresh breezes might have been sweeping out of a blinding blue sky, as the last of the grimy slush piled for months on street corners finally yielded to the promise of warmer days. Schoolchildren with brightly colored jackets, armed with homemade pinhole boxes to view the impending solar eclipse, would have already darted down this block to school, while their parents had made their procession toward the avenues just hours before to be carried off to work. The stone houses, gray and brown and uniformly graceful, were as always packed together, a line of impeccably outfitted soldiers at attention. I envision the events of the everyday: a baby in a carriage blinking and smiling at its nanny, a bird settled on a sill to consider its crumb, a wretched urban tree with its hopeful branch wound around its protective iron grate sighing in its way. And then, all hell broke loose.

A taxi driver slams to a stop, sticks his head out the window, and stares, shocked into stillness as a roar erupts eighty feet up the street to his left, the face of a townhouse contorted into a sudden and inexplicable scowl, the facade shaking uncontrollably and then melting in upon itself. A fireball of light and heat leaps heavenward as a deep hole opens wide below, sucking the entire building down into itself. Simultaneously a shock wave races down the street, shattering windows, setting up little tidal waves in the gutters and knocking the cabby's hat off of his head. It's over before he can grasp what it actually is. An explosion—fantastic alien thunder and a wall of flame.

Stranger still, young people, charred and shaken, clamber from the rubble, over the back fence, or out the front through the opening hole—one naked, bleeding from the nose; one with singed hair, all but gone. Neighbors appear with water and blankets, sweatshirts and old clothes. When the police arrive minutes later the survivors have already been carried along in the chaos, and disappeared.

The first news report describes a "gas explosion," then a blast of "suspicious origins." Soon the taxi driver would read in the *Daily News* that the demolished townhouse had been the "bomb factory" of a group of antiwar radicals. "The people in the house were obviously putting together the component parts of a bomb," said the chief investigator on the scene. "And they did something wrong." Two bodies had been recovered in the wreckage—Ted Gold, a spirited activist from Columbia University, crushed and broken, and Diana Oughton, from a prominent Illinois family, mutilated beyond recognition and identified finally from a fragment of finger. Authorities found several cases of dynamite and blasting caps, wires, clocks, and electrical tape; more of everything was expected. They never found Terry Robbins's remains, but he was, we knew soon enough, in there, too. He went out in the fiery blaze of glory he'd predicted.

The smoking ruin was a catastrophe of the exotic and the everyday—a gym shoe lying alongside a box of lead pipes, an open copy of *Catch-22* with a blasting cap for a page marker.

Many people, shocked by the implications, groped to understand what had happened in light of their own revulsion and rage at the government and the war. The *New York Times* editorialized about criminals in idealistic clothing, and much of the media was mocking and diversionary. The independent journalist I. F. Stone replied that to diagnose the trouble falsely was to move toward the wrong remedies, and that the wrong remedies would worsen everything. He worried that escalating statistics on antiwar bombings from around the country suggested that the first stages of an urban guerrilla movement were afoot, and he argued that a guerrilla movement is a political and not a criminal phenomenon, however many crimes it may commit. Until the war in Southeast Asia is ended, he wrote, and priorities revised to make racial reconciliation and social reconstruction the country's main concerns, the dynamite that threatens the country sizzles on a fuse that leads straight back to the White House.

The strangest thing.

22.

What the fuck? David exploded, mostly to himself, but also to the trees and the stars, to the wide world beyond, and now to us. What the fuck? His voice rose above the ruckus as he rushed to the battered Ford, slammed a green army duffel into the trunk, and hurried back to the rented cabin, scooping up belongings room by room, everything scattered from the days of waiting.

Rachel splashed rubbing alcohol everywhere—door handles, bed frames, countertops—frantically wiping the surfaces with paper towels, erasing the fingerprints that could betray us when the FBI arrived. We were sure they would, so better to be safe. The place reeked, and our eyes watered as we worked feverishly to pack up and get lost.

What the fuck? What the fuck? Like all of us, I suppose, David's devastation ignited his sadness, the shocking sense of waste and irredeemable loss; his grief agitated his anger and all of it bled inexorably toward a cold and draining fear. What will happen to me?

Alarms were going off in all of our heads—we're busted, we're dead—and I was fighting simply to stay upright and on my feet, to push the panic back far enough to regroup and get the hell out of there, all of us alive and in one piece and free. David was beginning to sound like a broken record.

Shut up, David, I said finally. Just shut up and get the shit into the Ford.

I'm getting it done, he shot back indignantly. I'm doing it.

Diana had been dead for days by the time I found out in that
unhappy phone booth on that desolate stretch of road. I was now
only twenty minutes away from the phone call, but an eternity from
all I'd known before. The force of the blast in New York, the deaths of
Diana and the others, hurled me—all of us—onto an uncertain
course. What had we expected? I was fighting to hang on to the
thread of my own life as the fire flared further out of control, blazing
like hell. The thunderbolt struck my chest and knocked me down.
Part of me was gone, but I wasn't entirely dead yet. Part of Diana
lived with me still, and I was on my feet, numb but moving. Fleeing
the abyss.

Inside I was filled with doubt, but I couldn't hesitate now. If I do, I
thought, we're lost. I was trying to do the responsible thing, to assert
my tattered leadership and to keep moving.

Andy was subdued and shaking; tripping over a pair of abandoned
boots in the doorway she dissolved into sobs. Daniel, grim-faced,
gathering the guns and locking them methodically into their cases,
helped her to her feet and held her for a moment. Everyone had gone
colorless. Fiona looked the most alive, her black eyes steady and still
as she conscientiously collected her things, moving deliberately from
room to room. You're doing fine, she said to me softly as we passed in
the hallway, and she brushed my face with the back of her hand.
We're all in this together, she said, and we'll get out of it together, too.
I felt a slight shift in her presence, like life restored. I was about to
jump out of my skin, she told me later, and since the moment cried
out for calm, I just clicked my thermostat down a notch. I was acting.

We'll meet at Dino's for breakfast tomorrow, I said. Seven sharp. I
was aiming for dead certainty, sounding, I'm sure, like a hollow fraud.
But since we were each acting a part, my fellow players gave me a
pass. I prayed a private little prayer for survival.

Dino's was a truck stop along Route 12, several hours' drive from
the cabins we'd been renting, and perfect for us—large and anonymous and transient, with showers, storage lockers, traveling supplies,
and, most important, long banks of pay phones out of sight in the

rear. We each knew the numbers of half a dozen of those phones by heart, and we could always use them to connect as backup if necessary. We'd hooked up here twice in the past few months, so everyone knew the way. Andy and Daniel would drive the gray pickup, David and Rachel the Ford, Fiona would come with me in the van. Seven o'clock sharp, I repeated, and in minutes we were all on the road, winding our wobbly way out into the wide, wide world.

That car ride is mostly a blur now, but even the next morning it was foggy, taking on the gauzy quality of a dream. I was exhausted, running on some high-octane mix of panic and pain, and perhaps I even nodded off at the wheel a couple of times. It wouldn't surprise me. What I remember most is talking, talking, talking, and Fiona following along mostly in silence. Whenever I glanced at her she was awake and watching me, standing a kind of careful vigil, her eyes embracing and accepting. She said nothing, and I rattled on.

I knew that something wide and monstrous had opened up, something I couldn't really name or fully understand. Diana had been so vivid a moment ago—her smell and her feel, her sound and her shape, the natural line of our love—so familiar and yet somehow so surprising every time. How could this simple intimacy be suddenly gone?

I began to feel sluggish. I wanted to stay still, but I drove on and on. I wanted everything to slow down, to stay unchanged. I'd lost my home, and I didn't want another.

I also wanted to know why, and I wanted to know what had happened. What had actually gone on in those last minutes? What did she look like, and what did she say? Who else was there, and what did they see?

We had no plan for what to do. We had been trying over the past months to build clandestine collectives of hard-core members who could carry out illegal and secret activities and then survive any repressive response, and, simultaneously, with the same people, maintain open organizations and a public presence. Foolish perhaps, but true. The hidden work was in ascendency and the leadership all tended to be going under, but this was still contested territory, and I hadn't been fully conscious of the split between the aboveground and the underground impulses. Part of the plan was for balance, for parallel efforts, for symmetry. Now that was all gone, and I didn't know what to do next. Brecht came back to me—indeed we live in the dark ages. The ground was shifting.

I remembered a story about a superhighway that cut through rolling green hills, and early on a Sunday morning in springtime a flooded stream collapsed a section of it. I imagined car after unhappy car swinging comfortably out of a turn and then off into the surprising abyss. You would be gone before your mind could catch up. I felt like that.

I remembered a dream, too, that I'd had while crossing the North Atlantic, a vision of falling overboard in the middle of the ocean and swimming as fast as I could as the ship steamed off and disappeared over the horizon. I had the feeling of total abandonment, of utter loneliness, and watching the waters close overhead, I realized that no one else could ever know this singular experience, and that the world, like the steaming ship, would go on entirely indifferent to me and my drama. I woke up drenched and cold.

I remembered the whole weird panorama of my life that night, and it played in dizzying flashbacks punctuated by headlights and truck exhaust and diesel horns. I was far away from my home by now, driving hard, moving farther and farther away. The place I grew up was straight off the cover of *The Saturday Evening Post*—my oak-lined street, the volunteer fire department, the Busy Bee Barber Shop. There was a universe beyond, of course, a place I even glimpsed occasionally, typically through the *National Geographic*. Friendly Filipinos, the cover instructed, Happy Haitians, and Sunny South Africa, each issue an exotic festival of welcoming smiles and native breasts, a world seen through the beneficent imperial gaze.

Even in prep school, I'd heard the advancing chords of freedom— This little light of mine, the voices sang at first, I'm gonna let it shine. Soon there were the sounds of war approaching, and then the mustering resistance. One thing was clear. The world was going, going, going noisily along, and I wanted to get going, too. I felt admonished.

There were turning points, breaks in the road, and I was sometimes aware of them, often unaware until much later. One event, one action engulfed another, and soon I was thrust into a world of consequences. The train was racing headlong downhill without regard to flashing lights or warning bells as the locomotive of my heart switched tracks. I didn't know where I would stop, or where I might be stopped, but there was already blood on the tracks and you could see it.

I was back in Chicago only days before and then, in a whirlwind, New York City, Washington, D.C., and rural Maine, where a small group raided a construction shed and made off with 125 pounds of high explosives.

It was illegal, yes, and dangerous, and the plans for the stuff apocalyptic. But we were freedom fighters, and we came to it in the spirit of John Brown and Nat Turner, in the name of liberty. We knew that others would brand us criminals, and then try to hunt us down to jail or kill us, but they were wrong, and anyway I didn't care anymore. We won't give up, we sang, louder and louder now, we won't turn back.

Only four days ago, Ralph Featherstone and Che Payne, who'd been friends from SNCC, were killed in a car explosion near Washington, D.C. The stakes for Black Americans were rising. I'd already seen the spectacle of tanks in the streets and troops shooting wildly into the night, bodies beaten and bloodied, stacked up in front of looted storefronts like firewood, the madness dragging on and on through days and weeks. Things were falling apart, an accelerating entropy everywhere, a shocking atmosphere of havoc, the evidence of fire and death. But then Fred Hampton was dead and it all became intensely personal—at Fred's funeral my eyes filled up, not with tears but with blood and with revenge. Now when we opened our mouths to sing, we could only scream.

A squad of cops in Cleveland had dragged Black men from a motel and shot them down in cold blood, and now we would, I thought, even the score. We'd walked into their precinct house several times, this time under the pretense of reporting a stolen bicycle. One of us unscrewed a vent down an isolated hallway while another stood watch; we crammed some dynamite with a crude cigarette fuse into a tight space, slipped around a corner where we met our set, and then we ran. How inevitable it all seemed then, how entirely impossible now, driving through the night. The device never went off—out of oxygen, it exhausted itself a millimeter short of an imagined modern-day Harper's Ferry—and I was unsure of why we were spared.

As I drove on, it began to rain, the wipers beating out a steady rhythm, and I thought about the blast, about the air sucked away with surprising suddenness, and behind the air, the light, the sound. Nothing left behind. Everything freezes for a flash, and then everything slowly rises. Wood splintering and the refrigerator collapsing in upon itself, and then quickly reversing direction. The toilet flying apart, sending shards of porcelain into the blue, blue sky. The toaster sailing across an open space with a long black cord for a tail flickering wildly behind. Clothes in the closet embracing, the TV tube spinning dizzily, pots and pans crisscrossing each other in maddening indecision. Books opening and closing, the *Times* disintegrating, a footstool rising through the debris like a paper airplane. Everything dying.

We had been playing at a deadly politics, it's true, and our rhetoric was filled with images of death. But not Diana's. Others were better candidates, darker and more suited to it. Daniel was distracted, David more exposed and clumsy, Rachel much more brittle. Diana was golden and fine, destined for a long and happy life. Why her? Let the others die.

Of course, her death could not be one of those pointless things that adds up to nothing. It had to have a meaning, a purpose I would fight for. I thought of her sister Christina getting the news, and of her parents, and I felt sick. How could they take any of this in? How could they ever understand it? They couldn't. I couldn't.

Oddly I wanted desperately to hold on to this heightened feeling of ruin, the magnified pain and my heated-up charge of loss, knowing that it would be a betrayal if I allowed the sensation to recede even a notch. Memory was a form of fidelity now. This stood for her life, and I clung to that sense of sweet devastation with both hands.

Dino's was abuzz twenty-four hours a day every day, ratcheting up the frenzy a notch between six and eight in the morning: locals and long-haul truckers, campers and salesmen jostling for feed—pancakes with bacon, three-egg omelettes with sausage, all the grits you could eat. Vats of noxious coffee were filled and refilled while corrosive fumes poisoned the air. Everyone's eyes watered as they gulped it down, stretched, erupted, and hit the road in a rank and swirling exhaust.

I pulled the van into a space between two semis in Dino's back lot. Fiona and I had made lists along the way: ditch the cars, sever any links from our open lives to where we were heading, get some usable ID, connect with old friends, and beg for money. Where were we heading? Never mind. Making lists was compulsive but also tranquilizing, and I arrived at the rendezvous more focused and aware, more determined and calm than seemed possible only hours earlier. Lists tightly in hand. Fiona told me later that she mostly wanted to hug me during that stormy night, but that she knew me well enough by then to know that more than that I needed to talk. That's what I always did with crisis or pain or anxiety. You're like a lot of bright people, she said. A talker. But I'd never known you to be as astute or as wide-awake as that night.

I was surprised she said that.

We walked into Dino's at fifteen minutes to seven, took a back booth, and got a head start on the coffee. Rachel and David followed by about ten minutes, looking bleary and beaten, but no Dandy. We ordered and ate without speaking—there was nothing to say until we were all together—but the symphony of breakfast at Dino's played full-up. At seven thirty, worried but following our backup plan precisely I went to the farthest bank of phones. Within seconds Andy called, still sobbing, still shaking. We're not coming, kid, she blurted out. I can't . . . I can't.

Andy, Andy . . . I tried to calm her, but it was no use.

We've already crossed into Canada, she said. You know me, kid, you know me . . . I will never, ever hurt you or the others. Never . . . But we've got to get out . . .

Andy, I said, get rid of the truck. There's nothing safe about Canada.

Don't worry about us, she said. We'll be OK. Oh, I'm so sorry, kid, so, so sorry. . . . I'm so sorry for Diana, so sorry for you. . . .

That got to me finally, and then I was sobbing, too.

To revisit the past is to become, whether intended or not, a crusading editor—selecting, correcting, disappearing, rearranging, cutting, and pasting. There is an insistent voice that urges subversion or, at the very least, caution: hide the bodies, it says, erase the tracks, clean off the fingerprints, yours and others.

David and I ditched the Ford in a desolate spot along the river, taking the license plates and throwing them into a Dumpster, leaving the keys in sight on the dashboard hoping it would be stolen by some wanderer and chopped up, but worrying that any self-respecting thief would smell a trap and move on. We sold the van for $400, and then fanned out to collect more money from friends. Tre handed me $200—It's all I've got, man. Please don't get killed. His eyes were moist and his characteristic playful expression completely erased—he looked scared. I couldn't imagine how I looked. The FBI's been everywhere, man, he said. Think about it.

Altogether we had just over $1,500. David and Fiona and Rachel took it to set up a new base area; I went to New York City to see the remains of the explosion.

23.

Gloria met me at the Port Authority bus terminal and whisked me away to a safe apartment she'd rented uptown. Gloria was a part-time actress and a medical student, but she was also a leader now in the shattered New York Tribe. She showed me the latest issues of *Time* and *Newsweek*, and there we were—rows of mug shots accompanied by vivid and dire stories about several of us, with the pointed warning that we were to be considered "armed and dangerous." It should say armed and terrified, she said, or armed and incompetent. This was true, but it sounded to me like heresy. No one in the last months chided our efforts. No one we listened to shared any sense of irony or humor.

Most of the pictures were fuzzy or dated. My youthful mug shot was from a 1968 arrest in Michigan—eyebrows arched arrogantly, lip curled, head slightly askance, every gesture suggesting an imagined cartoon bubble with the words "FUCK YOU" floating merrily in a corner, a comprehensive comment sweeping in the editors at *Time*, the mainstream culture itself, all convention and good manners and dominant assumptions, the cynical politics of privilege and control, the world in the hands of hypocrites and grown-ups. In 1968 I still had a sense of theater. Bernardine looked flirty and seductive, even on her wanted poster, the cold stare and the hard edge framed by her dark good looks; she was destined for the FBI's "Ten Most Wanted" list, and the caption taken from a comment by J. Edgar Hoover was perfect: The most dangerous woman in America, it said. La Pasionaria of the lunatic left. Jeffrey's picture was of a fresh-faced

surfer, but Gloria, thankfully, was largely unknown to them and off
their screen altogether, so there was no photo of her yet.

Gloria showed me a malignant editorial cartoon, too, with a
deranged-looking young man—sunken cheeks, eyes blazing, beard
blown to one side—with a bolt of lightning in one hand and a sizzling bomb in the other, "Weatherman" inscribed on his beret, walking through the charred ruins of a city labeled "UTOPIA." I thought
then of growing my beard and losing ten pounds—I already had the
blazing eyes.

In the wake of the Townhouse, my mug shot in *Time* magazine
seemed ho-hum. I glanced at it once and then set it aside forever. We
were in a different world now, and I was unsure of what to do, uncertain what to feel, doubtful that I would ever again feel much of anything with zest. I was mostly numb. I wasn't particularly frightened,
just vague and contrived, my emotions unreliable. Nothing spontaneous sparked up in me, nothing invested.

Gloria had gone to see the Townhouse right after the explosion but
before the nature of the thing was known, and she described the devastation to me in detail. It was horrible, and it loomed large and
would become even bigger in our mythology—we referred to the
explosion simply as the Townhouse with a capital *T.* Gloria said that
there were now police barricades everywhere, a police checkpoint on
each end of the street, and it would not be smart to go near the place.
Still, I wanted to see it for myself, and she knew I would.

I dressed up in a suit and tie, hat and trench coat, *New York Times*
folded under one arm, and Gloria put on a dress with a sweater herself. We walked arm in arm down Fifth Avenue affecting what we
thought was the look of a young couple who belonged in the neighborhood. It was after eight, and from the corner I could see the
somber remnants of one wall, the gloomy hole reaching away from
the street, and shadowy workers illuminated by powerful floodlights
moving about slowly in their melancholy tasks. It was a terrible thing
to look at.

Gloria, always adventurous and often unpredictable, suddenly
approached the cop in the little booth that acted as checkpoint. I

hung back trying to look casual. What's going on? she asked, and the cop assumed the role of knowledgeable and helpful tour guide, seemingly happy for the attention.

I realized that this was as close as I would get for a long time, and I had brought along a small package I'd unrealistically hoped to lay on the tomb—it had a bracelet of Diana's in it, a snapshot of the two of us, and a poem I'd written on a Vietnamese postcard that began: These abbreviated lines write themselves brusquely in blood, the vaulting hope, an overreaching gesture, a sudden, shattering fall. I pulled it quickly from my pocket, dropped it on the street, and kicked it into the sewer at Fifth Avenue and Eleventh Street.

I met with every orphaned member of the New York Tribe over the next few days, sometimes individually, often in small groups, and everyone was attentive and solicitous toward me. I became the aggrieved survivor, and I rather liked that, the object of special regard and unearned consideration. Everyone was kind, everyone caring. When I met with two of the comrades who'd come out of the explosion alive, burned and bleeding, the tables shifted—they had scurried from more than a metaphorical abyss. We talked about time before the blast, and I pressed for details, but they didn't know a thing beyond speculation about what had gone on in the last hour.

Everyone was also in some sense in shock and disarray, each living with friends or distant family or in newly secured apartments, each trying to keep out of sight and away from the mobilized police forces pursuing us now with accelerating fury. The pressure was ratcheting up, our faces featured regularly on TV, homes of known supporters raided, old comrades rounded up for questioning. We had a secret national leadership meeting set for the next week, and while I couldn't imagine what we'd unleashed or what was next, I wanted to survive long enough to reconnect. The specter of Diana and Teddy and Terry loomed over me every minute, and I felt the first cold fissures of possible betrayal spreading around me. Daniel and Andy had already bolted—who would be next? What if someone decided to roll over? Who could we trust? The void seemed real enough then.

We took new names and fashioned clumsy disguises and kept our living spaces hidden even from each other. We met up mostly at night in elaborately guarded ways, and then usually only briefly. Our precautions only fueled our paranoia and left us more vulnerable, the whole thing a vast self-feeding cycle spiraling downward, but we didn't know how to stop it.

Gloria worked feverishly to keep everyone in touch, to move us safely toward our rendezvous. I loved her then, her single-mindedness and her willful energy, and we held each other late one night, but in a way that was—how can I say this?—conservative and careful, tender bending toward therapeutic. It was just a great relief.

The New York Tribe had been led by Terry and CW, who were remarkably alike: intense and driven, each hot-tempered and quarrelsome, unassured in everyday affairs but with Big Brains for compensation. Each was fueled by some deep interior anger, and each assumed the angle of a tough guy—leather jackets and motorcycle boots, that sort of thing. Terry and CW one-on-one or alone could be irritating but not, it seemed to me, deadly; the two of them together sucked the air out of a room.

When SDS had split months before, it started a chain reaction that was not over yet. Splintering became a habit, and what constituted the big WE was getting smaller and smaller for everyone. We, too, swallowed the alphabet soup that seems to always choke the left—CP, OL, RU, YAWF, YSA. SDS had become two large factions, the Maoist Progressive Labor and the Revolutionary Youth Movement; the Revolutionary Youth Movement had split in two—a faction which would itself become Maoist and the Weathermen. And Weathermen, badly fractured since the Days of Rage, split into three, our geographic distribution mirroring the division perfectly. We agreed on the need to build a clandestine fighting force, but the East Coast Tribe championed the idea that revolutionary leadership had to be military, and Terry and CW set out to prove their point by creating the grandest possible gesture—chaos in the mother country, the bigger the mess the better.

The West Coast Tribe, led by Bernardine and Jeffrey, argued that while we all agreed that thought without action was sterile and hopeless, there was the very real danger in us now of action without thought, and that would lead inevitably to blindness and a repeating nightmare of blood and death. Revolutionary weapons are always led by politics, Bernardine argued, but she didn't win.

Terry and I had together loved the film *Butch Cassidy and the Sundance Kid*, a gaudy portrayal of the split of thought and action, mind and body, theory and practice, men and women. Terry thought of himself as Butch, the thinker, and he cast me as the dazzling and doing Sundance. That they died in a rain of gunfire was, for us, beside the point.

Bernardine disliked the film intensely and hated the other boys' favorite, *The Wild Bunch*, a gory display of going down in a blaze of glory. If we're serious about succeeding, she said, we have to keep organizing and winning people over, and we have to become aware of the coherence of thought and action. Thought is action in dress rehearsal, she said, and yes, in the beginning there is the deed, but followed as quick as an echo by reflection and deliberation and adjustment. Otherwise, nothingness.

Unable to agree, Terry and CW had gone east, Bernardine and Jeffrey headed west. The Midwest group was, well, in the middle. It was the smallest group by far, as well as the least distinctive, and I was—predictably, I thought—its leader.

I felt all the deep divisions vibrating inside myself, and I think others felt them as well—I was drawn to the escalating fight, to the need to hurl myself into war in solidarity and in sacrifice, and I was simultaneously sympathetic to the importance of keeping politics in command. I still felt myself to be a teacher and an organizer, but I increasingly thought of myself as a soldier. Terry persuaded Diana to join him for a time in New York, which I resented, and he urged me to build the military capacity in the Midwest. Bernardine disagreed, encouraging me to keep the Midwest group connected to the mass movement, and to meet up with her and Jeff on the West Coast soon.

Terry was gone now, and CW came out of his cave to sing to me like the Sirens. He embraced me and consoled me, pursued me in all things, and tried to stay by my side every minute I was in New York. Your loss is the greatest, he said, your lover and your best friend. It's up to us to uphold their memory, to fight for their vindication. Terry is our John Brown, Diana is our Tanya.

I didn't like it, all the coaxing, all the pressing, but I didn't know where any of it was leading, either, and I mostly wanted to get to the meeting at the safe house.

We had almost no money. Gloria and I took a bus to Baltimore and spent a day in department stores stealing wallets. We returned to New York with fancy clothes and a rented car. Brilliant! CW said when he saw it, and a group of us crowded in and zoomed off for the coast.

I was driving somewhere in South Dakota when a state trooper got behind me and followed us for over an hour. Everyone pretended to sleep while we had a frantic muted discussion covering every detail of our story—we were on vacation, we worked in restaurants or in bookstores, we lived in Philadelphia and our names were such and such. The city had seemed close and claustrophobic, but out here the wide open spaces provided no cover at all. We were ducks gliding in an open sky.

We thought that the car rented with stolen ID had a safe life of weeks, but now we were sure we were wrong. What if he was radioing in our plates? What if there was a roadblock ahead?

When I pulled off for gas at the first place I'd seen since he joined us, he pulled off, too, but just for a cup of coffee it turned out. He tipped his hat to the ladies; we filled up and pushed on.

We made phone contact with Jeffrey later that day, and our mistake with the car became even clearer. What you're doing is stupid and risky, he said, and criminal, not brilliant. Get rid of the car in the nearest city, and get the first bus out. Get rid of the fancy clothes, too. People like that don't ride the bus.

We split up the next day, Gloria and I on a bus toward the Northwest.

We arrived by night, dropped off at a little bus station that doubled as a grocery store and one-pump gas station in a small California town. Everything was closed down, and a single bulb illuminated only a tiny patch. The gravel pull-out was just big enough for the Greyhound as it heaved to a stop, discharged Gloria and me, and then roared back on the road.

It was after midnight and our bodies, stiff and creaky, ached in the cold. We headed to a fenced-in field a couple hundred yards away and spread our bags on the ground behind a ledge of bay trees.

At dawn we found a creek where we washed up. We hiked along a narrow road for three miles to a small town off the bus route and turned north on a highway that led toward the vineyards. Although we hadn't spotted him yet, we knew that Jeffrey had been tracking us from the moment the bus entered California. We were certain we were clean, that we hadn't been followed, but Jeffrey was responsible to clear us, and so the choice to make contact was his. If he didn't pull us in within the next fifteen minutes, something was wrong, and we would hitchhike out of the area and start calling our backup pay-phone numbers tomorrow at eight. Maybe we had missed someone tailing us, and we would be arrested on the spot, or maybe the police would continue some super-sophisticated surveillance and let us hang out until they'd roped all of us in. Or maybe Jeffrey and the others were already busted or killed and we were floating here ignorant and alone. Maybe we'd been set up, or maybe we'd been cast loose. We walked along the cliff's edge, silent with our thoughts.

Only a few minutes had passed when an old Chevy pickup loaded with hay pulled up next to us and Jeffrey leaned over to open the passenger door, smiling broadly. Need a lift? he asked, the thick red beard he'd grown in the past weeks changing his shape and feel dramatically. We leapt in as he accelerated down the road.

It was another two hours to the safe house, and Jeffrey zigzagged the mountain roads slowly, stopping to enjoy a breathtaking view of the vineyards or to try to identify a bird wheeling in the distant sky. Jeff's driving had always struck me as of a piece with the way he thought, the way he lived—a kind of improvisational genius, neither logical nor exactly visceral, but both of these all mixed up with cool self-confidence and hope. He seemed shockingly serene, and though he was sad, sad, sad about the deaths, and particularly attentive to me because of Diana, I think, he was in no hurry to explore any political issues with us yet. None of this had to happen, he said at one point, but when pressed, he said only that we would have plenty of time to sort things out. We should try to catch our breath for now, he said. We'll have plenty of time, he repeated, and that unremarkable phrase, a commonplace in most company, was jarring here because no comrade could have spoken it in the past several months without a barrage of derisive criticism. It was heresy, too, but it was calming, and I felt, oddly, that I wanted to cry.

24.

The safe house, rented for a year by a sympathetic doctor and handed
over to us as a hideout, was roomy and open, sunlight pouring
through wide windows into spacious rooms. When we walked in I felt
I could have been a mole crawling out of my dark little hole, blinking
and inhaling. Bernardine held me for a long time, then put on some
coffee and brought out a jar of chocolate chip cookies. I couldn't
remember my last homemade cookie, and what might have been
unremarkable elsewhere was something of a shock. Who had time to
bake cookies? Wasn't this just a bourgeois indulgence? On the other
hand, these were the best I'd ever had, thick and chewy, absolutely
choked with chocolate, and I had several.

The house filled up over the next days with the remnants of our
national leadership as well as some others gathered to help us think
through what had happened.

CW was wound up tight as a drum, and he took every opportunity
to lobby me and several others, but Bernardine and Jeffrey were in no
hurry to get down to business, and it was immediately clear that they
were controlling the tempo and the agenda. Instead of a routine
forced march of no sleep, bad food, speed, and endless meetings, we
took walks, prepared meals, and ate together all in our own sweet
time. It felt so odd, this normal life. We watched the sun drop into
the Pacific every evening, and then we drank wine or smoked a joint
together, inhaled deeply and slept the whole night through. The pace
slowed down, and I began to hope that here was a rescue ship I so
desperately needed. I felt myself coming back to life.

We spent a lot of time hiking the hills near the safe house. On one walk Bernardine told me in a hurry how she'd heard about the Townhouse, her quick descent into anguish, and then thinking of me and all that this would mean, and crying. She listened as I speculated on what had happened inside the Townhouse. What had it looked like? What words were spoken? What went wrong? Together we cursed Fate, and then moved on to easier topics, minor grumblings about Terry, flashes of anger at CW. She made fun of our inept barbs, our shaky aim, but inevitably we jumped back to the explosion, the cold, fateful moment of dread and loss.

I told her how I'd waited at the phone booth and my mounting anxiety. She said that she dreaded most the moment of bringing me the news. I could hardly breathe, she said.

We moved from the Townhouse to what would become of us. What brought you into the movement? she asked. We talked about Cleveland and the war, and even the Children's Community. We need to remember the most hopeful parts of our lives, she said. The basic things we've fought for and the fundamentals we long for.

I'll tell you one thing, she said finally. We need each other, and we need to help each other through the days ahead. We need to hold each other and to love each other like never before.

She's right, I thought. Of course she was right, but it came to me then as a revelation.

We've dissolved too often into barricaded and angry camps, Jeffrey said on another day. Easy but wrong. The challenge, he said, is to find ways to listen well and speak clearly, to weave our stories together—incomplete and interrupted, contingent and dynamic—and to seek always more knowledge rather than more evidence. We need to develop some skepticism, Jeffrey said, some doubt, and still hang on to our willingness to act.

Jeff had grown up in Southern California, and he fit my stereotype of a surfer perfectly—tall with straight blond hair that fell to his shoulders and the slim, athletic body. He had a face that made you want to stare; more than handsome, he displayed a kind of transparent innocence. He wasn't a surfer at all, but he was a strange West

Coast creature to most of us, and so the surfer myth prevailed, along with the myth that his dad, who was a technician at Walt Disney Studios, was in fact the voice of Donald Duck. When anyone challenged that biographical tidbit, Jeff would pipe up in a believable imitation of the duck and at least sow some confusion on the point.

Jeff was raised a Quaker—his dad did time for refusing to fight in World War II—and he embodied a kind of natural pacifism. You couldn't imagine him in war under any conditions, but by 1968 many committed pacifists like Jeff had concluded that even activist pacifism wasn't good enough to combat what was happening in Viet Nam—something more had to be done. For Jeff the step away from the clarity and purity of pacifism was painful. Hatred is hatred, he said to me then, feeding always on itself; perhaps our whole generation is doomed.

I had known Jeff when he worked in the regional SDS office in New York, when he ran with a group of cultural anarchists from the Lower East Side. The appeal was the irreverence, the stance, the fun, and the theater—they were forever opening fire hydrants for kids on the block or passing out free food, and during the New York City garbage strike, they collected neighborhood garbage and deposited it on City Hall and at gatherings of the wealthy. The anarchists were master disrupters, publicly disputing the suffocating cultural conventions. The downside was the sense of pointlessness, finally, of a kind of self-indulgent theater for its own sake, and the tyranny of structurelessness, a heightened individualism that worked to the advantage of the loudest and the angriest. I knew dangerous guys there, Jeff said, but they were armed mostly with brown rice and paintbrushes, less likely to hurt anyone fatally.

Jeffrey had traveled with a peace delegation to Indochina in 1967 and had met with NLF cadres in Phnom Penh. As it happened, those cadres were all actors, part of a guerrilla theater troupe—that's what they called it—and they put on a show at Olympic Stadium for ten thousand Cambodians. It was a lesson imprinted: guerrillas who were storytellers, armed mostly with ideas.

Jeffrey had developed a more modest metaphor for himself that suited his temperament and his outlook and which he never entirely abandoned: I just want to grow up to be a short-order cook on the Ho Chi Minh Trail, he often said, always with a whimsical smile. It was a bit preposterous, a little absurd, but it was also a smart mix of extravagance and modesty. The Ho Chi Minh Trail was, of course, its own metaphor—as many as ten (and in places dozens) of secret roadways snaking down the western border of Viet Nam—several thousand miles, some parts entirely camouflaged. For the U.S. military, the Ho Chi Minh Trail was sneaky communist subversion at its worst, but for Jeffrey, the Ho Chi Minh Trail was dedication and determination against technological terrorism. A third of the vehicles and machinery along the trail were destroyed by the Americans and 10 percent of the Vietnamese troops were killed or wounded, but that meant that two-thirds of the supplies and 90 percent of the troops made it through. A half-million workers maintained the trail, moving tons of supplies on bikes and backs, and Jeffrey imagined himself one of them. Just serving up the spring rolls with tea, he said.

Bernardine began the meeting forcefully: We're going to build a new political organization right here, she said, with a unified leadership, a capacity to survive, and the ability to organize people as well as to fight back. We're political people and we're organizers. We're not military men and we never will be.

We've come out of a burning house, she said, and on the ashes of that burning house we can build a new house, a safe house. But there's no way weapons or militarism can ever again be allowed to lead, because in the end every revolution and every successful resistance is first and foremost about consciousness, and then about popular action. Does anyone here believe that 125 pounds of dynamite will count for much in a contest with the Pentagon? Whatever action we decide to take, she concluded, the calculus must include its impact on people's thinking, people throughout the world, of course, but people here as well who are, after all, our responsibility.

We spent one whole afternoon and evening discussing the Townhouse and what went wrong there, and the lines of disagreement became tight and narrow. CW believed that the unsophisticated technology of these early efforts was inevitable—we didn't know about safety switches, for example, or warning lights—and that the cause of the disaster, the tragedy, was mostly technical. But by this point almost everyone disagreed. No, Jeff said. The cause was not technical, no matter how many technical mistakes were made. We blinded ourselves, we lied to ourselves. The root cause was political, and if we refuse to look at that fully we'll simply wander off the cliff farther along. I agreed with Jeff, but even after a lot of talk and speculation, no one really knew what had gone on in the time before the explosion.

When a comrade raised a small doubt about a peripheral point, Bernardine cut him to his knees, and hardly knew she'd done it.

Why did you crush him in there? I asked later. It was such a small point.

Did I crush him? she asked with real surprise. I only wanted him to hear me, she said. And I didn't want to say it twice.

And so we returned to politics—agitated though they were, overheated, and far-out, but politics nonetheless. No one at that safe house in those white-hot days wanted to surrender, and no one argued for surfacing or disbanding. No one even thought that we should turn away from violence on principle. There was, however, a consensus growing that our actions would be strongest as symbols, as inspirational to larger and larger numbers of people, a kind of overheated storytelling. The Townhouse was the result of militarism, we began to say, an aggressive and exaggerated sense of the power of weapons, a macho disregard for safety—our own and others'—combined with a fateful embrace of fighting as a test of courage and commitment and the dominance of a military class and its ideals. We had devolved from freedom fighters into criminals, from political radicals to minor technicians of illicit crafts, and we wanted to go back to basics. CW stood alone now, waving the bloody shirt.

In the months leading up to the Days of Rage, the collectives had engaged in bizarre competitions, little tests of will and courage. After the Days of Rage, a series of armed gut-checks drove at least some of the tribes. When a few of us stole a batch of dynamite, Terry had been ecstatic. We'll be doing this a lot now, he'd said gleefully, and then he pulled off an armed robbery of a Howard Johnson's restaurant in New Jersey. I was blown away that he'd actually done it, but it didn't unleash the predicted floodgate. On the contrary, the attempts to see if we could be gunslingers masked a deep disparity—even with justifiable rage, we simply didn't have it in us to harm others, especially innocents, no matter how tough we talked. And most of us were not convinced that a rapturous suicide mission, no matter how glorious it looked to a few, would move anything forward.

CW gave an impassioned speech about the importance of the road we'd now taken, the dangers of turning back, and the lure of American chauvinism even in us, and while trying to agree on our main points, argued intensely for the centrality of military leadership. We're all living on borrowed time, he said, and Jeffrey responded, But still living.

Where we're going, Bernardine said to CW on our last day together, you're not welcome. She said it slowly, formally, representing a consensus, and with that CW was expelled.

The earth split open then, sucked us down, down, deeper and again deeper into the widening world below. I had half expected to be dead by now, blown to bits or burned to cinder or crushed to dust, but no. I was still breathing, stunned but alive, and I experienced a kind of postpartum dizziness, the failure to plan beyond the big event. But here we were, without Diana, or Teddy or Terry, and so we paused. The everyday became more vital, more vivid, the air sweeter, the sky bluer. I looked myself over, and, more or less intact, got busy trying to survive another day, and then another. And step by step we built an underground society.

There was no maze of tunnels, camouflaged entrances and open-

ings, cross gates and traps, escape routes, false walls and hidden
rooms. I had imagined, perhaps, the drama of the black wig and
paste-on beard, an enormous Raskolnikov-type overcoat to hide in as
I slipped in and out of doorways, emerging only at night, back to the
grotto at daylight. It was nothing at all like that.

I caught my breath as our metaphor began to shift. I realized that
the underground had begun two feet from my own front door, that
the hidden world is a parallel universe somewhere side by side with
the open world. We learned to fashion survival along different
dimensions: timing and synchronization, the thoughtful use of light
and shadow, rhythm and pulse. We were seeking not liberated territory but freer vision, not a clash of armies but a battle of imaginations.
In Viet Nam there were the mountains and the jungle and the forest—we discovered that the secret path and the clandestine tunnel
had their equivalents in a good counterfeit identity and a safe house. I
began to wonder how we could resurrect the American underground
railroad of a century before—a protected space for uncompromising
resistance, audacious attack when necessary, and, importantly, survival.

We disappeared then not *from* the world, but *into* a world, a world
of invention and improvisation, a romance of space and distance and
time, an outpost on the horizon of our imaginations. We're not on
the fringe of society, I told friends, because society has no fringe and
no one is ever really outside of it. The underground was without borders or a point on the map, it's true, and it was as close to magic as I
would ever come.

In a sense it was so easy to find—we simply walked out into the
world and we were underground. In another way it was a leap away
from complicity and against accommodation. We stepped off the
hard surfaces of the everyday into a hidden room beneath the clatter
of the city, something to invent and then extend and protect. Our
mug shots were everywhere, every post office and police station,
banks and bus stations. The stakes became ourselves. Our disguises
were ourselves, too, concealed in the expectations of others. Look for
us in the whirlwind, I thought, happier and still happier to be alive.

25.

CW set off on his own to a life of the imagined underground outlaw—a shadowy underworld figure surviving through petty crime but always preparing for something big. The rest of us scattered to our base cities—New York, Boston, Philadelphia, Seattle, Portland, San Francisco, L.A.—to reorganize and regroup. Each of us took an alias, some of us several for different purposes, and over time our given names faded and became foreign to us, just as the open world was now far away. We hid even from ourselves, and soon we heard about the exploits of this or that comrade on the other coast, but we could never connect the news with anyone in particular.

Many took names from history's heroes: John for John Brown, Nat for Nat Turner, Harriet for Harriet Tubman. Others, from the worldwide struggle: Molly McGuire, Troy (Troi), Heidi (Haydee), Ernest O'Shay (Che), Emma (Goldman). Others adopted as names qualities they were seeking: Steel, Will, Love. We had among us a Ruby and a Carmen, a Hatchet, a Flint, and a Dawn. There was, of course, the need to hide and deceive in order to survive, but the game of naming and renaming also contained that old but still sparkling desire to reimagine and remake ourselves into new men and new women, to merge our identities with the movement. Bernardine became Rose Bridges, and I became Joe Brown. I loved those ordinary names, and whenever things got tough in the coming years, whenever we were feeling overwhelmed or defeated or terrified I kidded Rose, saying we should escape to Ha Noi and open a quiet little restaurant called "Rose and Joe's American Café."

Had we forgotten by now our real names? In a way, yes, but what's a real name anyway? Whose name is real? Almost every Black friend or comrade had by now shed what they called their slave names, and so we all adapted to a Jamal or a Lumumba, a Zayd, and many Maliks. I'd known Ismael Akbar and Afeni Shabazz; I'd known Ron St. Ron and Juan Chicago. And even Bernardine's father had played the name game—when she was thirteen he'd had enough of being a Jew in America, and he changed the family name from Ohrnstein to Dohrn, and his own nickname from Bernie to Barney.

People ask me now, Did you have trouble remembering all those names? Did you miss "Bill"? If someone had called out Bill in a crowded room in those years, I wouldn't have even looked up—I wasn't Bill anymore. I shed it like an old skin. And in those days I often met people more nameless than ourselves.

Rose and I, old friends by now and longtime comrades, fell in love slowly in that first year, the familiar angle of regard yielding to something new, shifting to reveal sweet dimensions and lovely edges never quite seen in this way before. It's true that when we'd first met years before at a conference with the funky name Radicals in the Professions, when she was still Bernardine and I was Bill, we had flirt-ed and danced deep into a hot and humid midwestern night in the pleasant haze of weed and wine. In the custom of the times we fell upon one another like musky, unkempt alley cats—scratching and biting, fur flying, howling down the city streets—and whatever the neighbors might have thought, no one threw a shoe or a bucket of cold water, and so we rambled on all night and became friends, stum-bling happily to the meetings next day, and then returned to our homes and to our partners. But now we were falling in love, and everything was changing.

We had been passionate and forceful together, and between us I had forgotten the differences of the sexes at first. We talked of all we had shared, and the things we had been before we were friends. Memories of Diana were never far away. Our friendship had all the important characteristics of love: a sense of a future together, intense shared experiences, vulnerability and agony and a fear of loss, a reluctance to name it with a word. There was desire, too, but not for exclusive affection. The emancipation of women and of the body was in the air, and while we wanted affection, it would have to be chosen every day. I moved to California, and I never thought of her as Bernardine anymore—Bernardine had become a creation on a poster. In our own bed late at night, bathed in candlelight, I whispered, I love you, Rose, and it was true, I was in love again. I'd fallen in love with Rose, and nothing else made sense. That sweet madness has carried us along a swift and dazzling river over exhilarating rapids and frightening drops, through gurgling undertows and treacherous canyons, hand in hand for three decades now. I tattooed a rose on my right forearm then. Rose gave birth to Zayd in 1977, to Malik in 1980, the year we surrendered to the FBI. By 1981 we were Bernardine and Bill again and we adopted Chesa, and then we were five, but that is another story entirely, and I'm getting ahead of myself.

We traveled a lot, underground, sometimes together, sometimes not. We built a little house in the back of our pickup truck, and when we were together we liked to take time to camp out, to cook dinner over a fire, to hike or swim on our way to our next rendezvous or meeting, the work ahead. When we were apart, we spoke on the phone every few days. Once when I'd been away several weeks, I got a card from her with a photo of two big hippos wallowing lazily in a lake. Times being what they are, she wrote, I can't imagine we'll grow old together, like these two happy souls. Still, when we're together I feel as close to contented as I have ever been, fat and full and floaty, and I thank you for that.

We invented all kinds of ways to obtain false identity papers, and got busy building multiple sets of ID for each of us and for every contingency. We stole wallets and purses at first without much concern for our victims, but it was a risky business that could reel out of control without warning. We were trying to learn artfulness and stealth, and stealing purses was definitely from the old school. More important, these papers were unreliable and had a short shelf life. As soon as they were reported missing, everything stopped working, and it could prove disastrous to buy a car, for example, or rent an apartment on a sour ID. Instant tracking. After the Baltimore fiasco, stealing ID was forbidden.

Instead we began to build ID sets around documents as flimsy as a fishing license or a laminated card available in a Times Square novelty shop called "Official ID." We soon figured out that the deepest and most foolproof ID had a government-issued Social Security card at its heart, and the best source of those were dead-baby birth certificates. I spent impious days over the next several months tramping through rural cemeteries in Iowa and Wisconsin, Illinois and North Dakota, searching for those sad little markers of people born between 1940 and 1950 who had died between 1945 and 1955. The numbers were surprising: two in one graveyard, a cluster of fourteen in another. Those poor souls had typically been issued birth certificates—available to us at any county courthouse for a couple of bucks and a simple form with information I could copy from the death announcement at the archive of the local paper—but they had never applied for a Social Security card. Collecting those birth certificates became a small industry, and within a year we had over a hundred.

For years I was a paper-made Joseph Brown, and then an Anthony Lee, remarkably durable identities. My on-paper official residences: a transient hotel in San Francisco and a warehouse in New York. There were tiny unknown risks in naming—the risk of being unaware of the lore or deeper meaning of a particular name, for example. One comrade named John was laughingly challenged by another John at a party: You're the first John I've ever met, he said, who's asked directions to the toilet using its Christian name. When I used the paper identity of an Eric Gourdanian to buy a used car, I mumbled something confusing and abstract when the salesman fixed my eyes intently, asking, What part of Armenia is your family from?

I thought of the baby Joseph Brown, deceased, and wondered if Mr. and Mrs. Brown would ever be proud of the part their little boy played in the struggle, or, more likely, furious at us for our blasphemous appropriation of his name if they ever found out.

There's more to it, of course. Some forgetfulness is learned, some forgetting forced, some studied. Forgetting and remembering become entwined, dependent, locked in desperate embrace. America's foundational myths—from our beneficent civilizing mission at the start through our pure motives and selfless sacrifices during World War II and beyond—are authorized amnesia. The U.S.A.—the United States of Amnesia, full of sham innocence and counterfeit virtue. Official history is choked with lies, a suppression of memory, but so is the pretense that the wheel of history is nothing but the details of a private life. Somewhere we might discover a life lived in history, grounded, distinct, pitching forward.

When the U.S. or any other author of conquest tires of the price paid to maintain the world order, they simply blow the whistle on themselves, wipe the slate clean, and begin again in some other form. They say, Forget about it, that's ancient history, even if it happened yesterday, even if the bodies are still warm. Let's move on. They insist it's already old news declaring it sour grapes and poor sportsmanship if their victims aren't immediately struck with the same afflicting amnesia. Great Britain is appalled by the IRA, Spain by the Basque separatists, Israel by the Palestinian resistance. And the U.S.? The U.S. is always hurt and shocked that anyone could even mildly dislike its charming presence in their lives. Let's forget the bad part. Can't we now just get along? A dominant historical theme, as Borges reminds us, something that just keeps popping up and popping up, is a perverse desire to forget the past. White people can never quite remember the scope and scale of the slavocracy and of rule by lynching, while Black people can never quite afford to forget.

Ours was the condition of change, of transport, of migration. We rushed along, uprooted, in our swirling motion toward the new, pausing only long enough to renounce the old, the experience of but

a moment ago, a predicament considered quaint by tomorrow afternoon at the latest.

Our lives underground, in outward form at least, resembled the
lives of a generation—moving from place to place, extending childhood indefinitely, entering and ending relationships, experimenting
with love and work and all manner of ways of being. Some of us
would move to rural communes, and some would go to work in mills
or mines or factories and join the industrial working class. Some of
us would marry, have kids, divorce, and remarry, and some would
discover—or decide now to announce—that we were gay. A few, like
Daniel and Andy, left for good, and a few new recruits joined up, and
so we were faced with the challenge—not unique—of inventing our
lives and our projects out of whole cloth, without support and without any tradition whatsoever. We were groping in the dark, and I
remember it coming on me with a flash like revelation: Since everyone around us is dislocated, elusive, and reinvented, we blend right
in. Each of us brought along fragments of our lives to the underground world, no one arrived brand-new, and each of us left a world
behind.

Renee brought a sweet smiling face and a huge heart filled with
Catholic love, homosexual desire, and a dogged attachment, it turned
out, to the confessional.

Harry hauled along decades of experience as a Communist organizer, including a stint in World War II flying American supplies over
the hump in China, time in federal prison, and then a period underground during the Smith Act trials of the 1950s. He left behind a wife
and a mortgage, but he brought a fully developed agenda and a book-
let he'd written called *The Object Is to Win*, which served as his guide
to daily living, his blueprint for contesting state power, and his Bible.
He eventually brought a huge amount of cash, and an abiding suspicion that he was the notorious skyjacker D. B. Cooper, something he
always denied with a wink.

I brought my self-confidence with me, my hunger for experience,
and my willingness to try everything at least once, along with Mom's

insistent creed that everything somehow would turn out fine. Rose brought an iron will and Apache tears, but she left behind her bulging address book with its 637 entries, making do now with runaway scraps of paper.

Linda brought her rollicking Janis Joplin swagger and her Jimi Hendrix albums.

Carolyn brought her notebooks full of poems and the equipment of the eternally poor student—a bed roll, a camp stove, a cast-iron frying pan, and a mixed set of plastic dishes.

Jamie Hawk left behind his mother's admonition to Be careful, and stay away from the *schwarze*, but he did remember to bring his warm coat and his asthma medicine and a bottle of tranquilizers. Jamie was high-strung. Rachel brought her acid tongue, her vitamin E, and a prescription for penicillin, and Caitlin brought her prosthetic left leg.

My brother Rick brought a diary and his army dog tags. Rick had burned his draft card early in the war and then run away to Vancouver where he organized a halfway house for American GIs deserting the army and making their twisty ways toward Europe and peace. He married a woman there who had a baby girl, and after a couple of years they returned to the U.S. where he joined the army, of all things, in order to organize a union of servicemen. Stationed at Fort Knox when the Townhouse was blown to bits, he deserted and we hooked up in Chicago.

He shouldn't have kept the dog tags, of course, but he did, and one day, a couple years into it, while laying cement with friends, he pulled out the chain, the little rectangles designed to identify the dead from the mess of a battlefield, and dropped them into the hardening mold. Rick was glad to be alive watching his name alone disappear into the cold gray lava, perhaps never to be seen again.

Rick brought a picture of his wife and baby, which he knew was a breach of security, but he wasn't a stickler for security and so he kept it and looked at it often and ached for them, so much so that you could feel something like a magnetic throb when you stood too close to him.

Fiona brought her whole feminist library, David his unfinished manuscript, and Sally her complicated wish to be both a woman and a little girl, a serious person worthy of true love and a sex object to be desired and pursued by every man.

Junior brought a gnawing fear and a little brother's eagerness to please, and Rory an Irish temper and a prodigious thirst so that he was perpetually angry or a little drunk, or angry and a little drunk at once.

Jenn brought knitting needles, yarn, and her mother, literally, who brought a teacher's patience, and a civil rights activist's courage. She also brought maturity, steadiness, and a minute-by-minute integrity for day-to-day living that took your breath away. She and Harry were of a generation, and they couldn't agree on a thing.

Jeffrey brought his pacifism, frayed and worn as it was, torn in some places but still remarkably intact. He knew he was a bad Quaker, but he'd decided to throw his fate onto life's great wheel, and to go to hell if need be to end this one nightmarish war. He brought his bird-watching binoculars, his favorite dope pipe, his astonishing sense of direction, his Buddha nature. What I mean is, Jeff trusted himself and carried a simple faith in the world—he could vibe his way through almost anything. Once when he was driving and we were stopped by a traffic cop, I felt as if I were watching the scene in *Star Wars* where Obi-Wan Kenobi uses his superior intelligence to mesmerize the police: We are not a problem, he said. You are not a problem, replied the cop. How did you get away with just a warning? I asked, and Jeff, with genuine innocence, said, I don't know, I just kind of gave in. He also deliberately picked his nose the whole time, and, he pointed out, no one looks a nose-picker closely in the face.

I brought my hay fever with me underground, and Jeff ended my suffering the Zen way. One August day when I was utterly miserable, sleep-deprived, sneezing and itching and dripping, eyes red and swollen, and high on antihistamine, Jeff invited me for a long run down a country road. Look at me, man, I whined. I can't breathe, I can't walk.

Maybe you should stop fighting it, he suggested. Breathe deeply, sneeze heartily, and just give in.

We went for that long run, after all, and I did sneeze loudly and often, and although I still have hay fever, I've never *suffered* from it since.

Rose brought attention, her great face on the "Ten Most Wanted" list. The list was a huge public relations bonanza for the FBI, and J. Edgar Hoover promoted it heavily as a way to garner support for his crime stoppers by featuring the "toughest guys" in America. Hoover's genius for PR included putting a long line of plug-uglies on the list, bank robbers, burglars, run-of-the-mill killers, blasting their fiendish faces across the land, then conveniently busting them within days, a couple of handsome agents leading each cur to justice on the front pages. Lo and behold, in 1971, six of the Ten Most Wanted were political activists, including Angela Davis and H. Rap Brown. The faces were no longer fiendish, and several of the "toughest guys" in America turned out to be young women, all wonderful-looking, but none as beautiful as Rose.

Zeke brought his medical education and a belief that his surgical residency provided the best possible training for revolutionary action. In the midst of blood and pain, he said, you learn to stay calm and steady, focused at once on the smallest detail and on the great humanitarian purpose.

Aaron brought his man-in-the-street countenance, his entire collection of Zap Comix, and 150 pounds of tools—socket set, welding kit, pipe wrenches, and more.

We all brought our distinctive ways of being, our little ticks and habits, and Rebecca brought the actual habit she'd worn as a Maryknoll nun and a crucifix squeezed into her hand by her dying father.

I brought my mother's admonition to pursue whatever I liked, but to try to rise to the top of my field, and Rose brought a sassy smartness, pieces of ivory lace, her musk and mascara—we were fighting the state, it's true, but she would still find time to put on her eyes.

And so, from just these fragments, and from the things we found and gathered along the way, we constructed our lives underground.

We each brought our longings and our desires, mostly intact, and we brought our homesickness, a memory of something whole, a sense of loss edged with fear and anger, rarely acknowledged but ever visible from the side. We were exiles inside our own country, and we experienced a kind of exile's identity shift, a sense of being both here and not here, of belonging and of not belonging. We were outsiders now, living unstable lives on the margins. Something was gained—a heightened sense of purpose, perhaps, the choice to throw ourselves wholeheartedly into this world—but something was irrevocably lost as well. We were evicted, and we felt that we could never go home.

Nevertheless, many of us soon reconnected with families—brothers and sisters, cousins and aunts and uncles, even parents who agreed to our sometimes strained security procedures in order to enjoy a picnic in the park with a son or a daughter now not *quite* so lost. Comrades returned from these family reunions with new underwear or shirts, and usually some money for food or a haircut.

Like other immigrants we were careful—no shoplifting, no food stamp scams, no sneaking into the movies. A great sin among us was breaking traffic laws, and I worked for months to slow down, having never obeyed a speed limit before in my life. Sometimes I ached to go eighty and my foot shook as I wrestled myself down to sixty-five for the sake of the work, for the good of the group, but it felt like a real sacrifice.

We developed a doubleness. More than a secret identity or a double life, we saw the world through distinct lenses. Like high school kids who are painfully aware of living simultaneously in two cultures, their own oppositional culture and a dominant, suffocating adult culture that must be mastered with more skill than that of the best-trained ethnographer, or like Black Americans who must know everything about the dominant culture while remaining in significant ways invisible to that culture, we had double vision. We saw the world as Americans; we saw America as revolutionaries. We were split, and we could not be whole in the same way again.

Seeking an alternative to jail and the courtroom, we'd abandoned our homeland, and with an immigrant's hope and an exile's fear we'd cast out for a new and different place to live. We would measure our success by our ability to survive in this alien new world, and we would build whatever provisional satisfaction we could on our actions, on our dialogue of the deed.

We found soon enough that our deeds and our words provided a voice to the old world we'd never imagined we would have, and they became a new world to inhabit.

We issued what we called a communiqué—a word borrowed from Latin American guerrillas—a "Declaration of War," signed by "Bernardine Dohrn" in May, filled with defiance and hyperbole. We threatened to bomb a major symbol of American injustice, and when, a little more than two weeks later, the promised bomb exploded in the New York City Police Headquarters on Centre Street, the Weathermyth was fully launched. The communiqué was reprinted widely and, oddly enough, through it we instructed the FBI, and through them police forces everywhere, on our reliability and our quirky authenticating signs. We were in communication.

There was a practice now of public storytelling, and the subtext was our own application of the metaphor of Viet Nam: you can't catch us.

We opened to a world of words and they tumbled from us in a crazy flash flood of awakening zeal. We wrote open letters to the militant Catholic left—and they wrote back urging us to temper our actions with a foundational compassion—and to the Black Liberation Army, who urged us to blast away at colonializing racist power, no holds barred, and to take no prisoners. We argued with both, and we agreed with both.

We scribbled to old friends—roommates from an earlier world, favorite teachers, brothers and sisters. I wrote to John Holt, an inspiring teacher and education writer, a deeply conservative man in some ways but a loving friend as well, and we linked up and corresponded for years. I communicated with my Aunt Sarah, a closeted leftie, and with Nathan Zuckerman, an old teacher who was now a failed writer but who slipped me money occasionally—our meeting place in back of a sleazy peep show off Times Square. Ruthie Stein, now a rising star in the New York art scene, wrote every month and we met up several times every year. Most of us wrote to our parents—careful missives meant to reassure, delivered discreetly and then quickly destroyed—and got letters full of relief and sometimes reprimand in return. We knew now that we were ill-equipped gunslingers, so we became word-slingers instead.

In that first year I moved several times, organized twenty-two hiding places I could use in an emergency, built eight complete sets of ID, held twenty-eight meetings with old friends—none of whom called the cops, most of whom offered support—and I was recognized on the street twelve times that I know of, and never turned in. Even though our numbers were small, each of us had dozens of reasons to feel connected and secure. I didn't feel isolated.

Our mantra underground, our endorsement of willful forgetting, was "need-to-know." What actions are being planned? There's no need-to-know. Where are the other comrades? You have no need-to-know. When will we regroup? We'll tell you on a need-to-know basis. It could become a habit, this everyday dissembling, as expected as the sunset. The protected veil of secrecy elevated our activities—mystery leans toward the marvelous. In the shadow, choices were also protected from critique. Need-to-know was adjective and noun, a sinister little slogan gesturing toward ignorance. Was it about survival? Always? That, too, was protected information; that, too, would be rationed strictly according to the need-to-know principle.

Whenever the police arrest a psycho-killer or a mass murderer—Son of Sam, say, or Jeffrey Dahmer—and the sinister glare of celebrity turns its baleful eye to the block, the neighbors can be counted on for two things: we will line up eagerly to put our faces right into the gaping cameras, and we will affect the cynical tone of tired disbelief as we mutter all the cliches of modern times—He seemed so normal, we'll say, and it just goes to show.

And what about the strange sounds, the howling and the thumping? a reporter might ask.

Oh well, the music they listen to these days, who knows anymore?

We were certain our neighbors would all call us normal in happy chorus, and just to be sure, we rehearsed them on the fine points. We had a dog, of course, and the newspaper delivered every morning. No visitors, and no sudden changes in routine. We left home each day at eight, and the frequent absences were explained by a sick mother in Seattle, a matter no one wanted to probe too deeply. It was all so perfectly scripted that a couple of times I almost wanted to get busted just to see how the neighbors would perform.

The goal was to fit in, to disappear, to become entirely obscure—Like fish in the sea, we said. We were on the run now, we were hiding out, and our camouflage would be, well, everybody else. The best place to hide a leaf, Jeff was fond of saying, is in the forest. Sea or forest, fish or leaf, we intended to pass unnoticed.

Yet for all our efforts to be indistinct, we quickly created a quite distinct Weatherfeel and Weatherlook. Wherever we went, wherever we found ourselves, we were accompanied by the artifacts of the culture we were creating. Take hair, for example. In the first days underground you could find the Weathermen in any group by the garish heads throbbing clearly from out of the murky crowd. We experimented with dying our hair, and for many the result was a blinding platinum or a flaming orange, for others a shiny black patent leather. We took to calling one another insulting nicknames: Carrot-top or Goldilocks or Shoe Stain. We all sported gaudy, vulgar heads, and we were completely conspicuous.

We soon moved along to other alterations—the men grew beards and long hair, way beyond shaggy, great manes curling to our waists. Some people called me Goat, short for Billy Goat, but also for the unmistakable resemblance, I'm sure.

The women mostly cut their hair short—little butchy do's or flattops. Rose had an adorable brush cut a quarter of an inch all around with a slightly longer, fetching flip at the front.

We dangled strings of Apache tears from the rearview mirrors of every truck or van or car we owned as we cycled rapidly through vehicles, avoiding long-term contact with the state at any fixed or followable point. We favored certain colors in cars, in clothes—forest green for a time and then smoky blue. The women had turquoise earrings and bracelets, the men denim vests with a rainbow patch sewn somewhere, and each of us carried lots of rolls of quarters for long-distance pay phone calls and, secure in back pockets, a K-55, the cheap but perfect little knife from Germany with a black panther etched into its sides and flat enough to elude detection in a pat-down.

We said Shoes, short for "brownshoes," code for the FBI: the Shoes were all over them after the Big Top; the Shoes took Rose's dad to identify a corpse—just to fuck with his head; those two guys lurking around Petrograd Restaurant? Shoes. A good code, like an obedient child, doesn't speak to strangers. We spoke in a language that was meaningless babble to outsiders, we hoped, but concise, clear communication inside the family.

Our language was one part necessity, a language of survival, and two parts youth-speak, an irreverent slanguage of sass with flavor. The Shoes signified that FBI agents were all dull, conformist bores, beneath contempt. And not only were they unstylish and plain, they were plodding and completely obvious. Want to find the agents in any room? Look at their shoes.

Calling them the Federal Bureau of Investigation would have bestowed too much dignity and power, exactly the qualities we wanted to explode, and the Bureau or the FBI was still way, way too respectful. George Raft and Edward G. Robinson might have called them G-men, and Al Capone, the Feds, but the contempt, while bitter, was still within bounds. Gumshoes was good, but brownshoes—yes, that's more like it. Our tongues were laughing at them, announcing that we were cleverer, smarter, and cooler in every way. We wanted to pierce their mythological image as a clean, efficient, well-functioning Swiss watch, to tar them as lazy bureaucrats wallowing ineffectively in their outdated metaphor. We would outsmart them, flip them the bird, and tell them, Go ahead, you fucking brownshoes, kiss my ass.

We were, of course, like everybody else, a bunch of signifying monkeys, more monkeyish than some, but of a type, hanging tentatively suspended in our interpretive jungle, sending shared meanings spinning along the dense thicket of language. We invented words; we constructed culture. And we were, like others, forever explaining, defining, correcting, implying, editing, translating in sometimes delighted, often desperate efforts to be understood. One person's gobbledygook is just another's graceful gift of gab.

We Weathermen were all talkers—we already loved words, most of us read widely, and groups of us were regular Scrabble players and Sunday crossword puzzle fans. The garble of Weatherese was mostly an intellectual game—clever, distracting, fun. But learning how to evade arrest had a serious purpose, a purpose that rode along on words, on talk tactics, mostly. When I blew an engine on the Golden Gate Bridge one day, the cop who pulled over found me not only respectful and engaging but charming, I hoped, open and grateful for his presence. I was practicing verbal jujitsu. Soon he offered to give me a push to the nearest service station, and I asked for his name so that I might send a letter of gratitude to his commanding officer. (He refused—the helpful push was outside regulations.) Again and again we learned what you say and how you say it has more to do with survival than guns, disguises, or even ID.

Dynamite became ice cream or pickles. So much easier to say I'm taking three pounds of ice cream to the Big Top than I'm putting a three-pound bomb in the Capitol.

The preface "Weather" had become as prominent among us as "Mc" is in the wider world, and just as colonizing. We talked of Weathermen and Weatherwomen, Weatherkids and Weatherstories, Weather documents and Weathersymps. The leadership was, of course, the Weather Bureau, then the Weather Eye, then simply the

Eye. A longtime comrade was Weather Beaten, a leaflet was a Weather Balloon, and the anti-imperialist struggle was the Weather Going Tide. Recruits went through what amounted to an informal Weatherman Berlitz in order to become functionally bilingual.

When we began doing secret and illegal work we needed a word that cloaked our intentions, and so we spoke of the North Star, and then of the Dash—I'm spending this morning on the Dash, someone might say, implying both a censor's beep, a word unspoken, as well as the mad dash we anticipated to the underground railroad, following the North Star toward freedom. When we were actually on the run we inoculated ourselves from fear and called our status, our fugitiveness, the Joke—Have you told your new boyfriend the Joke? Or: I don't think anyone here knows the Joke. Our organization, publicly the Weather Underground, became the Eggplant, from an obscure rock lyric about "the eggplant that ate Chicago."

We expropriated an entire lexicon of Weather words from the music—"You don't need a weatherman to know which way the wind blows," of course, from Bob Dylan, "Bad Moon," our code word for the Haymarket statue, from Creedence Clearwater Revival, and the "Place" for the New York Police Headquarters from "We Gotta Get Out of This Place," by the Animals. "Rescue" from Fontella Bass's "Rescue Me" was the name for a two-year effort, finally successful, to break a Black Liberation Army comrade from jail. We drew on "Kick Out the Jams" by the MC5 for names and codes, "Purple Haze" in tribute to Jimi Hendrix, and "Volunteers" from the Jefferson Airplane. The Pentagon was called "Maggie's Farm," again from Dylan, because we were planning to put a bomb in it and then, we said simply, "I ain't gonna work on Maggie's farm no more."

Homegrown, as American as Mom's cherry pie, the underground was in other ways a foreign country—we spoke patois and did things differently there.

26.

I remember nothing. For us memory was the ally of our pursuers, a danger to our survival, to our lives and our insurrection. I repeated the practiced phrase—I remember nothing. I remember nothing. Forehead glistening, red-rimmed eyes bulging, little twitches and trembles dancing erratically across my face, through my temples, I imagine the coming shock or blow or burn. I don't remember the safe house, the secret path, I don't remember the names on the false IDs. I retain nothing. I really don't know. It's gone.

Forgetting can be confused with remembering—the fictions we force ourselves to carry replace the facts we are hiding from the world, facts buried within fictions. Memory can become a way of forgetting the things I don't remember hiding inside the things I do, my secrets, the underbelly of the facts.

A good cover stays close to the real story, but veers off just in time. I was raised in Chicago, for example, not Missoula or Biloxi, because I have experiences with Lake Michigan, untapped reservoirs when it comes the Cubs or the Bulls, but I know nothing of catfish or crayfish, copper or cattle. I can hold my own with Chicago lore—from Al Capone to Big Bill Thompson, Nelson Algren to Jane Addams. Now there's a key detail to blur: my name is Joe Brown, like a million other guys. I live through the disguise of my desire, the mask of my experience.

When Diana was killed I wanted to die, too, but I was alive, and now I was relieved, and starting to like the idea that death would wait, would wait a year, might wait for more. Death would wait.

We should try to help those who had followed us to the lip of the precipice, Jeffrey said one day, to warn them, to help them stop a moment and step back. We were learning to acknowledge fear again, to permit it as human and sensible, to welcome it back from exile. We were learning to permit doubt again, too, even to value it. The FBI was hunting us frantically, noisily, and so our continued freedom was its own triumph, we thought, something to cherish and protect.

But our survival had to have meaning beyond the narrow and the particular. For me, and for most of us, we would only find meaning in participating fully in all aspects of life, and we would try to understand everything in order to make ourselves subjects in history and not passive objects to be used and discarded. We would make history, act within it in order to enlarge people and contribute to humanity. We would fight unearned suffering and undeserved pain, all the ways people oppress and exploit and dehumanize one another. We would affirm every gesture toward social justice and liberty, everything that honored each human being as irreplaceably worthwhile and the whole of humanity sacred.

Our actions should speak for themselves, Rose said. They should be immediately understood and timely, fire the imaginations of young people, inspire the movement, and make anyone of goodwill secretly smile—even if they denounce our tactics.

That our efforts would be stained by mistakes was, we now knew, inevitable. We could never see fully or far enough, we could never know all things in all ways. We were limited as is everyone, our theories flawed, as they all are. Still, I believed the greater crime would be to do nothing. Inaction was impossible for me now. Stepping into history, we would make errors; staying aloof from history would be its own choice and all error. And so, believing with all my heart in the immense power of people to challenge fate and accomplish the unthinkable, holding on to a profound sense of personal responsibility, I plunged ahead. We would fight, of course, but in new, imaginative ways. We would bring the war home as we had planned, but with measured force, with precision. We would draw an angry sword against white supremacy, retaliate for racist attacks, and fight alongside our Black revolutionary comrades, but from a new and liberated space. And with care.

We were slowing down. It might not have been noticeable to those outside, but to those of us who'd been inside that hundred-mile-an-hour gale, a sixty-mile-an-hour wind was a breeze.

Within months we had established a pattern of action—retaliation for what we believed were attacks on the Black struggle and offensives against the war machine. Our signature was a warning call to some sleepy guard inside the building or to the police nearby or to a journalist with calm and detailed instructions to clear a specific area, and then letters of explanation—sometimes exhorting, sometimes threatening, sometimes still barely decipherable beyond the knowing—claiming credit and publicly defending our actions as politics by other means, signed and delivered simultaneously to several major newspapers in different cities across the country seconds after the blast. The FBI and the big city police knew our signature, and separated what they came to know as the authentic Weather nuts from the variously weird.

Each letter had a logo hand-drawn across the page—our trademark thick and colorful rainbow with a slash of angry lighting cutting through it. New morning, it signified, changing weather. Oddly, as intense as it all looks and sounds, it was in our minds then cautious and responsible, a huge de-escalation from the apocalyptic plans of just months earlier.

I wanted to be a Weatherman forever then, a revolutionary outlaw, and I loved the symbol of peace and reconciliation balanced by the hot bolt of justice. I eventually tattooed the rainbow and lightning on my skin, discreetly out of sight.

We geared up for survival and fanned out across the country in search of lost comrades, autonomous fighters, militant youth who, strong-willed and lighthearted, were, we knew, on the loose in the world. Our hope was to build some unity of purpose, to prevent further disasters like the Townhouse, to talk politics, argue strategy and tactics, and to disarm the crazies.

We had claimed half a dozen bombings, each one hugely magnified because of the symbolic nature of the target, the deliberate and judicious nature of the blow, and the synchronized public announcements suggesting the dreadful or exhilarating news that a homegrown guerrilla movement was afoot in America. A positive wave of violence and despair blew up, but we had few illusions now about our own real capacity, and we could see what was happening in the wider world. Bombings of ROTC buildings, Selective Service offices, and induction centers had been escalating for at least two years, and targets of political violence now included corporate giants most clearly identified with U.S. aggression and expansion: Bank of America, United Fruit, Chase Manhattan Bank, IBM, Standard Oil, Anaconda, GM. From early 1969 until the spring of 1970 there were over 40,000 threats or attempts and 5,000 actual bombings against government and corporate targets in the U.S., an average of six bombings a day. All but two or three of this orgy of explosions were aimed at property not people; to me they were entirely restrained. Five thousand bombings, about six a day, and the Weather Underground had claimed six, total. It makes you wonder.

Still, we dreaded the possibility of two, three, many Townhouses, and we hoped to use our celebrity in the lunatic left as well as the gathering Weathermyth in the larger world to persuade others to pull back. We knew where to find a few organized groups—the Red Family and the Proud Eagle Tribe, for example, the Motherfuckers and the White Panthers—and we held several secret summits where we had the traditional frank exchange of views and hammered out some kind of new formal understanding. Only once, in a dingy basement hideout near Houston, were guns drawn, but it was based on a misunderstanding—the crazies thought Jeff had said, "We can turn you shits in in D.C." when he had actually said, "We can turn you into fish in the sea"—and we laughed about it later as we passed a joint.

Jeff and I drove into Denver one night, too late to call the one contact we planned to look up, the place we would start our search, and took a room in a fleabag hotel downtown. There were a lot of old comrades in the Denver area, most of them open radicals working and living as they always had, but a few had slipped from sight. An escalating string of bombings in the last months drew us here to search for whatever autonomous cells were moving in and out of Denver doorways, to try to connect up with them, perhaps redirect or possibly disarm them. It was a tricky business, to be sure, but to us it had become a kind of calling.

Next day I phoned Lizzie Egg at her job. Lizzie was the older sister of a high school friend of mine. She was political but not flamboyant, and we'd been in touch off and on for years. She worked now as a legal secretary, and she was likely off the main radar of the FBI.

Hey, Lizzie Egg, I said when she answered. It's your beautiful baby brother, Robert. She connected right away—I sounded nothing like Bob and he hated the longer form of his name. But she knew me well enough, knew my voice, and responded as if we'd rehearsed it: Hey, hey, kid, I've been waiting for you. How's Mom?

I told her I was in town and asked how soon we could meet up. I can take an hour right now, she said, and I told her I'd meet her at Helen's Sunny Spot, a coffee shop we'd checked out a couple of blocks away.

Jeffrey stood where he could see the entrance to Lizzie's building, and watched as she came out the door a few minutes later, heading north. She was alone, no tail. At the corner, she turned west and immediately went down a wide staircase to a lower-level street, still alone. Jeffrey signaled me and then circled back to pick up the truck, while I watched Lizzie from below. At the bottom of the stairs she continued west, toward the dark corner where I stood. Helen's was a block away. I came out of hiding as Lizzie swept past and took her arm, steered her into an alley. Oh my God, she said, smiling as I grabbed her arm. Come on, I said, and we walked briskly through to the next street where Jeffrey waited, motor purring.

Ten minutes later we were miles away at a truck stop, drinking coffee and catching up—I'd mentioned Helen's on her phone, so that was not an option for us. We were prepared for a sustained stay and a serious search in Denver—in some places we had spent days or weeks hanging out near campuses or in youth ghettos until we found someone who could guide us—but Lizzie knew everything: Quinn, an old SDS friend, went under right after the New York explosion, she said. They've built a small armed group, and they're the ones who hit the federal building and all the draft boards. They called themselves the Red Hawk Tribe, and they considered themselves part of the Weathermen. Since they had no capacity to find us—as Abbie Hoffman said at the time, I'd like to send them some money, but I don't know their address—they were conducting themselves as they thought we would want, an autonomous action group working independently, one piece of a mosaic impossible to completely destroy, an entrenched, entirely leaderless resistance. Lizzie was their main support and contact, although she had no idea where they lived. Quinn's scheduled to call me at a pay phone tomorrow before work, Lizzie said. And so we were in.

Quinn fell into Jeffrey's arms late the next day at the meeting Lizzie had set up. His face was a picture of relief. We talked for hours—we had time and we were learning patience. By next morning we were in close agreement: the Red Hawk Tribe would stop the armed actions for at least a month and concentrate all their energy on building up a base of survival—clean up their ID and develop a few deeper sets, establish a couple of new safe houses, find some new pay phones and meeting places. I showed Quinn how to create a trajectory leading to a meeting with aboveground comrades, people like Lizzie, that involved a scheduled and preplanned route with switchbacks and breakaways observable from afar, and then entering a movable pickup zone in which only the clandestine comrade could initiate an approach.

The backdrop of our discussions was an unprecedented explosion of political violence and mass resistance everywhere, particularly on campuses. When the U.S. widened the war into Cambodia, extending the agony and expanding the murderous American adventure, students seized university buildings, poured into the streets, and organized strikes in massive numbers. At Kent State, National Guard troops, without warning or provocation, fired on unarmed students killing four (the nearest was 100 yards away), wounding nine others, and everyone everywhere, we thought, saw the ugly face of repression unmasked. Mass action escalated to new highs: 100 major demonstrations a day, 536 schools shut down by student strikes. Half of the colleges and universities were up in arms, and violent confrontations marked the largest and most prestigious campuses, with brutal clashes between students and police and close to 2,000 protesters arrested in two weeks. A student in San Diego imitating the Buddhist monks of Viet Nam immolated himself in protest of the war, and dozens chained themselves to the doors of induction centers. A hundred thousand people then poured into Washington, and 400 were arrested for blocking traffic and trashing buildings. When white state troopers opened fire on unarmed Black students at Jackson State University in Mississippi, killing two and wounding twelve, we felt that finally America was on the edge of chaos, its violent core exposed for all the world to see. President Nixon, predictably, blamed the victims themselves: When dissent turns to violence, it invites tragedy, he said. How can the president get away with that? I thought. This is crazy.

I watched the demonstrations on the TV news and I read the articles in the newspapers. I was miserable to miss the action. I knew how to run in the streets, and I could hardly stand seeing others advance and retreat, attack and regroup, feeling sadly on the sidelines. I ached.

The sheer size of the upheaval was stunning—the multitude was up in arms, a host of rebels, a legion of potential revolutionaries. We would build our red army on hope, I thought, and not despair, reconnect with a popular opposition, and convince the other armed militants that attention to and responsibility for the mass resistance had to be part of our work and their work. We would reconnect.

We trained in the desert several times, but the trips took on the character of campouts more clearly each time. Jeff was in charge. On our first trip, he and Rose and I camped at Joshua Tree, met up with a half-dozen others in the morning, and found an isolated canyon to fire high-powered rifles and 9mm pistols at paper targets for a couple of hours. But our attention wandered to coyotes and sagebrush, and we marveled at the subtle beauty of the place.

We put a huge bomb in the rusted shell of an abandoned car down a gully on our next trip, then retreated two hills away to watch the thing blow sky high, and, dazzled, spent the next several days exploring the land, admiring the Indian paintbrush and the blooming cactus and, one evening, coming upon a herd of wild burros, sturdy and beautiful, galloping toward the setting sun. The desert—wide and peaceful and mysterious—captivated us, and Rose and I returned again and again, for picnics, not practice.

We were taken with words, as I've said, and practically taken over by words on occasion. Our most ambitious project by far engaged our entire organization, pulling in the whole network of friends and supporters including the most far-flung contacts, going through a thousand readers and a zillion drafts, and taking over two years to complete. In the process we established a Clandestine School for Cadre with regular teachers and a formal curriculum, a complete print shop hidden in a garden apartment named the Red Dragon Press, a newspaper called *Osawatomie*—taken from John Brown's nickname in Kansas—and a large, and we hoped sophisticated, secret national distribution network. The book we created was *Prairie Fire*, but when we began, we called the project "Manzanita," named for a bush running wild on the hills near our house.

"Manzanita" was an attempt to sum up our thinking since the "Weatherman" paper and especially since the Townhouse. Through it we hoped to consolidate our political organization and to forge unity with progressive activists. I wrote an early draft in 1972, searching for new directions while holding on to the threads that remained true— the importance of national liberation movements and the central place of Viet Nam, the decisive nature of the Black struggle inside the U.S., the sense of history as a drama of human beings thrusting forward, a product of people's activities.

In "Weatherman" we had been insistent in our anti-Americanism, our opposition to a national story stained with conquest and slavery and attempted genocide. In *Prairie Fire* we discovered the steady resistance that pursues the official story, Osceola and Cochise, Nat Turner and Marcus Garvey, Emma Goldman and the Grimke sisters. We located ourselves in history and found a way at last to have a little niche at home.

Group writing is always a danger, the tendency to accommodate everyone leads almost inevitably to the death of style and the collapse of character. But we weren't writing for style or character, and we had agreed upon strong lead writers for most sections—Jamie wrote the history section, Rose wrote on internationalism, Jeffrey on Viet Nam. The book was readable.

The constant reading and rereading, editing and revising did build the desired unity, and often a seemingly small correction led to days of rethinking. Rose had written at one point: In spite of the Holocaust, Jews must understand the suffering of the Palestinian people. Jenn's mother, Abby Stern, insisted on a fundamental correction: Because of the Holocaust, she wrote, because of their historic suffering, Jews have a special responsibility to understand the predicament of the Palestinian people.

Perhaps the most fundamental difference between "Weatherman" and *Prairie Fire* was visual—"Weatherman" was tight and angry and tough to embrace—it was meant to be read only by the most committed, preferably standing in a drafty ill-lit hall. *Prairie Fire* was all color and space, pictures and, we hoped, engaging graphics. *Prairie Fire* included songs and poems and whimsical decorative touches. Its deep red cover—actually it came in two separate covers, one blank and without any incriminating marks, the other blaring its name in black block letters—made you want to hold it. Or so we hoped.

Prairie Fire was dropped off at hundreds of bookstores across the nation on a single night, and the next day thousands of copies were passing hand to hand. An extended conversation was under way, and I was elated.

27.

Remembering is also a way of forgetting, a way of filtering.

The fullness of that fugitive world lives within me still with a kind of fierceness like first love, urgent and absolute. I remember the primitive emotions and tingling anticipation underground, the dread, the devastation, finally, and the pain of loss.

I remember new sounds and smells and tastes, the surprising sweet sensation of being suddenly everywhere, alive. There was something new and invigorating underground, so different from anything I'd ever known before, a kind of triumph perhaps. There was a sense—although this territory is claimed with such suffocating authority that I hesitate—of being born again. But, yes, it's true, I was born again, born underground, awakened to new ways of seeing and hearing, and new openings of human possibility. The rupture was so sudden and so absolute, the gap so unbridgeable, and my longing for a place so intense that this became life itself, all there was. The underground gave me a whole new world, and I gave myself to it wholly and without reservation.

We learn to hold back, to moderate, to temper our enthusiasm as we grow. We become less childish, and we learn to sound less foolish and less absurd. We gain perspective, perhaps, but we risk becoming sterile old cynics. We are unhooked from ignorant love, but we can also unhook then from hope, from deep desire. The world can become a place without color or texture, boring and predictable—we've seen it all before—and the distance we've achieved has the effect, finally, of a shrinking us. We become more absurd than the kids.

I hold on to that bliss, to the memory of those first commitments and the possibility of those primal affections, not because I'm blind but because it's a necessary echo—whatever energy I might muster still for something good always draws ambient heat from that first fire. Knowing now that thoughts of Elysian fields can lead to the garrotte and the guillotine and the gulag, I still can't imagine a fully human world without utopian dreams. Why would anyone go on?

We dwelled in possibility, and we built a simple structure of semi-autonomous cells called tribes, each responsible for its own survival and support systems, each free to initiate activity, each encouraged to recruit members and build relationships with movement friends and families. Tribes were pulled into this or that activity by a leadership that exercised influence mainly through the power of argument and persuasion—the leadership had no independent ability to enforce its will, and its most dramatic sanction had been banishing CW. Still, as the Weathermyth grew, and the string of successful actions extended, a corresponding internal myth evolved, acceding more and more authority.

The Weather Underground reared up as a pole of possibility, an extreme example against which others would measure commitment and courage. We defied the state, we survived, and, like Muhammad Ali, we imagined ourselves floating like a butterfly, stinging like a bee. We ran free in our parallel underground world, re-creating ourselves, and holding out an invitation to others: JOIN US!

The safe house of my imagination is filled with sunshine and fresh air, and it opens to a meadow of red clover and wild flowers. In the mornings the deer, quiet but alert, graze along the tree line, and in the evenings two familiar red hawks sail out of an indigo sky wheeling in great circles overhead. Stars throb and spin in their coronas while the creek whispers steadily from its bed, and underneath it all we hear the pulse of the earth, beating the rhythm of life. We can sleep the whole night through.

In reality our safe houses were a motley lot: "garden apartments" in the Tenderloin or Uptown, a scabby boardinghouse near the waterfront, a coach house in the Mission District. Mostly we found anonymous apartments in modest neighborhoods off the main thoroughfares.

Where we weren't, ever, was Berkeley or Madison, the Lower East Side or Hyde Park. By leaving our Vermonts and Ann Arbors behind, we plunged into working-class neighborhoods, less likely to bump into anyone from before, more likely to begin again.

Out of sight was mostly a figurative state, mostly metaphorical. We saw our landlords, our neighbors, the nearby shopkeepers, and they, of course, saw us. We got jobs, mostly where large numbers of workers flowed by steadily, mostly where Social Security cards were glanced at casually and withholding taxes were considered inconvenient, mostly where you controlled your own schedule. I worked out of temporary hiring hails and day-labor "slave markets," I built swimming pools for a while and slaughtered chickens, I was a baker and then a chef in an upscale French café. And over time, on our jobs and in our neighborhoods, we made new friends.

I remember Ned Killian vividly from a hiring hall I worked out of for a couple of years. Ned grew up on a farm, dropped out of high school to join the navy, and married a Haitian girl named Matilde with whom he had five kids. He wore a dark stringy ponytail that poked out of his smudged Jamaican beret. Now retired, Ned was waiting for the last of the kids to finish high school and saving money to add to his navy pension so that he and his wife could build their little dream house in the Caribbean.

Ned and I met at 5 A.M. several mornings a week, and if we didn't have any work by nine, we'd get breakfast together at the greasy spoon next door and then go shoot some pool or spend a couple of hours reading in the library. Ned could fix anything—furniture, cars, toilets, refrigerators—and he loved to read, pursuing eclectic and esoteric interests with a passion: Chinese history, bee biology, Native American mythology. I liked him a lot for all of this, but our friendship was cemented by two incidents from our first days together.

I'd been working at the hiring hall for months, and I knew all the regulars—Old Dan, the child of former slaves, a lifelong communist who'd fought to organize the waterfront in the 1930s and who hung around the hall because there was nowhere else he wanted to go; Alice, forty years old and always smiling, several teeth gone, one of only a handful of women in the hall, a tiny grandmother of eight, born in Belize, where she had worked as a registered nurse, demoted to "hospital worker" in the U.S.; Murphy, an unreconstructed racist of the old school, small pink eyes, a perpetual blue scowl on his doughy face and a large oafish chip on his shoulder.

Murphy and I found a reason to chide each other, to tease or argue about something almost every day, but one day things spiraled out of control. Murphy had been lobbying the business agent to move him ahead on the board, whispering that certain work should be reserved for certain people and that women, and Alice in particular, could not be reliably sent to do a man-sized job. Later when Alice and five other workers were called for a large cleanup, Murphy exploded: Oh, come on, man, he groaned. Alice, you don't want that stinking job, do you? Here, sell it to me for five dollars and take my slot on the board.

Alice, still smiling, walked quickly and quietly to the window to claim her papers, but Murphy was on his feet now, blocking her path. I shouldn't have done it, I know that, but the scene became panoramic in my eyes, sweeping and all-inclusive: the fat white man obstructing the path of the small Black woman, and what did she want? A simple, honest job. I never gave it a thought, but flew across the room and blind-sided Murphy, sending him sprawling across the floor, banging his head into a chair.

Murphy was a big man—I'd have never knocked him down in a fair fight—and now he was enraged and struggling to his feet, blood on his mouth, in order to kick my ass. Just then Ned, whom I'd known for about two days, stepped in front of Murphy saying, Break it up, break it up. He was clutching a foot-long oak bludgeon.

Break it up? Murphy whined. That bastard attacked me.

Sure, sure, said Ned, I know, but now it's over. And it was.

Later Murphy and I were dispatched together to a job thirty miles away, and in his car he passed me a joint which I innocently took to be a peace offering, but which was in fact a Mickey spiked with angel dust and it almost killed me, but that's another story. Years after that, when my first child was born and I was walking around dazed and starry-eyed and enthralled, I remember saying over and over, Everyone has a mother, even Murphy, but that's another story, too.

Ned turned out to be one of those decent guys who tried to be good in his own life, but more than that saw it as his human duty to oppose injustice and especially to fight racism every day in each and every way. This had gotten him into trouble more than once, in the navy when he contradicted his commanding officers in bars from Manila to San Juan, when he challenged the prevailing sentiments back home with his father and his brother. It had also earned him a private sense of integrity that shone through in other areas, a complicated reputation on all sides, and special affection from some quarters. Ned could quote from *The Autobiography of Malcolm X* and the poetry of Langston Hughes, and he and I spent hours talking politics and swapping stories.

The second incident took place a few days later while the two of us were shooting pool. I think I know you, Ned said, and I froze. He looked at me for a long time and then nodded to himself. I thought so, but what I meant, he said finally, is that I know your heart, I know you're a good man, but you're running from something. You don't belong in that hiring hall, and that hair color, well . . . you're running from something. Don't tell me anything you don't want to, he said, staring into me, but if it'd help to talk, well, here I am.

I'm really just a hippie, I said.

No you're not, Joe, he said in a serious tone. You're not a hippie.

How can you say that? I've got long hair, I smoke dope, I'm a hippie.

No, you're not.

Why not?

You work here every day. A hippie doesn't work ever.

Rose and I began to see Ned and Matilde a lot, to eat together and then go to the movies, or to organize a barbecue in the park or a trip to the beach. Matilde cooked in a Haitian restaurant, and Rose would sometimes babysit the kids or bring them to our house overnight.

We brought the underground with us wherever we went. We didn't tell most people the Joke because we didn't want a wide range of people wandering around unreliably with a truth they couldn't handle, or facts that could blow up on us. Ned and Matilde presented an entirely different problem. We trusted them completely as friends, but we didn't want to tell them the Joke because we thought it would be a burden and a nuisance. On the other hand, our deepening friendship demanded some accounting, in part because friends don't lie, and in part because we were potentially exposing their family to danger, and it seemed wrong to deny them access to the Joke and the right to choose this relationship freely for themselves.

What is a safe house anyway? A safe house is what you seek when your home has turned into hell, when you conclude that your homeland has become a place of lies and deceptions, a giant justification of murder and mayhem. You want to escape from the burning house to find a safe house.

A safe house could be any place rented anonymously, unlisted and unknown. An unsafe house might be rented by "Bernardine Dohrn," say, and feature a big picture of her in the front window with the headline: TEN MOST WANTED, and then a cheery WELCOME HERE, all in capital letters. We saw just that front window by surprise one day on a city street, and Jeff and I were so delighted we insisted on cruising past it three times while Rose cringed between us in the front seat.

An unsafe house could be a place where the realtor asks too many questions or demands too many references or just feels too uptight. Or it could be a place where any other shady business is under way—drugs being dealt from next door, for instance, or hookers in the apartment upstairs.

Our first safe house was a houseboat at Gate 6, Slip 58, a grimy tenement swimming in a shallow cesspool but with a million-dollar view of the city. For a time we lived in a perch above a goat shed on a commune, and later in the groundskeepers' quarters of a mansion near Laurel Canyon. We occupied a penthouse in Manhattan for a few months, and a basement room in a monastery in Mundelein for the balance of that year, a flimsy shack near Watts, and a stone house on the Olympic Peninsula. My favorite place was a sunny room above a noisy Irish tavern patronized by off-duty cops—the landlord was forever apologizing and leaving us little remorseful gifts of food or drink.

Wherever we were Rose put a piece of lace on the window, her treasured little quilt on the bed, and it was home. A safe house was a house from which you remembered other houses, from which you imagined other homes. We were nomads, and we moved a lot; like snails, we learned to carry our houses on our backs.

I knew that there were parallel undergrounds and I'd even participated in several—illegal abortion networks, for example, pathways to Canada or Europe for deserters, characters and minor outlaws like Ron St. Ron—but searching for safe houses I discovered a thousand undergrounds, a million, an entire culture of undergrounds. And while each was different and in important ways distinct, they shared a couple of edges, which made them suddenly, surprisingly visible to me.

I had found a perfect pay phone for receiving calls—the telephone was our enemy and I still feel an odd aversion to it, but this was an important discovery because pay phone–to–pay phone communication, always paid for with rolls of quarters, was the main means for the diaspora to be in contact. It was a time when Rose and I were on separate coasts, and fell into a pattern of regular use—she called me every other day at 7 PM. The phone was downstairs, between the washrooms in a bustling Howard Johnson's at the intersection of two busy highways twenty minutes from where I was staying. It was not a single phone but rather two separate booths, so that if one was busy or out of order there was an easy and instant backup. All of this made it a great phone for us, but there was one other thing which I'd never found before that made the phone ideal—the hallway featured a bench covered with neon orange and aqua Naugahyde, long enough for three people to sit comfortably.

I'd been using the phone for a couple of weeks when I arrived to find two tough guys the size of trucks, arms folded, filling the whole bench. My heart dropped, but I nodded lightly and cruised right into the men's room. Shoes, I thought. But, slow down. They were each wearing sharp Italian loafers and expensive wool suits and, by their expressions, no underwear. One looked like my old friend from high school with the Frankenstein head, the other had the face of Manny the Masher, a professional wrestler who'd experienced way too many headlocks. To be safe, I thought, I'll stay long enough to take a piss, and then go back out. It was one minute to seven.

Suddenly both phones rang simultaneously and I heard the bench groan as the two trucks rose to answer. Yo Frankie, they said in unison. Silence, and then the men's room door eased open and Manny asked, You Joe? It's for you, Joe.

Thanks, I said, taking the phone, and while the guy with the square head rambled on to Frankie in some kind of coded message that sounded a lot like a weather report—degrees and directions, velocity, highs, and lows—Manny sat back down smiling and I made a plan for another call at a different place. Then I got out of there, quick.

Once when we were looking for an apartment and a rental agent was showing us through a big building, we stumbled accidentally upon a really unsafe house. The agent, young and eager, was opening doors manically in a gesture of the hard sell as we followed casually along, when suddenly we found ourselves in a tiny bedroom converted into a crowded electronic surveillance station—windows shaded, two cameras pointed at a first-floor apartment across the street, tape recorders whirring. Oops, the agent said with an embarrassed laugh. I forgot about that, but they'll be out by the end of the week.

After dark I rang the buzzer for the first-floor apartment across the street—it was marked "Jackson." Package for Jackson, I said, and the door opened a crack. I don't know you, Mr. Jackson, I said quickly, and I don't want any trouble, but you're being watched from the second floor across the street. The door slammed shut and I ran, never knowing if I'd just warned a Soviet spy, a drug smuggler or a kidnapper, a good guy or some really foul low-life. At the time I didn't much care.

We built alliances with several other fully realized underground groups for specific purposes or goals or actions—for example, the Brotherhood of Eternal Love, a dope and acid network, in order to break Timothy Leary out of California prison, and the Black Liberation Army for all kinds of insurgent mischief. But the most interesting alliance to me was struck in the first months underground, and it was with a kind of eccentric shadowy group that would become fast and reliable friends for decades to come.

The group was without a name, counted hundreds of members in half a dozen cities, and was organized by a charismatic leader and psychologist who called himself Kaz. They were all former heroin addicts, former beatniks, former hustlers and prostitutes, five, ten, twenty years older than us, living now in luxury and working downtown, but thinking of themselves primarily as deep, deep underground, a kind of fifth column waiting patiently for the revolution.

We've been expecting you, Kaz said, embracing me warmly when we first met, his eyes twinkling and his trim gray beard shining. We were in a penthouse apartment on the Gold Coast, surrounded by Persian rugs and Asian vases, overstuffed sofas and modern paintings. Kaz embraced our activities, too, and before long he was providing us with money and safe houses and more.

Whenever we met with other organizations or with characters from the movement—and we met with hundreds—Rose and I would tell our story in two-part harmony, a practiced duet that nonetheless sounded fresh to me each time.

I might begin talking about the lessons learned from the Town-house and the need for a broad unity of purpose against the war and racism that would transcend tactics. I might talk through Rose's interruptions or I might yield, and she'd pick it up, talking about the need to build strong bridges to all sectors, to women's groups and international groups and the elders, and, of course, with a strategic focus on the Black struggle here.

I'd wait and then take it up again, and together we would shape a rap, a story with understandable dimensions and a happy safeness to it. We said the same words in the same ways, and over many months it became soothing and familiar.

I worked in a health food bakery for a couple of years, and one night on the late, late shift I encountered a parallel underground that almost killed me.

The bakery was a small neighborhood storefront—three shifts of young people humming from six in the morning until midnight, cranking out massive amounts of granola and oatmeal cookies, carrot cake and eight-grain bread. Late on a hot summer night two of us— Paula, a young woman in medical school, and I—were left to clean the shop after closing, and we propped the front door open so we could breathe.

I was mopping up when I heard the door slam shut; I wheeled around and saw a silver pistol the size of a baseball bat just inches from my head. The pistol was shaking and the youngster holding it looked as if he was going to cry. I don't want any trouble, he said, and his voice cracked. Back up. The gun was bigger than his head.

I tried to speak and my jaw moved mechanically, but nothing came out.

He corralled Paula and me into the bathroom, and just before he locked us in, I recovered enough to say, Take the money, take anything you want.

We sat on the floor holding hands and trembling. The bathroom had a phone on the wall, but we didn't dare use it until we heard the front door slam again. Paula quietly called 911, and then the owners, and when they arrived she burst into tears.

We each went home, but neither of us could sleep that night, and next day the cops picked us up at the bakery and drove us, weary and still shaking, to the 20th Precinct to look at mug shots. Paula didn't know that I was a fugitive myself; my nervousness looked to her like a result of the shock of the night before.

We sat in a small room as a clerk brought us book after book of pictures to look through, each one thick and heavy, each labeled BLACK MALE, 18–20, ASSAULT, ROBBERY, WEAPONS. An hour into it, all I could think of was the tragedy of this anarchistic and nihilistic quasi-underground, the wasted courage and the senseless sacrifice.

Paula and I never saw our guy, and if we had, at that point I'd have just turned the page.

We got a snow-white Samoyed puppy named Lolita (for Lolita Lebron) that first year who disappeared one night, and soon we inherited an Afghan hound named Maddie, short for madrone, a tree we loved. Jeff later got a spirited Irish setter who accompanied him everywhere, named Red Dog, or sometimes Under Dog, short for Wonder Dog. Now our safe houses all had to be dog-friendly places as well.

Owning a dog for most people was a commonplace—completely unremarkable. For us, having a dog marked a dramatic new direction. Months earlier it would have been unthinkable, an irresponsible indulgence, derided and ridiculed. The time it takes you to walk that damn dog is time stolen from organizing, a comrade might have said, and another would have added, The food that thing eats could feed five Vietnamese for a week. But now, whenever Jeffrey showed up with Red Dog, someone, or several people together, would romp around with him in dizzy excitement. It was strange, but the dogs, too, changed our lives.

Working on the waterfront I ran into dozens of shady operations—gambling rings, smuggling crews, screwy little gangs of thieves—but I didn't even see the most prevalent and the most obvious underground network until one day in late summer when it exploded in my face.

It was before four o'clock, shift change, and the work crew finishing up crowded onto the deck near the gangplank. The game was to get near the top soon enough to be one of the first off the ship, but not so soon that a shift foreman would send you back down—quarter to four was way too early, five to four way too late. It was a tricky calculation.

In any case, we were assembling on the deck, smoking, joking, jostling one another, and I was thinking about dinner with Rose and no smoke or sparks or welding arc for sixteen hours—freedom— when the corner of one eye caught a plainclothes cruiser easing behind a storage shed. I don't even know how I knew what it was, but I did, and my antenna shot up instantly. I was on full alert.

I was suddenly aware that the big shipyard was crawling with cops—at least two with rifles on the roof of the locker room, four more lingering by the gate, a couple with radios standing just away from the gangplank, and unmarked cars at every angle. Two minutes to four. My heart was racing; my mind closed in on escape. I measured the distance across the blacktop from ship to fence—no good— and through the water to the next pier—I'd be crushed or drowned in the open space. The best choice was a ditch that ran under the fence just beyond the locker room.

The horn blew and I hung back, head down, as the crowd funneled forward. If I could just get beyond the spotters with their radios, I'd be only sixty seconds to the ditch. At that moment somebody hissed *La Migra*, and the running and the chasing began, the shouting and the cornering, the blackjacks and the handcuffs—and it had nothing at all to do with me.

Every Mexican was lined up as I cruised untouched to my locker, and then home, free. I'd misread every sign. That day, like so many days, my white skin was my passport. My freedom was stained with shame.

28.

We were going forward, but on a modified path now, and at a different pace. The change was subtle and might have appeared trivial to an outsider, but to us it was marked and obvious. Again we'd been in the hundred-mile-an-hour gale, and sixty-miles-an hour was a relief.

We were still susceptible to occasional gut-checks, to charges of not doing enough, in part because we knew that we weren't doing enough, since doing enough was an unachievable goal. The war had to end now, the racist system had to be destroyed this very minute, and every day we looked to tomorrow was in part a failure, and we knew it. In part our rhetoric was still way out in front of our capacity. But three of us were dead, and soon we would organize a prison break and a series of high-profile bombings using dynamite—that most romantic of nineteenth-century radical tools—in government buildings, most dramatically the Capitol in Washington, in response to the widening war, an action code-named the Big Top.

To our left were the anarchists and the terrorists, many of them wonderful people but with the ideology of a ten-year-old, convinced that we were accommodationist reformers and soft intellectuals playing at revolution, quiet now because we had lost three comrades and because the drama of the event overtook them and was so beyond them. To our right were the peace movement and the social democrats, also silent, some because their dire predictions of doom and repression never panned out, some because we were a useful lever, an implied threat if peaceful reform failed, and some out of respect for the price paid.

Each year came on charged with possibility. When Timothy Leary's band of merry men approached us in 1970 to break their guru out of a California prison, their timing was perfect. Months earlier we would have found it laughable to work with these guys and impossible to justify a single prison break—what about the hundreds of thousands left behind? Until we could go through the front gates with a tank and a red army prepared to liberate the lot, we'd be simply jerking off.

The Leary break—code-named Juju Eyeballs from the Beatles' "Come Together"—featured elements we were striving for—artfulness, for example, subtlety, and indirection. It was practice for a second line of action we wanted to perfect—jailbreaks were in our future. Juju Eyeballs was a matter of thinking mostly, planning, attention to detail, mobilization, and then a moment of determination and courage. The Old Man himself took the biggest risk—he'd done hundreds of push-ups a day motivated by a single thought: on a night in September when the prison camp was blanketed in thick white fog he would scale a wall and work his way for one hundred feet hand over hand suspended from a wire. When he dropped in the trees beyond the fence he would make his way to a railroad spur and then follow it north until he found the sign we'd left him: a smiling six-inch Buddha carved in wood. At that point he would plunge into the brush and find the road.

A second Buddha welcomed him to his hiding place—the nook of a shady tree at the far end of a turnout. Every fifteen minutes a comrade named Ernie pulled into that turnout, flashed his lights, and then circled back around. He would have done it all night if necessary, but on the second pass the Old Man bounded from his tree and leapt into the back seat. The hard part was over.

Ernie gave the Old Man a joint, an ID, plaid and polyester clothes and spray-on hair dye, and drove twenty miles north to a campground where the Old Man joined a family—two blond kids sleeping in the back of a camper, Dad driving and Mom next to him in the cab, the Old Man stashed safely in the overhead. The kids, incidentally, were the best secret keepers, instinctively getting the game. Ernie took the Old Man's prison clothes to a rest stop thirty miles south and left them on a counter near the sink, splattered some blood around for dramatic effect, and went home. The Leave It to Beavers headed north, and within days Timothy Leary was united with his family in Algeria.

We were negotiating an in-between: holding on to the special, edgy underground life we'd invented but angling toward a sustainable life with some conventional dimensions and ordinary boundaries. Our underground life could be undermined or even destroyed—externally or internally—if we fell into too much habit, too much complacency. But our sustainable life required just a bit more pattern, and we were searching now for balance. It didn't seem too much to ask—a world with strong sides, the basics somehow intact: home, society, food, sex. I wanted little things to be secure, to give off a sense—an illusion, of course—of permanence, or at least of normalcy. When our patterns betrayed us, we were quickly outsmarted and encircled, boundaries collapsed, and we almost lost it all. But we ran and, almost miraculously, we escaped. We yanked ourselves forcefully then into a mission of repair. Here's how it began.

We ate mostly in neighborhood restaurants. In San Francisco, we loved the St. Petersburg, which we'd code-named Petrograd, a run-down place owned by a remarkably cheery old lady whose family had escaped the Bolsheviks and gone to China, only to flee the Maoists en route to Cuba, and then to run from Fidel, landing right here in the U.S. where, we hoped, if the pattern held, she was merely awaiting another revolution. She made a hearty borscht and the best chicken soup ever, which featured fresh spinach and huge chunks of burned garlic floating everywhere.

I liked the US Restrant (*sic*), featuring mounds of pasta with pesto or cream and a staff that spoke no English; the Dents de Lion, with a fresh basil salad that bit with the teeth of the lion; and the DMZ, the first Vietnamese restaurant in town that advertised "We don't go north, we don't go south . . . We stay right here in the DMZ," and whose chef drove a car with a pointed personalized license plate: UNCLE HO. I liked Yet Wah and, even better, Wing Fat's, a gloomy room with an unmarked entryway a few steps up Eternal Happiness Alley, crowded with locals and with the Fat Man himself hovering over the sizzling woks like an Asian volcano, sending waves of pungent smoke billowing overhead and stinging your eyes.

We'd planned to meet at Wing Fat's at six thirty, but when I got there at six fifteen, Jeff and Rose were already squeezed into a back booth, looking frazzled, Rose's face tight and red and worried. Are you OK? she asked, and I thought, Oh, no. Those were her exact words after the Townhouse, and they signified disaster. Whatever was next, it was nothing nice.

Kaz, who had developed a complicated and safe way to send us money, had missed a drop, and we agreed, just this once and because we were desperate, on a shortcut. Kaz sent $200 through Western Union to "Tom Stewart," an ID Jeff had built up. I now heard that when Jeffrey went into the downtown office, red lights and warning bells started going off in his head. There was an older looking hippie—beads, headband, scruffy beard—lurking near a phone booth inside. Could be nothing. The transaction went smoothly enough, but the clerk kept glancing over his glasses at Jeff. Again, maybe just a nervous clerk, acting the way he always did with everyone.

Outside Jeff hesitated, then walked around the corner, jumped into the pickup truck, and Rose started it up. There was an old guy dressed like a hippie watching you from a doorway, she said.

Shoes, Jeff said. The place was staked out.

A car pulled out behind them—a beat-up Ford—and Rose knew he was right. Shit. She took two quick turns and then went into a one-way street, three lanes with heavy traffic and timed lights. Shit.

Before they could move a moment forward the Ford eased up on the passenger side—Rose was holding steady in the center lane—and two carbon-copy hippies like the ones Jeff had seen close up—triplets now—stared up at Rose. The passenger smiled and held up a peace sign. Rose slammed the brakes, swerved left across two lanes, and plunged onto a side street as the Ford shot through the intersection trapped for another block at least.

Where's Suzy Q? I asked, referring to the pickup.

It turned out she was abandoned in an alley beneath the underpass near downtown, and Jeff and Rose were, for the last hour, trying to figure out what had happened and what to do next.

We left Wing Fat's and two hours later met up at a safe house with two close aboveground comrades. We rehearsed the events in reverse again, and then again, and agreed, finally, that Bert would walk up to Suzy Q first thing in the morning, open the door and get in, wait a minute, and then, if nothing happened, leave. Ernie would watch the alley and then guide Bert through a complicated route to reconnect.

Next morning at eight we got a call at a pay phone from Ernie— the moment she opened the pickup door Bert was surrounded by a dozen Shoes, guns drawn, a no-bullshit show of force. She was in custody. Suspicion confirmed.

We worried about Bert, although she told us later that it was strictly pro forma. They were inefficient and lazy, she said, working from some outdated script: Are you a member of any secret societies? Do you know others who are? Are you in contact with any foreign agents? It all sounded so naive. She saw her job, she said, as miscuing whenever possible, steadily disrupting the scene: Foreign agents? You mean like the Rolling Stones?

Of course, Bert's fate bore no resemblance to the fates of poor people caught up in the judicial system. Lawyers were quickly dispatched, resources mobilized.

The bigger problem dawned on us slowly. The "Tom Stewart" ID papers linked to a transient hotel we'd used for two different sets of ID, and the second ID had been used to rent an apartment and open an account with the electric company. One of our cars, registered to another ID, had been ticketed outside that apartment recently, and, come to think of it, Jeff had been stopped in Suzy Q on a traffic safety check a week ago and the cops wrote down information from a clean ID he was carrying that linked to a bogus address, home to two more sets. And so it went. By eleven we realized that every vehicle was gone, every house unsafe, every ID tainted. We were back to nothing.

The circles of danger emerged clearly, and each was resisted by someone. Jeff hated to part with Suzy Q, but there was no argument there. The occupants of one compromised apartment couldn't believe that it was really lost, and so Rose had to persuade them to stay away for a day while an aboveground cadre staked it out from a nearby laundromat. The block was swarming with Shoes, and Carolyn cried thinking of the books, letters, diaries left behind. None of us wanted to give up the little ledges we were perched on.

We fell back and the enemy, his blood up, began a new and frenzied round of searching. We retreated further and further, convinced that retreat was wisdom, that retreat at this time was not defeat.

Rose and Jeff and I abandoned the rocking houseboat and moved in with an artist, a childhood friend who heard and understood the risks and said yes. We struggled to contain the losses, but finally gave up and fell back.

Ernie made doubly careful contact with my brother Tim, a filmmaker and a generous soul who never hesitated. He took two days off work, loaded us into a VW bus, and drove us out of state where we could begin again.

The encirclement taught us an important technical lesson—keep a firewall between every ID and every resource, and call it compartmentalization. It also underlined a theme already in the making: every day we could survive was itself a victory, and our energy should, then, be directed to safety. Our existence underground, we thought now, opened a world of possibilities.

What passes for memory is more often memento—a little souvenir dangling on a chain, some commemorative keepsake for the mantel, the gold paint flaking off by the time you get it home.

This was the first of several times I lost everything, every possession, all the notebooks and papers and books and little personal treasures I had collected. My stores could never be replaced.

I'd had apartments broken into in previous years, always, I assumed, by the police or the FBI. Papers would be rifled, much disruption and some items stolen, but this was more serious. The whole stock was gone.

The experience, hard and difficult though it was, had a positive and liberating effect. I was never crushed by losing stuff, and over time I became indifferent to material things. Standing naked I learned that I could do without.

There are always hardships in life, and life underground had its share—our employment was marginal and making a living was tough, and, living outside the law, we had no rights and no protections whatsoever. When our apartment was burglarized—twice in one year—and the wave of paranoia passed, who could we call? The red army?

But there are benefits to displacement as well. We were free of straitjackets; there were no expectations to conform to, no lines to follow to make a career. The upheaval of life broadened my perspective, cast me among people I never would have known in the narrower course of life. I could be all things—a slum-dweller, a migrant worker, a day laborer, an itinerant traveler. I was an internationalist in my heart—nowhere a stranger but everywhere an outsider. I saw everything and felt the great pulsing unity of all humanity.

Emile de Antonio, the radical documentary filmmaker famous for his *Point of Order* and *Painters Painting,* sent word through friends that he'd like to meet with us to discuss the possibility of a project that would bring the Weather Underground to life in the media. I love your courage, he'd written us, and your commitment. I'm here to help.

We were flattered. And intrigued. But a film would be tricky, and a meeting difficult.

Contact with the open world was where the hidden world came into sharpest focus, and we built elaborate little mechanisms for connection. Here's how Jeffrey and I met D the first time.

Our contact person—an aboveground movement ally—received a preplanned route, a trajectory, that he and D would walk before contact would be made.

I watched from half a block away as they stepped off the sidewalk at Van Buren Street heading north on Michigan Avenue, and within blocks they were already going under. It was 8:15 AM. Nothing had changed on the outside and so anyone observing them but me, casually or intentionally, could not have known that they were now in liberated territory—they looked to all the world like just a couple of folks in the throng swarming up a crowded city street in rush hour. But from the start they had been in what we called the set, and halfway across Adams Street, click, they entered the underground. This part of the passage was called the tunnel, and from here on, every move was monitored by Jeff and me safely out of sight.

Just south of Madison they headed down a flight of stairs leading to the Grant Park Garage, cut into the second aisle, and then quickly walked north two blocks, never looking back. This was the trap, because any tail would become instantly visible. They surfaced then at Michigan and Washington, headed west to Wabash, into Marshall Field's, and made a quick diagonal through the store to the exit at State and Randolph. The breakaway. North on State to Lake Street, underground again, a second breakaway, west to Clark, up and north to the river where a steel staircase led down to Wacker Place. Along Wacker was the pickup, and it was Jeff's and my responsibility to make contact. I signaled Jeff, he nodded, and they were in. If the pickup had been missed, they were finished for the day, and that trajectory would be scrapped. They were not to reenter the tunnel, but to head to a prearranged pay phone that would start ringing in exactly six hours.

It's odd thinking back to that hyper-aware, meticulously worked-out method of contact, because everyone we met, everyone from the open world, went through just such a passage. Journalists, lawyers, prominent donors, occasionally parents. It didn't matter, everyone walked a trajectory. The first words spoken after a handshake or an embrace were also part of the pattern: Who am I? Who are you? Where are we going? What's our tale? We called this "the conspiratorial minute," getting our story straight in the event of a traffic stop, an accident, an unforeseen encounter with the law. More talk tactics.

We hid inside the circles of an ordinary life, masqueraded as a smiley face, and our safe houses were so normal they squeaked.

Anyone who paid close enough attention, however, anyone who thought deeply about our meaning-making and our motivation, might have picked out the tiny cultural artifacts that boomed from the walls like the telltale heart. There were no bombs or guns anywhere, but inside every safe house the atmosphere of revolution was on red-hot display.

The bookshelf was an immediate giveaway—every Weatherman read Malcolm X, the poetry of Ho Chi Minh, Amilcar Cabral, and Mari Sandoz's marvelous biography of Crazy Horse. Harry Haywood was on our reading list, and so was Amiri Baraka, C.L.R. James, and James and Grace Lee Boggs. And somewhere, usually the bedroom, was a modest, framed black-and-white photo of Che.

Our refrigerators stocked Vietnamese fermented fish sauce called *nuoc mam*, which we loved, even though the smell would make us gag, to be used on rice or stir-fry, and we kept a living sourdough starter for bread or pancakes given to Rick by a Native American comrade in Canada, passed from hand to hand, and reputed to be over a hundred years old. Every Weatherman considered forks uncivilized and ate with chopsticks, and most of us kept a large container of Dr. Bronner's Magic Soap, a cruelty-free liquid made in Escondido from hemp and eucalyptus that claimed eighteen different uses from shaving to shampoo, from mouthwash to dishes, and had a label so jammed with Dr. Bronner's small print "All-One!" crackpot religious philosophy that next to it "You Don't Need a Weatherman to Know Which Way the Wind Blows" looked like a children's book.

I remember one evening in particular, the details as alive today as if it were yesterday—no, more vital than that, for yesterday is already a blur while this has the fine lines and tingly feeling of forever.

Rose and I met up for dinner at a simple place we liked called Yet Wah. This was the original site—before the great success and the explosion of Yet Wahs into every district—an unadorned room with twelve tables and a genius in the kitchen. We had just ordered fried dumplings and tofu with string beans when two old friends from the movement, from the open world, walked in unexpectedly. A moment of frozen indecision, then a discreet nod, and they took a table on the far side of the room. We went on with our conversation and with our meal, and when our check came I paid and then impulsively ordered a bottle of cabernet sauvignon sent to our friends' table.

Perhaps it was our primitive circumstances or our vulnerability and then taking hold of ourselves, perhaps it was the ancient gesture, formal and honorable, but I felt then, for the first time in my life, grown-up. Yes, I was an adult suddenly, with all the knowledge all people have ever had, and I felt fully the days of my years, the years of my life. I am alive right here, I thought, and Rose is here, too, in this place, at this precise and perfect time. We are in the going world, life exactly as it should be.

29.

Everything was absolutely ideal on the day I bombed the Pentagon. The sky was blue. The birds were singing. And the bastards were finally going to get what was coming to them.

I say "I" even though I didn't actually bomb the Pentagon—*we* bombed it, in the sense that Weathermen organized it and claimed it—but I've had difficulty writing this, and I thought if I just said it boldly—"I bombed the Pentagon"—that might liberate me to go on.

There's a necessary incompleteness in this account, an incoherence which is in part an artifact of those times and that situation. Some details cannot be told. Some friends and comrades have been in prison for decades; others, including Bernardine, spent months and months locked up for refusing to talk or give handwriting samples to federal grand juries. Consequences are real for people, and that's part of this story, too. But the government was dead wrong, and we were right. In our conflict we don't talk; we don't tell. We never confess.

When activists were paraded before grand juries, asked to name names, to humiliate themselves, and to participate in destroying the movement, most refused and went to jail rather than say a word. Outside they told the press, I didn't do it, but I dug it. I recall John Brown's strategy over a century ago—he shot all the members of the grand jury investigating his activities in Kansas—but we weren't there, and so we built a strategy of noncooperation: don't talk.

Even all these years later I look at it—a bomb inside the Pentagon—and my breath catches, I tremble a bit. I used to say,

Those who tell, don't know, and those who know, don't tell. It was a clever way to keep the bastards guessing. But I do know this, and I'm going to tell. In my way.

Why did you bomb the Pentagon?

My dad wants to know. He was once offered a cabinet position and was once considered for Secretary of the Army. He knows that I bombed a lot of things—Those were crazy times, he says, better forgotten—and he knows, too, that Diana, whom he liked, is dead—She was older, he says now, and she led you astray. He's stuck in other patterns as well—You need a haircut, he says automatically, and, You'd better cover that tattoo in front of Mother—and now he wants to know why I bombed the Pentagon.

I didn't really think that three pounds of dynamite would knock it down or even do much damage—although it turns out that we blew up a bathroom and, quite by accident, water plunged below and knocked out their computers for a time, disrupting the air war and sending me into deepening shades of delight. I didn't think that our entire arsenal, 125 pounds of dynamite, would actually count for much in a contest with the U.S. military, but I was never good at math, and I did think that every bomb we set off invoked the possibility of more bombs, that the message—sometimes loud and clear—was that if you bastards continue to wage war, we'll go into places you don't want us to go, places like the Pentagon, and we'll retaliate, and soon—who knows?—you might completely lose control.

It was a story we told ourselves, and a story we spun out into the world. Armed anecdotes. Explosive narrations.

The Pentagon was ground zero for war and conquest, organizing headquarters of a gang of murdering thieves, a colossal stain on the planet, a hated symbol everywhere around the world. Do you know what the word for Pentagon is in Chinese or Korean, Arabic or Haitian Creole? Pentagon.

We went back and forth, not only between us but within each one of us. I called up all the courage I could summon in order to take the next risk—to bomb the Pentagon, say—and then I ran my commitment through the severest tests. And then I thought, enough. There must be another way. And then the ferment stirred and the demand to do more, to go further, again issued forth. Back and forth. Without end.

I thought about the justification for each action. Sometimes I answered technically: we worked hard and did our best to take care, to focus, to do no harm to persons and no more damage than we'd planned. The psychological answer, I think, was that we were young with an edge of certainty and arrogance that I would be hard-pressed to re-create or even fully understand again. The moral justification requires remembering the context of the times. I could barely justify eating my own breakfast because it seemed a kind of inaction or a kind of moving along blindly, as if normal life included unending slaughter. I went for days on end with nothing to eat, no money of my own, no change in my pocket, thinking only of how to stop the war, how to make the price for continuing the war great, how to reach out to the victims of the war and stand alongside them and experience something of what they were experiencing. I wanted intimate knowledge of their situation, of their suffering.

I'd marched on the Pentagon more than once, scaled its walls, confronted armed troops there, and even peed on its side. If I could have, I'd have duct-taped it shut, or put it in a trash compactor, but the closest I could come was a tiny bomb in a toilet drain.

We'd already bombed the Capitol, and we'd cased the White House. The Pentagon was leg two of the trifecta.

Millions of people had died in the war by now as the United States rained millions tons of explosives on Indochina. Where was there room for all those bombs? I imagined I could taste the ash in my mouth, smell the acrid smoke from something still smoldering in my chest. Ho Chi Minh had said long ago, "Neither bombs nor shells can cow our people and no honeyed words can deceive them. We Vietnamese are resolved to fight till not a single U.S. aggressor remains on our beloved land." He was right.

We were mostly into armed propaganda then, propaganda of the deed, guerilla theater, invisible resistance. Our bombings were less frequent, but we were not done with bombs. We reserved big attacks for big targets and big moments. We knew they would come.

President Nixon ordered the systematic bombing of Ha Noi and the mining of the port of Hai Phong in an operation code-named Linebacker, a nod toward the president's preferred football metaphor—It's just a game, folks, and we're playing defense. Over two hundred B-52 sorties dropped fourteen thousand tons of bombs on the capitol of Viet Nam. So we decided to answer that terror bombing with a tiny surprise, this one inside the Pentagon itself, the five-sided behemoth serving as the nerve center of American military might, the most hated symbol throughout the world, we thought, of America's bloody global mission. Some of us wanted to flatten the place outright, sick of our restraint until now.

We pulled together a special group that scouted the Pentagon irregularly for months. When a new escalation in Viet Nam became imminent, Anna and Aaron and Zeke got a storage locker outside D. C., moved some explosives in, and then found a cheap apartment nearby and rented it by the week. Their reconnaissance led them deep into the bowels of the Leviathan, and they soon knew every hall and stairway, every cul-de-sac and office and bathroom. Everything was elaborately mapped, and their apartment began to look like an alternative war room, the dark mirror-image of the Pentagon itself.

Anna, her fingertips painted with clear nail polish to obscure the identifying marks of her naked hand, and heavily disguised in suit and blouse and briefcase, dark wig and thick glasses, began entering the Pentagon every morning with hundreds of other workers. She walked the halls, ate breakfast in the cafeteria, and left by eleven. She was never challenged.

I can do it, she said finally, pulling out her sketches and maps. Here—she pointed to an isolated hallway in the basement of the Air Force section—I've been here four times, never seen another person, and there's a women's room halfway down, right here. She made an X on the map. There's a drain on the floor, narrow but big enough, I think, she said. One more visit was planned in order to unscrew the cover and take the dimensions of the space.

Anna was in the next day at 9:00 AM, and was in the women's room and the stall by 9:10 AM. She locked the door, hung up her jacket, and pulled plastic gloves, a screwdriver, and tape measure from her briefcase. The grated cover was gunky but easy to pop off once the screws were out, and there was a comfortable 4-inch diameter that ran down for over a foot. Anna replaced the drain cover, wiped the area down and was back at the apartment by 10:00 AM.

A delicate and complicated series of phone calls built a consensus from all quarters to go forward. Aaron was a specialist, and Zeke assisted as he customized a sausage twelve inches long and three inches around, with a tiny timing device at one end and a suspension arm fashioned from fishing line and hook at the other. Aaron packed the thing into a briefcase beneath official-looking papers and personal effects. Zeke walked Anna to the train, hugged her, and went off to a bookstore for the two hours before they would meet up in a trajectory far from the target, and far from home.

When Anna appeared in the trajectory, making her way slowly down the street, Zeke's heart leapt, but he calmed himself, waited, and watched. Switchback, turn, switchback, breakaway. Certain that she was safe, he practically jumped into her arms. They were back on their block by nightfall.

All that long day Aaron worked to close down the Washington operation, emptying the storage area, cleaning out the apartment, and paying the remaining bills. Aaron was stocky and muscled, close-mouthed but even-tempered, deeply confident without a hint of arrogance. He was also the backbone of the group—entirely committed and trustworthy, hardworking and dependable. Aaron had been an emergency room nurse and a lumberjack, a guy we all believed could easily survive in the Australian Outback or the Siberian wilderness for weeks with nothing but a pocket knife, or the streets of Greenwich Village with only a couple of dollars in his pocket. Aaron was smart but never showy, steady and able to improvise when necessary—the model middle cadre.

At eleven, Aaron pulled on plastic gloves and taped a statement about the impending attack beneath a tray in a phone booth across from the *Washington Post* offices. He then moved across town, and at eleven thirty called the Pentagon emergency number. In twenty-five minutes a bomb will explode in the air force section of the Pentagon, he said calmly. I'm calling from the Weather Underground, and believe me this is no prank. Clear the area! Get everyone out! You have twenty-five minutes. Viet Nam will win!

He moved two blocks away and called the local police station, repeating the message, and then moved once more to call the *Post*, directing the night operator to the statement in the phone booth explaining it all. Comrades in New York, Chicago, Los Angeles, and San Francisco simultaneously directed local newspaper operators to copies of the political statement taped neatly in nearby phone booths. And then Aaron, too, was off.

Although the bomb that rocked the Pentagon was itsy-bitsy—weighing close to two pounds—it caused "tens of thousands of dollars" of damage. The operation cost just under five hundred dollars, and no one was killed or even hurt. In that same time the Pentagon spent tens of millions of dollars and dropped tens of thousands of pounds of explosives on Viet Nam, killing or wounding thousands of human beings, causing hundreds of millions of dollars of damage. Because nothing justified their actions in our calculus, nothing could contradict the merit of ours.

The president said our action was the work of cowardly terrorists.

The morning after the Pentagon action, Rose and I talked to Aaron, pay phone to pay phone, gathered up the newspapers, and headed happily to our apartment for breakfast. Just after ten the doorbell rang—it was our landlord coming to fix a leak in the bathtub. We lived then in an apartment above Sylvan's Night Café, and Syl, in his mid-fifties, tended bar late into the night, owned two or three other apartment buildings, and was rarely seen in sunlight. He struck us as a small, struggling capitalist, squeezed from all sides with a narrow, embattled outlook on life. But he was friendly enough to us; he'd said he would come by this week, and here he was.

This won't take long, Joe, he said to me.

Fine, Syl. Take your time.

Syl went into the bathroom with his tools, clicked on his transistor radio, and set to work. We could hear the radio humming beneath the sounds of pipe wrenches, nuts, and washers, and just as Syl was finishing up, the news came on. The lead story was the bombing of the Pentagon, and Rose gave me a look.

Syl emerged chuckling and wiping his hands. You hear about the Pentagon getting blasted, Joe? he asked.

Yeah, I said, fighting to sound casual.

You gotta hand it to those guys. The bastards in Washington— 'scuse me, Rose—don't listen to the people, and those guys might just open up their ear-waves!

You're kidding, I said. It's illegal, what they're doing, and violent.

Fuck that, said Syl. 'Scuse me, Rose. They're about as violent as a bee sting. Sure it's illegal, some property gets destroyed, big deal— same thing in the Basque country, no? Same thing at the Boston Tea Party, and that was also great.

Who knew Syl was Basque?

But, Syl, I said, enjoying this sudden reversal, if those bombers are so great, why do they hide themselves? They should have the courage of their convictions and just come forward to admit it and take the consequences.

No, Joe, no, Syl responded. Impossible. That's an invitation to their own funerals. Those guys gotta hide out. They're not hurting nobody but the bastards—'scuse me, Rose.

I can't agree, Syl, I said, and Rose now gave me a stern, disapproving look.

When Syl left and we heard the downstairs door close we grabbed each other, laughing and rolling around and around, shrieking. Syl was only one person, of course, and probably in a weird, sleep-deprived mood that day, but still, to us he became an instant symbol and a barometer—the forecast was sunny. We took the day off to rejoice and congratulate ourselves and laugh some more. From then on whatever we did, the winking question we asked one another was, What would Sylvan think?

The papers were full of stories describing the Pentagon bombing as an action of the "terrorist Weather Underground." But we're not terrorists, I thought, no matter how many times they repeat the charge. We came close, it's true—whenever there are guns and bombs, the line narrows between politics and terror, between rebellion and gangsterism. We were part of a movement, and then of a tendency toward armed struggle. We crossed the line and came back. Everyone wasn't so lucky. I hoped we'd learned some things.

To me the distinction was huge. Terrorists terrorize, they kill innocent civilians, while we organized and agitated. Terrorists destroy randomly, while our actions bore, we hoped, the precise stamp of a cut diamond. Terrorists intimidate, while we aimed only to educate. No, we're not terrorists.

The lynchings in the South for more than a century were the work of terrorists. A tiny minority of hard-core terrorists—some prominent officials in the light of day—actually donned the white robes, lit the fires, set the bombs, and threw the heavy ropes over the branches. But many more white people were called upon to witness and celebrate the events, to identify with the actions, and to see their favored fates linked to those deadly deeds. The message to Black people was that at any moment and for any reason whatsoever your life or the lives of your loved ones could be randomly snuffed out. The intention was social control through random intimidation and unpredictable violence.

The wrongdoings in Viet Nam had all the markings of modern-day terrorists. The air war, the artillery, the naval barrages, the bombing campaigns targeting whole populations, entire regions. Crops were destroyed, bridges downed, roads ruined. There was often a ritual feeling to the destruction as witnesses were flown in for optimal viewing. The slaughter was the work of a small hard core, but all Americans were called upon to identify, to celebrate, to link up. The suffering was often entirely random. The intent was control through intimidation.

In a war without fixed positions, the calculus of success was always murky. Body counts became the slippery shorthand for the war's progress, and it was not uncommon for the U.S. to report twenty enemy dead and one weapon recovered in one patrol, or ten enemy dead, no weapons recovered, no American casualties in another.

The U.S. created an elaborate environment for terror in Viet Nam, and terrorism became the way of the war every day. When a military jury made up of combat veterans convicted Lieutenant William L. Calley Jr. of three counts of premeditated murder and one count of assault with intent to commit murder for his role in the My Lai massacre, a small light was turned on and shined on the murky underbelly of American terrorism. But the moment passed, and the light was put out.

"Rusty" Calley was the commander of Charlie Company's first platoon, assigned to Quang Ngai Province, an area the U.S. military designated "Pinkville." The soldiers called it "Indian Country," meaning it was hostile territory, controlled by the National Liberation Front, a place without "friendlies." Between 1965 and 1967 tens of thousands of tons of bombs and napalm were poured into northeastern Quang Ngai Province. Artillery was randomly fired into the area, and planes with excess bombs often just haphazardly unloaded here. The U.S. military destroyed 70 percent of the dwellings and relocated some 150,000 civilians. Calley told a reporter that, "Everyone there was VC. The old men, the women, the children—the babies were all VC or would be VC in about three years. And inside of VC women, I guess there were a thousand little VC now." The justification for terror was established.

U.S. search-and-destroy missions in Quang Ngai were frightening, difficult, and deadly. American soldiers were killed by snipers, mines, booby traps, but somehow could not engage the enemy in a straight-up fight. Soldiers began beating civilians in frustration, torturing and murdering prisoners, raping villagers. Units created "Zippo squads" to torch hamlets after a combat sweep. A culture of terror built up and took control. Eventually everyone tolerated aspects of terror, witnessed it, and shared in its mission, even those who didn't actively participate.

In early 1968 U.S. planes dropped leaflets into the area telling civilians to leave or the Americans would consider them VC. Now, the military told itself, everyone was the enemy, and their job was to engage and destroy the enemy. As they prepared for battle, officers reminded the soldiers of comrades lost to booby traps and snipers—now they could get the revenge so richly deserved.

The first platoon entered My Lai early on March 16 in several small groups, shooting at anything that moved, killing buffalo, pigs, ducks, dogs. As the American soldiers swept through the village they motioned people out of their homes and herded them into large groups. Dwellings were torched, swept with machine-gun fire, or destroyed with grenades. Some civilians were shot. Families huddled together shrieking and crying. Gunfire could be heard from all parts of the village, and it created a kind of frenzied chain reaction. The terror grew. Groups of men, women, and children were pushed down into bunkers and grenades thrown in after them. Women were raped, sodomized, and mutilated, stabbed or shot in their vaginas. People were clubbed, bayoneted, and beheaded. Some GIs carved "C Company" into the chests of the dead. One GI reported finding a twenty-year-old woman with a four-year-old child in the midst of the chaos and forcing her to perform oral sex on him as he held a gun to the child's head.

Calley came upon a young soldier guarding a group of elderly people, women, and children, and said, "You know what to do with them."

When he returned a short time later he was visibly irritated: "How come they're not dead?" he asked. "I want them dead." At that, Calley started shooting. "He burned four or five magazines," according to the soldier, who added, "I helped shoot 'em."

Heads were shot off, arms and legs, pieces of flesh and bone exploding in all directions, people screaming and moaning. The young soldier dropped his gun and wandered off, but later saw Calley at another ditch blasting away into a tangle of people. At the end of that ditch a priest with folded hands and bowed head rocked back and forth pleading, No Viet, no Viet, and Calley smashed him in the mouth with the butt of his rifle. As he fell back, Calley shot him point-blank in the face and half of his head blew away.

Someone shouted that a child was running back toward the village. Calley ran and grabbed the child, flung her into the deep end of the ditch and shot once into her chest.

Company C received no enemy fire and no resistance at My Lai. There was one American injury—a GI shot himself in the foot in the frenzy. Three weapons were reportedly recovered, and 128 VC were reported killed. The attack was described as "well planned, well executed, and successful," in the official report of the action, and General William Westmoreland, commander of U.S. forces, sent a telegram to the unit praising them for inflicting "heavy blows" on the enemy. In fact, 347 Vietnamese were killed.

Calley's comment on the affair was to the point: "As for me killing those men in My Lai, it didn't haunt me—I couldn't kill for the pleasure of it. We weren't in My Lai to kill human beings, really. We were there to kill ideology. That is carried by—I don't know. Pawns. Blobs. Pieces of flesh. And I wasn't in My Lai to destroy intelligent men. I was there to destroy an intangible idea, communism. . . . Those people are monsters, and they have no qualms, no hang-ups, no holding-backs to the extremes they'll go to. I mean butcherings; that is what communism does, and we were there in My Lai to destroy it. Personally, I didn't kill any Vietnamese that day. I mean personally. I represented the United States of America. My country."

On September 5, 1969, William Calley was charged with the murder of 109 "Oriental human beings." Twenty-four others were also charged with offenses from assault to murder to dereliction of duty. A decision to hold separate trials—one mass trial would surely suggest Nuremberg and a deliberate policy of terror or genocide—meant evidence and attention was severely limited. Vice President Agnew noted that "the Communists have committed many atrocities and the . . . difference between us is that in the Communist case they were carried out with the direction and consent of their leaders," and President Nixon insisted that My Lai is "an isolated incident."

Calley's trial lasted seventy-seven days and involved over one hundred witnesses. Convicted of three counts of murder and one count of assault with intent to murder, he was sentenced to life at hard labor.

The next day President Nixon ordered Calley released from the stockade and returned to his apartment. On August 20, 1971, Calley's sentence was reduced to twenty years by the Commander of the Third Army. On April 15, 1974, the Secretary of the Army commuted Calley's confinement to ten years. On November 9, 1974, Calley was paroled by the Secretary of the Army.

Was My Lai and its aftermath typical? It was not the kind of event that happened every day, not the kind of thing most guys participated in regularly, or ever. But in many ways it was to me the absolute heart of the matter, and in its extreme and unvarnished horror, it exemplified the whole affair, exactly as the slaughter of Native Americans at Wounded Knee in South Dakota only eighty years earlier embodied the U.S. military mission then.

That, to me, was terrorism.

When the U.S. signed the Paris Peace Agreement, it at long last admitted military defeat. A first. The U.S. said it would fully withdraw from Indochina, end all aid to the puppet government in the south, and pay reparations for the destruction caused by its aggression. We thought there was certainly more pain and suffering to come—imperialism never really means its withdrawals, we said—and that we would be called upon again. But we were also overjoyed, and spent several days celebrating, laughing, and crying in gathering after gathering.

Who can ever forget the desperate images of Americans lined up like ants atop their own embassy in downtown Sai Gon, climbing aboard helicopters that ferried them in great feverish circles to safety on warships far out in the South China Sea as the enemy closed in? Or the frenzied throngs of Vietnamese who had cooperated with the Americans and been promised safe passage, waiting hopefully in the embassy compound, eyes skyward, for rescuers who never returned?

Rose and I curled up on the couch together and watched the scene on our little black and white TV. Neither of us said a word. There was nothing to say. We could hardly remember a world without war, and it was much too late to shout and cheer. The killing would end. We were right. And I still didn't know what had happened at the Townhouse. We watched and we watched, and when I finally looked at her, she was covered in tears.

30.

In those years people will say we lost track
of the meaning of we, of you
we found ourselves
reduced to I
and the whole thing became
silly, ironic, terrible:
we were trying to live a personal life
and yes, that was the only life
we could bear witness to

But the great dark birds of history screamed and plunged into our per-
sonal weather.
They were headed somewhere else but their beaks and pinions drove
along the shore, through the rags of fog
where we stood, saying I
  —Adrienne Rich

I don't remember, but I imagine.

March 1970.
    This, then, is the dream of a death.
    The place, an elegant townhouse on West Eleventh Street in
Greenwich Village, New York City. Death is never spoken here, never
looked at. The neighborhood is elegant, as I've said, a place where the

sidewalks are kept clean and the junkies and the pushers swept to some other avenue far away. Much is taken for granted. No one is paying too much attention.

On the nearest corner, a street sign: Fifth Avenue, Eleventh Street. On the house, a number in refined calligraphy on polished stone: 18.

When I went there for the first time I gave it only a fugitive's glance, ducking into the basement entrance ahead of an elderly woman and her noisy little dog, a blondish pug with an alarming bark dressed up in a neatly woven jacket. I'd turned off the avenue with a package of supplies and realized with my third step that I'd entered another country. Power—confident and restrained, muted yet obvious—boomed from every broad front window and echoed down the street. A certain indifference was everywhere in the air. And the last time I was there? Just days before all this.

Now there is a nasty hole and a tomb at number 18.

She was, of course, a child of privilege herself. The street where she died, not familiar specifically, but surely recognizable in a general way. It was coded in class.

She was twenty-seven.

Her name is engraved on a gray concrete slab in a family plot near her childhood home in Illinois. There are no names here. This is prime real estate, and a new house already going up. A mausoleum.

Some—the leading newspapers, the paid pundits, those who didn't know her at all—called her terrorist and bomber after the event; small, persistent adjectives that clung to her like a title until their nasty little embrace became part of her name. With that new naming she was orphaned, cast loose.

She'd attended boarding school in Virginia, a kind of temporary orphanage for the rich. She went on to college in Pennsylvania and became a Quaker and a pacifist. She reinvented herself and, with others, enlisted to help the poor. It was, she said, an unburdening. She went to Guatemala, to the Mayan market town of Chichicastenango in the Western Highlands. She worked with Catholic priests embracing the theology of liberation. She studied Thomas Merton and the holiness of suffering, the obligation to discover God on the threshold of despair. She walked the mountain paths and read Simone Weil and pondered the gift of affliction. She came of age there.

In the last minutes of her life, as she saw what was coming, she moved deliberately, calmly. She was a prisoner of that basement room by then, a captive to her own dreams and the endless echoes of desires. Yes, she was a prisoner all right, but she was on the verge of escape. If only she could have found the words, the key. A pain stabbed her in the stomach, her mouth was chalk, her head oddly clear. She fell into death, illuminated on all sides with the radiance of her hope in full eruption.

For many days the people on West Eleventh Street could not believe their eyes. A smoldering hole on their very own block. Collapsing brick and mortar, twisted steel, black flames. And worse than that: a terrorist. An aberration from Africa or Asia or Palestine. Not America. Not here. Surely, never here.

She is still there mostly, in that hole at number 18, West Eleventh Street. Her death—and the deaths of Ted Gold and Terry Robbins, perhaps others—remains, persists.

On March 6, a year later, over three hundred people came to the site to lay flowers and light candles. Many cried. Others spoke quietly. Everyone felt much, much older. The police and the FBI photographed everything; I watched from a distance that I thought might be safe. I wondered and wept. Her death began again on that anniversary, as it begins again each year, and then goes on and on.

I saw a dead body once, as I said, when I was ten, during the Korean War. It belonged to Jimmy Paulus, a neighbor, eighteen years old, and he was wrapped in a white sheet, the blood from his temple going black, thrust hurriedly out the front door on a stretcher borne by two tall and pale carriers lurching toward the ambulance, his right arm lolling aimlessly, brushing the ground, his mother stumbling close behind, her face twisted red and wet, her moans deep and lingering. My only child, she sobbed, he didn't want to be a soldier, he was a gentle boy—and he shot himself once in the head and he died instantly. In that one bright and frightening moment all that he was and anything he might become vanished. Everything stopped. Jimmy will always be stuck right there, at eighteen, cried over forever by his mother. Always eighteen.

Diana's body disappeared. It was her own one minute, straight and strong and beautiful and twenty-seven, forever. She had known work, the joys of jobs well done inscribed upon her body, and she had been loved, traces of desire engraved everywhere as well. And then, in the next moment, her body blasted into the opening air of the wide world. Gone. And still strangely here.

In Viet Nam the bodies piled up forever. Mass graves, pictures of pits full of bodies, nameless heaps of human beings. No names. Bodies belonging to no one. I remember the photo of a trench where thirty or forty lay in a tangle, overlapping and grotesquely anonymous, but in one place a hand jutting up in the posture of a whimsical wave. I say thirty or forty, because how could I know? Thirty or forty, what does it mean, anyway, how can you even cry? They were a tangle, as I said, and a mess. And they were twisted into one long stinking human swamp. An American tractor pushed dirt over them, and they disappeared, thankfully. Later a monk said a prayer for the dead. But not for each distinct life—how could he?—rather for the dead in general.

How quickly they became anonymous, how quickly death claimed them and collapsed them into nothingness. But one knew somehow that they were human beings once, the waving hand, the bit of scarf, the sandal, the crucifix.

Diana had also seen death up close by now. A two-year-old dying of pneumonia in her mother's arms while family and friends stood watching, helpless. An Indian baby, Mayan, poor, unimportant, and unnoticed to those with access to the means of survival. A nameless death–like those in Viet Nam–outside the village. A violent death, Diana said, quietly executed. A complete death nonetheless. A death to enter into a ledger. But where?

We had our own love, we two, our shared fondnesses, our distinct affections, our fugitive acts and criminal desires. We were never blameless, never entirely innocent. We talked of death, of course, for we were on fire and in love in a time of dying.

We had heard a story of a friend of a friend, a man who plunged fearless, smiling, to his death. He had been ice-skating on a frozen pond in Maine with his five-year-old daughter. She wandered off a moment and disappeared suddenly beneath the ice. He screamed and ran toward her, and, as the ice gave way, sucking her in deeper, he never wavered, never reconsidered, but dove ahead, offering comfort and solidarity, a father's embrace to his love who, at least, should not have to die frightened and alone. Those who saw his face at the end said he looked entirely at peace. And then they were gone. We imagined a death of purpose and peace for ourselves, a purity in death.

We fought back against death as well, death from afar, nameless death and faceless death, against quiet death. And there were costs. There would be bombs, yes, carefully placed, thoughtfully detonated, or so we thought, so we'd planned, and so it began. Bombs against death. Bombs for peace.

I studied a triptych by Ruth Weisberg called *In Memory of Diana*, a massive oil painting in three panels. In them Diana sits at a meeting, hunched forward, arms on knees, face intent, full of passion and yearning, dressed in jeans and work shirt just as I remember her. She is twenty-seven, seventeen, thirty-seven, ageless. She begins to blur, and then, in the third panel, dissolves into the wide world, into the heavens, into the galaxy. Gone.

Terry is the one who knows how to build the timer and arm the device. This one was huge, many, many sticks of dynamite stolen from a railroad shed, taped together in a briefcase destined for the army base nearby. It was primed with heavy cotton, packed with screws and nails that would do some serious work beyond the blast, tearing through windows and walls, and, yes, people, too. This one was huge and would vomit death and destruction. This one will be noticed, goddammit, he proclaims. In a minute he would blow them all to hell, but not yet.

In the corner, five wooden boxes piled high—"Hercules" stenciled neatly on each one, "Monster" and "Giant" scrawled in grease pen by a railroad foreman or a worker, and the latest entry, this one from the comrades, "Revolution!"; "Justice!"

Each stick was about a foot long and an inch and a half in diameter. Terry held one, examined it in his hands, rolled it over slowly, returned it carefully to its case. A case might cost seventy-five dollars, a box of blasting caps—tiny little silver bullets with two curious wires dangling out one end, more volatile, harder to carry, always handled away from the big stuff—maybe forty-five dollars.

We can buy the stuff, but it's a danger, he said. We would have to fill out form 5400.4 of the Bureau of Alcohol, Tobacco and Firearms, which asked for name, address, height, weight, race, and a lot else: What are you going to use it for? How will you store it? And then: Are you a fugitive? Are you an unlawful user of marijuana? Are you under indictment? What can we say? Yes, yes, yes? No. So though it's all pro forma bullshit for the most part, Terry said, there's a record of it, and who knows? So let's just steal it.

This is as easy as falling off a log, Terry continues. In front of him, no logs, but the imminent possibility of falling—a workbench with wires, a clock, batteries, a blasting cap, needle-nose pliers, some screws, fast-drying glue, a large mug of steaming black coffee, cigarettes. A box of carpenter nails to transform this into something deadly, something unspeakable. The briefcase at his feet. Here—in the briefcase—is the big motor, the good stuff, the real damage, but we need a little motor to crank it up. If I hit this stuff with a hammer . . . if I hold a match to it . . . nothing. Probably . . . I need a starter motor. I need a cap. He reaches for one. It's called the principle of initial ignition, but why get technical? He is accelerating.

OK, electrical current gets the cap going through these leg wires, and then heats up a bridge wire and it all starts tumbling along, but no current flows unless a circuit is complete. Nothing happens until we close that circuit.

The week before Terry had found an ancient editorial from *Alarm!*, the nineteenth-century anarchist journal of Haymarket martyr Albert Parsons that began:

> **DYNAMITE! Of all the good stuff, that is the stuff! Stuff several pounds of this sublime stuff into an inch pipe ... plug up both ends, insert a cap with a fuse attached, place this in the immediate vicinity of a lot of rich loafers who live by the sweat of other people's brows, and light the fuse. A most cheerful and gratifying result will follow. In giving dynamite to the downtrodden millions of the globe, science has done its best work.**

Cartoon images of pale-faced, longhaired anarchists with bushy black beards and eyebrows came to mind, each holding a perfect black globe aloft with fuse sparkling, rushing erratically toward the stock exchange. Terry had copied it out longhand, drawn a little cartoon of the imagined anarchist bomber, and taped it to the wall above the work bench. An inspiration. He called explosives "stuff" forevermore.

Tomorrow, I'll deliver this stuff myself, Terry says. Diana's assent is wobbling, and he begins to lay out the wires, the clock, the batteries, the cap in a neat sequence, explaining as he goes. He is perspiring now, gulping big mouthfuls of coffee, blazing toward glory. I'm not sure, Diana murmurs, but she is unheard. We have to be sure, sure, sure, beyond a doubt. Action, action, action. Audacity and more audacity. I'm not sure, she says again, a bit more loudly this time. Here, I'll start again, Terry says, looking up briefly and then back to the bench, replaying the deadly sequence.

Diana swoons briefly, comes back to herself and sees suddenly in the clearest and severest light, as if for the first time, and she remembers her unburdening, the epiphany of the martyred.

I wasn't there so I can never be sure. I don't know what happened, and really no one knows. It's possible, even likely, that Terry in his eagerness to spark a revolution took shaky aim—our aspirations way, way ahead of our capacity. We wouldn't be the first students or intellectuals to join the working class and then get the shit kicked out of us, or to pick up a gun and accidentally kill ourselves. Terry crossed the wires, the place blew up. End of story. It's a cliché. I can easily imagine him cocksure, Diana subdued or passive or unthinking or simply going along. Was she dismayed? Did she make reply? Was she just another ordinary soldier, into the Valley of Death?

I can imagine her in full agreement, too, grim-faced and tight-jawed, full of fire and fury and a lust for vengeance. Every one of us was torn between our loving dreams of Elysian fields and the killing fields we would work through to get there. Every one of us was brimming with idealism and futility, not always so delicately balanced. It's quite possible she, like all of us, pushed her prejudice away one last time and rode willingly on the glory train.

But this is what I wish had happened; this, then, a dream of how she died.

It is in an elegant townhouse in a windowless basement workshop. The killing floor. Murder is in the air, death and destruction, the site of preparation for slaughter and decimation and she wants, suddenly, out. She is disconnecting.

But she is a prisoner of that room, convicted by her own bright hopes and vivid dreams. She is a captive of every little step and choice that brought her, lurching, to this point and place.

This minute hand has to come off. Terry snips and pulls with the needle-nose pliers. And this wire connects to the hour hand which will, at the appointed hour, complete the circuit. And then . . .

She listens and looks at Terry—sweating, smoking, chattering—and realizes slowly that she cannot hear a thing. How can we stop? she wonders. We are way beyond words now, beyond discussion. There are only echoes, so how can we stop? He moves on, oblivious, firing methodically on all available cylinders, supercharged willful energy steaming from his head, speaking of connection and completion. She, however, is disconnecting, as I've said, and reconnecting. Is she still a prisoner? Is it entirely inexorable after all? She is glowing now, smiling slightly, and Terry looks to her like an angel, beautiful in his blessed hope. Misguided, perhaps, but so righteously beautiful. She reaches toward him, but he neither sees nor hears. He is beyond noticing, bent upon his task, and hers is veering away. She remembers, too, the gift of affliction, the importance of sacrifice.

She takes a wire lightly between her thumb and her long first finger—no, wait a minute—and blue discovers red. Circuit complete, compass in motion, disruption under way. Upside down. And so it ends, and so it begins, and we were, all of us, short-circuited, going under.

Memory

Memory is a mystery.

There seems so little continuity in my story, so little that is linear or logical or aligned in a life. I've been a firefighter and a soldier and a tree planter; a welder, a teamster, a baker; a community organizer and a longshoreman. I've been a teacher and I've brought up children, and I also wrote a book about juvenile justice. I was a revolutionary anarcho-communist, small c, intent on overthrowing the government, a worthy if immodest goal.

The first fiction is to conceive a straight line of battle, a steady string running through this chaos of life. Accidents will all be explained, confusion made clear, the wild shambles tamed—this, then, will not be like any life at all, certainly not mine.

Roz Chast sketches a cartoon vision from "Inside One's Memory Bank" with a white-coated doctor in front of small neatly stacked containers indicating that "all available drawers are completely filled" by the time you're forty—local zip codes, for example, bus routes, the plot of Anna Karenina. *I'm well over forty now.*

Of course, forgetting is more powerful than remembering. Every day there are five hundred forgettable moments for any happy instant that sticks—and in the end oblivion trumps memory.

On March 6, decades after the explosion that ripped apart the big house in Greenwich Village killing Diana Oughton and Ted Gold and Terry Robbins, I stop at a fruit stand on Fifth Avenue to buy a big bunch of fresh flowers. I walk down to Eleventh Street and turn right. The street is practically deserted, a lone garbage truck working its laborious way down the block. Eighteen West Eleventh is a lovely townhouse again—all restrained elegance, with a distinctive front window jutting out gently like the prow of a yacht. In the window Paddington the Bear sits on a table, his whimsical outfits changed seasonally and for special occasions. I pause in front for a long moment, eyes closed, remembering the black hole of long ago and I arrange the flowers along the low cast-iron fence.

Two hundred miles away, at this same moment, three veterans of the Viet Nam War are honored in a solemn and emotional ceremony near the granite walls of the Viet Nam Veterans Memorial in Washington, D.C. The three—Hugh Thompson, Lawrence Colburn, and Glen Andreotta—happened upon the My Lai massacre on March 16, 1968, landed a helicopter between Vietnamese civilians huddled in a bunker and marauding American soldiers. They trained their guns at the advancing Americans, and Andreotta (who was killed three weeks later) and Colburn provided cover for Thompson as he confronted the leader of the American forces. These three pointed guns at their countrymen to prevent further atrocities, and when the soldiers stood down, they ferried the surviving Vietnamese villagers to safety. It was the ability to do the right thing even at the risk of personal safety that guided these soldiers to do what they did, Major General Michael Ackerman said at the ceremony. It took more than twenty-five years to imagine their actions as heroic, to remember something moral in doing the unthinkable right thing in war, even when it seemed like the wrong thing.

How much longer for the three who died on Eleventh Street? How much longer for Diana? When will she be remembered?

I walk beside the Viet Nam Memorial in Washington, remembering images of Viet Nam—a girl burned by napalm running naked down a highway, a suspected Viet Cong being summarily executed in the street, the American CIA fighting to retake the U.S. Embassy in downtown Sai Gon. I focus now on a girl with pigtails here at the memorial, crying. Why? She is with a woman in her fifties who is touching a name on the wall, and she is crying, too. Is this her brother? A husband? Childhood sweetheart? What does it mean to the girl in pigtails? There are flowers and notes and artifacts left everywhere along the wall. Two men are making memorial rubbings for a long line of people, solemnly locating a name, holding delicate white paper to the wall, and transferring the image from wall to paper. The wall is a living drama. It seems to grow out of the ground, and the names of the dead are animated by all the human motion and action taking place around them, because of them. Walking along the wall, I can feel spirit and passion swelling and then throbbing from the granite. It goes on and on, and still there are no Vietnamese names here. I write "Diana" on the sidewalk with chalk.

Viet Nam shows us things about being human, some of which we don't want to know and don't want to see. We live now and forever in a post–Viet Nam world, as well as in a post-Holocaust, post-Hiroshima world. We live in a world marked by genocidal warfare and irregular warfare, psychological warfare and economic warfare, a world that has known desert warfare, guerrilla warfare, mobile warfare, mountain warfare, naval warfare, aerial warfare, open warfare, position warfare, bacteriological warfare, chemical warfare, underground warfare, nuclear warfare, robotic and "smart" warfare, and so much more. Standing against it all is a wall, a monument, simply peace, the hope of a movement. We know something of catastrophe and precariousness, it's true, and something of indifference and narcissism as well. And memory.

I started out from Cody's Book Store in Berkeley—an auspicious beginning, I thought. I was on tour, promoting my third book on children and teaching. For this one I had spent a year in the juvenile detention center in Chicago. I decided to read from the foreword and then to speak for a few minutes. A plump baby crawled across the floor; someone passed a petition for legalizing hemp; a young man walked by with no clothes on. I felt right at home. Later, while I was signing books, an obese guy with a gray ponytail and dirty red bandanna, his large head glistening with sweat and his smudged bifocals slipping off his nose, leaned toward me, smiling. Remember me? he asked conspiratorially. He must have changed in thirty years. I was sure my memory was shot.

Bank Street Book Store was a tiny, intimate affair. Several reunions with old friends and lots of catching up over dinner.

Vertigo Books was small as well. Two very nice middle-aged women asked in unison, Remember us? Yipes!

Albany was fun because I was with dear friends who hosted a delightful dinner, and the bookstore signing went well until a severe fifty-something woman cornered me: Remember me? Not really. The night we trashed the South Vietnamese Embassy in Washington? Oh, yes, of course. Later that night? At the collective house? A complete blank. I'm Vicki Russo. Still nothing. I became a lesbian that year, and that was the best decision I ever made. Whew!

The evening at the Chicago Foundation was great. I was joined by two teachers featured in my new book and Alex, a former juvenile delinquent now running his own personal fitness business. It was a glittering gathering—three judges, the U.S. attorney, two university presidents, the state's attorney, and on and on. Among friends I referred to it as the Ruling Class Party, and on the way to Madison, Alex asked me why I called it that. I explained a little about the means of production and the labor theory of value. He asked, But you like Doris, right? Sure, I said, I like all those people, my dad included, but why do we need charitable organizations? And would they fund work that would make their existence irrelevant? And what would a fair society look like, anyway? In the long run, I argued, when the crisis deepens, those of us who neither own nor control the means of production or communication can join hands with our allies, demanding justice not charity. I got kind of excited, and Alex asked, Well, should I keep building up my business?

Absolutely.

But which side am I on?

You'll be on our side.

All the radio was good: *Fresh Air* a real treat, Studs Terkel great. The most moving moment came during a drive-time show on WVON (Voice of the Negro, originally). Cliff Kelley, former alderman, former inmate at Statesville, brilliant, all-round charismatic and thoughtful good guy, praised the book heartily. Phone calls came from professionals and working people, the editor of *The Final Call* and worried parents. The last caller was named Humphrey. He said he had followed my career since the sixties and had always admired what I did. Thank you, Humphrey. Then he asked how my dad was doing.

OK.

And your mom?

Fine.

How about your sister and brothers?

I began to worry.

Well, please tell your dad Humphrey says hello. He'll remember me. I drove a car for him thirty years ago.

An American moment.

The Learning Alliance was a shock. The event was billed "Subterranean Homesick Blues," and I anticipated an audience of four—two outpatients from St. Vincent's psychiatric, one homeless, embittered Weatherman, and a right-wing assassin. But fifty people showed up, several with books for me to sign, and we talked for two hours. It was exhilarating in a lot of ways—thoughtful, deeply political, engaging, provocative. One young guy, from ACT-UP, made a short speech about the need for militancy and then asked me to share anything I knew about getting false ID, smuggling, and making bombs. I demurred. He made another little speech—sharp, angry, aggressive—and people asked him to calm down. He told everyone to get fucked. As I was leaving an old woman asked, Remember me? By now I was practiced and so I replied in a kind voice, Yes I think so, but it was a long time ago and my memory's wobbly. And, of course, we've all changed a lot. What's your name?

Eve, she said. Eve Marychild. We were married in a previous life. Oh, of course. Now I remember.

So we found ourselves alive and awakening into a going world, a world that was moving fast, and then faster and faster—and we ran to catch up. We took it up as a challenge and a demand. We thought, rightly it turns out, that the notion of continuous progress in human affairs—an idea heavily promoted by the favored and the wealthy—was a blinding myth, and the idea of science and technology as neutral and forward-looking and advancing, equally unreal. We stood against the pillars of privilege, the fictions of the master narrative, the authoritative Western Voice of America. Having looked to the Vietnamese, we were thrust into a perspectival world, a landscape of lenses and angles and points of view, the ones we inherited particularly mystifying and self-serving, the others we later adopted bearing their own fatal pitfalls.

I don't look at us now as heroic guerrillas, nor do I feel misty-eyed and wistful. I don't think we were particularly crazy or demonic, either, although the madness of the times cast a huge screen as backdrop. So I don't want to stand smugly on the high ground of middle age and look scornfully down at the romantic fools in the fields of youth, nor to get even, nor to settle accounts.

Still, it was the end of life for some, the end of innocence for many others—the recognition that happiness is not an entitlement, the sense of cataclysmic forces in play, the great mysteries and events of life illuminated with intensity and clarity in a time of revolution. Choices were made, the valiant side by side with the foolish, the selfless intertwined with the selfish. We took the words of the old war resister, A. J. Muste, literally: "Those who undertake a revolution are obligated to at least *try* to see it through." And the hero of the Cuban revolution, the eternal internationalist Che Guevara, spoke to us every morning from a huge poster above our bed: "In revolution one wins or dies." The stakes were ourselves, we thought, and so we lived inside the resistance, facing each other every day as free people with neither road maps nor guarantees, building an exciting space of possibility underground. We wanted nothing more—and nothing less—than to claim our own lives.

Memory is mystification.
At its silver anniversary, Starbucks Coffee issued a series of napkins under the heading "25 YEARS AGO." One morning quite by chance I picked up this one:

> **The astronauts of Apollo 14 went for a drive over the moon's surface, and brought back a four-billion-year-old rock ... Radicals from the Weather Underground exploded a bomb in the U.S. Capitol to protest American involvement in Viet Nam ... And the Baltimore Colts beat the Dallas Cowboys in the final five seconds of Super Bowl V.**

Yes, yes, another perfectly American moment—the moon, the bombs, the Super Bowl—and the commodification of memory.

Emile de Antonio made his film about us at the height of the resistance. Viewing *Underground* years later with a group of young people, I had two distinct reactions. I thought the politics—the analysis of war and aggression, the understanding of racism as a main instrument of division and control, the vision of a world based on justice—held up remarkably well; I was embarrassed by the arrogance, the solipsism, the absolute certainty that we and we alone knew the way. The rigidity and the narcissism. I saw again how the impulse toward community, too, can betray us. We can, as well, be carried along toward an easy belief, toward the decisiveness of our dogma.

In Monty Python's ridiculous and hilarious *Life of Brian*, a reluctant messiah appears before an eager crowd and proclaims, I am not the savior.

They respond dutifully, You are not the savior.

You are free . . . you have minds of your own, he cries frantically.

We have minds of our own, they respond eagerly.

Funny, says a stranger in the crowd, turning to those around him, I don't feel free. I don't think I have a mind of my own.

Shut up, they shout. You have a mind of your own.

It's silly, of course, because it's so familiar, so utterly and universally human. We all want to believe in something, and most of us long for a solid surface or ledge to grab on to in the swirling, slippery shambles of our going experience. We seek some pattern or frame, some structure to provide meaning and purpose and direction to our lives. We want a solution to every problem, a vaccine for every virus. We human beings—most of us—want clear and definitive answers, something certain in our extraordinarily uncertain world.

But beyond being silly, Monty Python bites for anyone who has lived in a land of credulousness and absolutes and easy belief, and has moved away—or been thrust out or escaped—and then looked back from a distance. We see ourselves, suddenly, in the posture of the faithful, headstrong and moon-faced, looking a bit addled, mesmerized perhaps, in perfect dogged step with our sect, all marching for a just cause. And the cause is always just. We see ourselves, as someone said, living in the clean, well-lit prison of a single idea.

A few years ago a young mother asked me to attend an open house at a Montessori nursery school she had in mind for her son, and in a mild benign setting my own *Life of Brian* rushed back to me. It was a perfectly fine school, but on that day at the open house, I felt a shock of recognition as the school director guided us from room to colorful room—each filled with the sounds of happy children, each a workshop of purposeful play and productive projects—and opened each description of what we were seeing with the identical phrase: Maria Montessori would say that the children are . . . She would then point to a particular interaction or some set of materials.

Maria Montessori would say that the children are . . . began to take the familiar annoying place of Musak, a strict, insistent background buzz, disorienting and blurring. Eventually I could neither hear nor see the children; the space had been filled with white noise and eyewash.

At a break, drinking coffee with a group of prospective parents, the conversation turned to psychology, and someone mentioned the names Rogers and Jung. I noted that Carl Jung once said, I'm glad I'm Jung and not a Jungian because I can still change my mind. The director didn't miss a beat, responding eagerly, Maria Montessori said the same thing.

When you're untroubled by doubt, when your orthodoxy is full up, it resists all irony or interruption, all modification or reflection. By now I had become allergic to groupthink and inoculated against doctrinaire behavior. I had taken the live virus and survived. Still, I was awed by the familiar patterns, troubled by the ease with which normally thoughtful and aware people make moral commitments and simultaneously surrender something irreducibly precious: their minds. HO, HO, HO CHI MINH! I heard the echoes in my mind.

Of all those fugitive days—of all those terrible, exquisite years—I regret nothing for myself; I am sorry only for those who are perpetually blind to the cruel side of the world, those who never feel stirred to fight for something infinite, for humanity itself.

This story is a version of events, not definitive by any means, neither authorized nor authoritative, certainly not a pretense toward history. I warn everyone of my bias; I warn you of my mistakes. Still, this account feels honest enough to me. I've come to see, in any case, that fiction does a better job with the truth in almost every instance, and that being there is a dubious credential since "being" is so layered and full of movement, and "there" is a place bristling with interpretive possibilities.

For over a decade I was on the run, an American fugitive fleeing what the government winkingly calls justice. My purpose then, following years as a community organizer and movement activist, was utter defiance—to blaze away at the masters of war, the purveyors of death, the perpetrators of hatred. I wanted to penetrate what they posited as impenetrable, to pierce that smug veil of immutability, to open spaces for unimagined choices. Propaganda of the deed. My weapons were explosive words at first, slowly replaced by actual bombs. That is, of course, a troubling aspect of the story. Among my sins—pride and loftiness—a favorite twinkling line to comrades and acquaintances alike: guilty as hell, free as a bird—it's a great country. There were a few virtues: confidence, passion, optimism and hope, some humor. And I was not alone.

The important questions, of course, remain unsettled: What does the dream of social justice ask of us? What are the obstacles to our humanity now? And how shall we live?

I can't quite imagine putting a bomb in a building today—all of that seems so distinctly a part of then. But I can't imagine entirely dismissing the possibility, either. To say, We want justice, makes utter sense to me as it always has, but to add, But of course not by any means—is, it seems to me, to put your neck right on the chopping block. As a tactic, perhaps, but as principle, no.

Say the unjust are particularly powerful, as they so often are in our world, and enforcing a wide range of painful social relations, and say they make it clear that any serious opponent will be jailed or shot. They insist on only "peaceful" protest, prescribed and entirely in-bounds, and they enforce that dictate with clubs and guns and rockets. They grant themselves a monopoly on power, an exclusive franchise on violence, and they use it. What then?

I think back to my childhood, to the houses in trim rows and the identical lawns and the neat fences; I remember everyone sleeping the deep American sleep, the sleep that still engulfs us and from which I worry we might not awake in time. We are living our isolated lives in our shattered communities, and in our names the U.S. project shatters community everywhere—in the Middle East, in Colombia, in the Philippines. The world roils in agony and despair, the catastrophe deepens, and our ears are covered, our eyes are closed. Perhaps only the bark of bombs at our doors will shake us up after all.

Besides, the democratic project is always a contested space in America, forever confronting opposition, resistance, and crisis. The

forces for democracy have accordingly been called upon in every generation to rise up to meet various challenges. Looking backward, we
can easily accept the importance of the Boston Tea Party, Shay's
Rebellion, Nat Turner's uprising, Denmark Vesey's revolt, John
Brown's attack, the Deacons for Self-Defense, the Freedom Riders, the
theft of the Pentagon Papers, and the bombing of the Pentagon—
well, maybe not the last, not yet. But the others, certainly, are examples of democratic-minded people crying from the margins for a
democracy that is deeper and truer, lustier and more vibrant. And
looking backward is pretty painless—most of us can imagine ourselves throwing tea into Boston Bay or even throwing ourselves in
front of that fateful bullet flying toward Martin Luther King Jr.

But that settles nothing for today; the difficult questions remain.
What challenges the democratic vision today? What is to be done?

Bertoldt Brecht asks: In the dark times, will there also be singing?
The answer: Yes, there will be singing. There will be singing about the
dark times. I find myself again and again singing about the dark
times.

I assert a future, a vision of tomorrow, and the cherishing of possibilities against a grim and harsh background. The modern predicament is borne of nuclear bombs unleashed on civilian populations, of
holocaust and annihilation and the attempted extinction of whole
peoples. We are wracked with terror—the fallout includes numbing
insensitivity, narcissism, violence, repression. We awake suddenly to
see that technically proficient men, powerful and controlling men,
seem ready to destroy the world, that existence and continuity cannot
be assumed or guaranteed and must, therefore, be imagined and chosen and fought for.

We are not living, to be sure, in mountain times, in revolutionary
times, and that is as it is. We live in valley times—times of uncertain-
ty and confusion, times of endemic hopelessness and deepening
despair. These are times to stay awake and aware, to gather strength,
to study and build our projects, to make whatever modest contribu-
tions you can, to blow softly on the embers of justice—and to
remember.

My models remain civil rights champions like Ella Baker and Myles Horton and Septima Clark, each an activist community educator. They were workers in literacy and voting-rights projects, in community organizations and educational institutions. Their every work project was linked to a larger life project of community empowerment for liberation. Each was a teacher then, in the largest and best sense: a dreamer, a builder, a creator of intellectual space and ethical action, an enabler of individuals, and a midwife of a new society. When history is being rewritten in the interest of a smoother, less troublesome tale, a story more tailored to an era of selfishness and perceived powerlessness, these teachers remind us that in spite of humiliation and opposition, resistance continues. Though there are periods of quiet and confusion, people find a way to rise again.

When America lost the war—miserably it turns out—it failed, predictably, to admit defeat, to remember and to face reality. And because the powerful couldn't admit defeat, could not say they'd been wrong, America couldn't take responsibility and couldn't overcome the loss. America said, instead, that it quit or it left or it lost only the will to win. Military men in starched khakis said that their hands were tied by gutless politicians who weaseled and whimpered. We were never defeated on the field of battle, they intoned, and some other strategy—bombing the dikes, perhaps, or bombing China— would have done the trick. Presidents and senators and political pundits added that nobody really won the war, that the whole thing was an inexplicable mess, that we'd best move on. All of this was dissembling bullshit. The truth is the U.S. lost the war in Viet Nam. The truth is the other side won.

It's hard for America to admit this sad, dishonorable truth, running as it does against a solid American myth of might and invincibility. Harder still, because it pushes toward something deeper: we were dead wrong. Not only was all the bleeding and sacrificing and pain and sorrow irredeemable, it was in the service, finally, of a rotten and unjustifiable project. So the Vietnamese won, and it is right that they should have won, and that leaves us the losers.

Bernardine and I went on a pilgrimage to Viet Nam twenty-five years after the American defeat, returning to the scene of the crime, so to speak. We went to remember, to recover some parts of our lives, and perhaps to put our imaginations to rest. We went to see the war.

Whenever you go abroad, if you are a westerner in the East or a northerner going to the South, the first thing you encounter at the airport or the train station or in front of the hotel, is the onslaught of the children. There are dozens of them, hundreds, thousands, and they all have dark eyes and beautiful open faces, they all know a few lines of your language: Hello, they repeat, smiling. How are you? What's your name? These are the famous street children of the world, the gutter snipes and alley urchins, the garbage eaters, the kids Gloria Emerson referred to in wartime Sai Gon as the *bui doi,* or the dust of life.

They might want to sell you something—a bit of pineapple or banana, perhaps a trinket. You might buy some coins or a sweet. One might ask, Where are you from? America, you respond, and the smiles spread. They think you are rich, and after a time of doubt and apprehension and reassessment, you guess they are right. You are rich—fabulously, extraordinarily, inexplicably wealthy. It's a surprise and a wonder.

We met a few *bui doi* in Ha Noi, all of them peddling nuts and postcards, English-language editions of the antiwar *Sorrows of War* by Bao Ninh and Graham Greene's 1955 novel *The Quiet American*—particularly eerie reads in Ha Noi fifty years later. Ten years before the American war was actually under way, Greene foretold it all, the lies and delusions, the cruelty and ignorance and murderous consequences.

We saw a few other Americans while we were there: one big guy who simply cried the whole time. He would meet someone and start sobbing. Crying in his noodles, sobbing on his cyclo. Poor bastard. Another weird guy gave out dollar bills to everyone he met. He bought one of everything being peddled on Bat Dan Street walking from his hotel to the lake, or he just dribbled them out like wrinkled green exhaust in his wake. Reparations, he would mutter. Healing the wounds of war.

We lined up to see Ho Chi Minh's mausoleum with a huge crowd of jostling schoolchildren here on a mandatory field trip. Ho had begged his comrades not to put him on display, but they apparently hadn't listened. I thought of the young Nguyen Ai Quac—only later Ho Chi Minh or "he who enlightens"—participating in the founding of the French Communist Party in 1920. French intelligence characterized him then as awkward-looking, mouth constantly open in a stupid smile. You can look that up. I just ached, imagining the colonial functionary who penned that contemptuous and patronizing line, perhaps as an old man, witnessing the French debacle at Dien Bien Phu. On the French rubber plantations, workers died young, their small bodies buried in the orchards under the rubber trees where, the Vietnamese say, they became the melancholy fertilizer for the French affair—every time I see a Michelin tire I think it is haunted with Vietnamese souls, the very heart of the rubber formula.

In the tomb Ho looked waxy and bizarre, an icon, I suppose, to connect today's bureaucratic and mildly cranky government to its revolutionary past and its friendly, energetic, and propulsive people.

Khe Sanh was hard to get to, out along Route 1 near Laos and then up some rust-red rutted dirt roads and a slippery walk in the rain to a spot that is mostly lush jungle again, of coffee and rubber plants, although it had once been home to six thousand Americans—in 1968 the U.S. dropped sixty thousand tons of explosives on positions around Khe Sanh, killed between sixteen hundred and fifteen thousand Vietnamese, and lost two hundred U.S. combatants. The war there is an old scar now, the relentless jungle bit by bit, day by day erasing the Americans.

Everyone in Viet Nam calls the period between 1965 and 1975 the years of the American War, a brutal decade in a history that stretches back thousands of years and has been followed by two other wars. In the U.S., Viet Nam is unresolved, a cleft, a jagged rent in the body politic.

A couple of Viet Nam-era vets we spoke to had come to revisit Khe Sanh and Hamburger Hill. Ernie Parisi spent three months retracing every step he'd taken in Viet Nam thirty years ago, from Da Nang to Cu Chi, including the step that took off most of his left foot on Highway 8 in the Highlands. Jake Brightman spent two weeks in Hue scribbling furious notes in a spiral notebook. We never lost a battle here, he said. What the hell in the world went wrong?

In Hue we went to an Internet café and exchanged e-mail letters with our children. Dozens of youngsters crowded around us, eager to practice English, to play with the computers, and to eavesdrop on our messages. They were friendly and helpful and funny, and we realized again the power of the passage of time—over 65 percent of the people of Viet Nam were born after the Americans ran away.

The great ones—Henry Kissinger and Daniel Patrick Moynihan of Harvard, for example, or the "whiz kid" Robert McNamara from Ford, the great thinkers, the Bundy brothers, the mental giants and moral midgets—remember little. The logic they follow is fantastic: We destroyed that village in order to save it.

Of course, in the common rewriting of history, we are served up a steady diet of monsters and rogues, each uniquely horrible and beyond explanation. Each the greatest criminal ever known. Adolph Hitler, Saddam Hussein—or take Pol Pot, who, in the three years and eight months he clung to power, led the annihilation of perhaps a third of his nation's people. Who can forget the fragile-looking piles of skulls, the bones gathered into ghostly mountains? A nightmare holocaust, a mass murder as extravagant as this extravagant century would see.

And yet. And yet who will remember that it is the U.S., blinders firmly in place and frantically denying its steady losses in Viet Nam, that invaded neutral Cambodia in 1970, allowing Pol Pot a pretext and a tool that led to the seizure of power? In the early 1970s, U.S. intelligence identified supply depots in Cambodia. Bombers were deployed and perhaps three-quarters of a million Cambodian peasants were murdered cleanly from the air. During six months in 1973, more bombs were dropped on tiny Cambodia than were dropped on Japan during all of World War II—the equivalent of five Hiroshimas. Cambodia was bombed into chaos, driven into the waiting arms of a very happy Pol Pot. Later, after the mayhem and the murder, when the worst was done and Pol Pot was gone from power, we—the U.S., that is—rushed to the side of Pol Pot, the ultra-nationalist, militarily, economically, diplomatically, because he now opposed the Vietnamese. At the Ha Noi airport, we were startled to look up at a live CNN broadcast to see Kissinger being deferentially interviewed as a senior statesman—supporting the U.S. bombing of Iraq. No irony, no drawing of lessons, no trial as a war criminal, no memory.

We were exhilarated in Viet Nam, breathing in the whole experience in big gulps, unable to sleep, walking from early morning to late at night through crowded streets that flow like human rivers in Ha Noi, stopping at little stalls to eat rice and sauce and something grilled at the table. We talked to everyone we met, and everyone greeted us with enthusiasm. The Vietnamese assumed I was a veteran, and I felt I was a veteran of a sort. At one shop, the proprietor questioned us about America, discovered that we had been antiwar activists, and told us of his life as a soldier. We had cookies and tea together in front of his shop. More family joined us with photo albums. As we prepared to leave his wife appeared with a gift—a small tin box with a battle scene etched on its front, made, she told us, smiling shyly, from the wreckage of an American plane she had participated in shooting down as a girl. We thanked them and gave them a relic of our own—battered copies of our wanted posters. They insisted we autograph them and we wrote short messages of solidarity. Their smiles widened.

On April 26, 1977, at 8:41 AM, Bernardine pushed Zayd Osceola into our world in a rush of blood and joy after a long, long labor. Zayd, named for a Black Panther comrade murdered by the police, was born in our bed in a third-floor walk-up in the Fillmore district, the big red comforter folded on the floor, the sun slanting through the lace along the window, and he was perfect. So was Bernardine, laboring so long, only once, at 3 AM and thirty hours into it, whimpering and bewildered, screaming to the heavens, I can't, I can't; I'm messing it up. Zayd was huge—nine pounds and twenty-two inches—with one elf's ear, a burgundy wine stain on his side, and a pigeon chest.

Malik Cochise, his first name after Malcolm X, was born in a fifth-floor Manhattan walk-up February 1, 1980, at 12:48 PM. He came faster than Zayd, but the cord was wrapped around his neck and he was blue-faced. The midwife clamped it off decisively and cut it, and then there he was on Bernardine's belly where I massaged his back and chest, and he spit and breathed. Zayd had had a bath with Bernardine hours earlier, and watched the last minutes wide-eyed from a friend's arms before scrambling onto the bed with us, holding Malik in his arms as we whispered his name into his tiny ear. Zayd then laughed and announced to all, The grownups call this baby Malik, but I call him Garbage.

Later that year the four of us drove to Chicago to surrender to authorities, and a certain kind of fugitive life ended for us. In a restaurant on the Ohio Turnpike, while Bernardine changed Malik in the rest room and I got yogurt and oatmeal from the cafeteria line, Zayd told an older couple at the next booth, We're going to Chicago so my mama and poppy can turn themselves in. They smiled and nodded their silver heads beneficently, their bifocals flashing in the sun. It would be our last security breach.

The federal conspiracy charges which had put us on the FBI's most wanted list were, ironically, dropped because of extreme governmental misconduct. It came out, in the wake of the Watergate affair, that the Bureau had recklessly tapped phones, broken into people's homes, even written a plan to kidnap Bernardine's infant nephew.

On December 4, 1981, at 10:30 AM, Chesa Jackson Gilbert Boudin joined our family. His parents, old friends and comrades from SDS and Weatherman, had just been arrested after a bloody Brink's armored car holdup, and his grandparents were caring for him. What would happen to our sweet boys if we couldn't raise them? Bernardine asked, and we agreed to take him. For days leading to his move, Malik, twenty-two months old, walked around our apartment saying, Chesa can't have my bed . . . Chesa can't have my blocks. . . . And as Bernardine dressed him one morning, Chesa can't have my pants . . . Chesa can't have my shoes . . . Chesa can't have my mommy. And yet, when Chesa came to us, Zayd and Malik became his champions and his pillars, astonishing and devoted brothers.

This was not any family we could have imagined a decade earlier, but it was the family we now had. To call it dysfunctional would be both unnecessarily cruel and redundant—aren't they all? I mean, when you say family, isn't the next thought all the strange little secret lore, all the stories and eccentricities? We had our ways and our weirdnesses, but that, too, is another story.

When Mom died of Alzheimer's disease, she looked just like a small animal who'd been hit by a car, eyes half open, curled up and panting. And then she was gone.

I kissed her good-bye and drove over to see my guy Dave, a Chicago tattoo artist. I wanted a memory of her cut into my flesh forever, and I asked him to draw a red heart with the script "Mom" in a retro design evoking the 1940s.

As he gouged the thing into my skin, wiping the blood and carefully fixing the dyes, digging deeper and deeper, tears sprang to my eyes. I tried to concentrate hard on the remains of the other tattoos, to take my mind off the pain. The big red star had fared the worst—faded now to a harmless pink—and the rainbow and lightning bolt between my shoulder blades was wrinkled and sadly dim. My permanent reminders had all proved unreliable. Everything changes, I said, pointing to the star.

You're right, Dave said. And what brings folks to me is that elusive wish to hold on forever. If I can carve the sensation of permanence into their bark, he continued, brand it onto their hides, they get excited with thoughts of eternity. It's heaven's gates here, a permanent memorial, they think, and cheaper than church.

Stories get retold, I thought, the young become the old.

But over time, he said, tattoos start to look like some grimy inkblot, a terrible mistake of sagging skin, an oil slick on the street. That's just the way of time; nothing—and no one—stays the same. Dave's art of the skin goes the way of all flesh; his is an aesthetic mostly for the worms.

Outside the street life pulsed indistinctly forward—blurred now by my tears—that driving, mysterious energy I always want to be a part of.

Acknowledgments

Many books are born in love and struggle, hope and pain, this one perhaps more literally than most. I acknowledge a blood debt to all those who traveled these fugitive roads with me and whose stories I've interpreted here.

Thanks to Chesa Boudin, who listened eagerly to every word and asked a seemingly endless stream of thoughtful questions, and to Malik Dohrn, whose love and resolute confidence encouraged me always to go on. Zayd Dohrn provided persistent insights as well as an important first edit to the whole book; he was smart and incisive as always and I'm deeply thankful to him. I'm thankful as well for the reflected light and warmth of these three spirited and beautiful young men.

Jeff Jones and Eleanor Stein have taught me a thousand things for more than thirty years, mostly how to be friends for life, and I am forever grateful.

Thanks to the Chicago writing circle: Hal Adams, my model of an effective community educator; Caroline Heller, a talented writer and sweet, sweet soul; Mona Khalidi, whose love and friendship and politics enrich my life; and Therese Quinn, my colleague, docent, and longtime guide.

Thanks, too, to my talented teachers, the artists and writers of Bennington College.

Helene Atwan has been a brilliant and dazzling editor throughout. The entire Beacon Press tribe is an inspiration, and I thank them for their wisdom, commitment, and plain hard work: Erin Clermont, David Coen, Tom Hallock, Pam MacColl, Christopher Vyce.

I'm indebted to others who generously read the manuscript in various forms and drafts and offered their thoughtful comments: Rick Ayers, Harriet Beinfield, Vicki Chou, Sunny Fischer, Michael Kennedy, Susan Klonsky, Mark Larson, Mary Larson, Glen Lyons, Bart Lubow, Carole Saltz, Bill Schubert, Tim Shanahan, Bill Siegel, Malcolm Terence.

I am deeply grateful to Diana Ruiz for her steady work, her intelligence, and her determination in all things.

There are not words enough to thank Bernardine Dohrn for all she has been and done, but she knows that I know.

Finally, my heart and my hope is with every freedom fighter who is, even now, imprisoned for speaking out fearlessly, for acting on a passionate conviction that we might work toward a future of peace and justice: Sundiata Acoli, Jamil Al-Amin (H. Rap Brown), Herman Bell, Anthony Jalil Bottom, Kathy Boudin, Marilyn Buck, David Gilbert, Mumia Abu Jamal, Raymond Luc Levasseur, Sekou Odinga, Anthony Ortiz, Leonard Peltier, Oscar Lopez Rivera, Michael Santos, Carlos Alberto Torres, and the list goes on and on.

Afterword

Emancipate yourselves from mental slavery; none but ourselves can free our minds.
—Bob Marley

A constant theme of this book, first published eight years ago—a refrain that plays on almost every page—is the inescapable responsibility each one of us has to live our lives purposefully, to choose who we want to be and who we want to become in a shifting and complex world, to name ourselves and construct our identities in the noise and chaos of the whirlwind. One of my earliest teachers put it this way: Live your life in a way that won't make a mockery of your values.

Of course, that injunction settles nothing in the everyday world we inhabit: we still have to make our choices operating largely in the dark, we still live without guarantees regarding the outcomes of our choices or our actions. But the admonition has as well some positive spark: It assumes that we have values that we can access and assess; it asks us to use those values as guides and goals; it challenges us to live a life that ties those values as closely as possible to our behavior every moment of every day. This book chronicles my complex read of how we did that in the frenzied decade 1965–75.

There's a telling exchange in *Wonderland* between Alice and the Cheshire Cat. Alice begins, "Would you tell me, please, which way I ought to go from here?" "That depends a good deal on where you want to get to," says the cat. As the saying goes, if you don't know where you're going, any road will take you there. Making our values explicit and accessible is one way to begin to create, if not a detailed and completed map, at least a sketch and a dream. This is what freedom looks like—it asks us to act with courage, to operate without a safety net to confront the horrors as well as to celebrate the joys of living, and finally, to choose.

In the 1999 Brazilian film *Central Station* we find a woman who makes a meager living writing letters for illiterate people in the Rio de Janeiro train station. One day a man comes to her with an astonishing offer: he will pay her a significant amount of money if on the following day she will pick up a young boy at a certain address and deliver him to an American couple on the other side of the city so that the boy can be adopted. She, of course, takes the job, collects her money, and on the way home stops off to buy a new television set. Later, happily watching her new TV, a friend stops by and hears the story of the boy. Her friend scolds her: Are you crazy? she asks. Don't you follow the news? She explains that children all over Rio are being kidnapped, sold, and murdered, their organs harvested for an international market in such things. The woman sets off immediately to try to find the boy and save his life.

When the woman took the job, there was no burning ethical issue involved. But when her eyes were opened, she had to either act or choose indifference and therefore immorality. A first step, then, in making a moral choice or taking an ethical action is to open our eyes to reality. We must see the world as it is, we must act on the world, and we must also then question whether our action was completely correct. And we act again.

During the time of slavery there were undoubtedly honest slave traders, loyal slave-catchers, and plantation owners who told the truth, paid their bills, and lived up to their promises, but in what sense were they acting ethically? In order to be a moral person then and there—it seems so obvious now—one would have had to work for abolition. Not many did, but we find some comfort today in telling ourselves we would surely have been among the courageous and the righteous few. But is it true? How do we know? We know that a slave society undermines goodness every moment in a million different ways. And since we know that it is very nearly impossible for individuals to live virtuous lives in a slave state, it becomes essential to end slavery—or, in these times, to work toward a more just and peaceful world—as part of leading a moral life. A just society creates the conditions for more of us to act more often in a moral way. Are there any injustices here and now that we take for granted for which the coming generations might indict or condemn us? And, most important, what social and community standards would allow or invite more of us to do the right thing?

I'm writing this on July 4, 2008, in the heat of the summer presidential campaign, with all its attendant bells and whistles and spin, all the diversion and dissembling that happens every four years when the big election carnival rolls into town. I just saw a bumper sticker with a large colorful peace sign—all tie-dyed and psychedelic, so sixties—with an accompanying slogan: BACK BY POPULAR DEMAND. And on the radio John and Yoko implore us: "All we are saying is give peace a chance." Déjà vu all over again.

Every candidate claims the mantle of change, and why not? None can afford to run on a platform of war without end, illegal and aggressive occupations draining the wealth of the nation, an expansive use of indefinite detention, extraordinary rendition, torture, and extrajudicial murders, all undermining and destroying traditional humanist values. None wants to own job loss and economic dislocation combined with corporate corruption and unprecedented shifts in wealth to the rich and the superrich. Eight years of catastrophe and crisis, a time that echoes in important ways the national and international crisis I describe in this book.

Senator Barack Obama, asked during the primary campaign whom he thought Martin Luther King Jr. would support, responded: Reverend King wouldn't support or endorse any of us, but he'd be in the streets building a movement for justice, and holding our feet to the fire. Exactly right. Lyndon Johnson, the most effective politician of his generation, was never involved in the civil rights movement, although he did pass far-reaching legislation in response to a robust and in many ways revolutionary Black freedom movement in the streets. Franklin Delano Roosevelt was not a labor leader, and yet he presided over important social and pro-labor legislation in a time of radical labor mobilization in shops and factories across the land. And Abraham Lincoln was not a member of an abolitionist political party, but reality forced upon him the freeing of an enslaved people. Each of these three responded to movements on the ground.

There are a few marked similarities between the era of Viet Nam and the era of George W. Bush's so-called global war on terror: Invasion and occupation look remarkably the same wherever and whenever they occur; the U.S. government—like all governments—lies about intentions and outcomes; the illegality and immorality is similar; the people of the world readily see through the charade, and even the American people require only a few years to come to oppose wars of aggression even in the face of steady, screaming, jingoistic propaganda. Three million Iraqi wounded and a million Iraqi deaths—more than three hundred thousand killed directly by U.S. troops—attest to the nature of the conflict.

The American people are indeed opposed to the war raging in Iraq in this summer of '08. The opposition does not express itself in mass demonstrations, but that doesn't make it any less real. In fact, in some ways the mythologizing of the 1960s is now a brake on progressive struggles, and we should not expect to replay that moment in exactly the same terms. The vocabulary of resistance and the drama of protest today will necessarily be new, and it will—in a world as out of balance as this one, a world of such screaming and unnecessary pain—no doubt burst onto the scene in unpredictable ways. The powerful and their propaganda organs will be "Shocked!" but injustice is inherently unstable, and people who are systematically pressed down will always rise up as they come together to name themselves in opposition, and as they begin to sketch the outlines of a better world that could be but is not yet.

Fugitive Days was initially published in early September 2001, and on September 11, just hours before the bloody events that would transform that day into what we now call 9/11, I woke up in Ann Arbor to a page-one story about the book in the arts section of the *New York Times*. The angle of the *Times* account was captured in its headline: "No regrets for a love of explosives." That's neither my narrative nor my sentiment, but the idea was seized upon by the neocon media machine: I was an unrepentant and violent terrorist.

I'm nowadays often quoted as saying, "I don't regret setting bombs. I wish we'd set more bombs. I don't think we did enough." I never actually said that I "set bombs," nor that I wished there were "more bombs." I said that I regretted many things—for example, in the political movement, I was deeply sorry for the turn to dogmatism and the slavish devotion to a rigid set of ideas that led to the terrible intolerance and splitting that was so characteristic of the Weather faction in 1969, and I deplored the macho posturing and destructive male-supremacist practices that passed for leadership. I regretted the deaths of our beloved comrades and wrote about the subsequent and contested Weather decision to engage in purely symbolic actions. But I killed no one, and I harmed no one, and I didn't regret for a minute resisting the murderous assault on Viet Nam with every ounce of my being. Over a thousand people a week were being annihilated, and the antiwar forces couldn't stop it. We weren't effective enough, we weren't strong enough, smart enough, experienced enough, quick enough. Eventually the U.S. was defeated, and everyone remembers the humiliating pictures of people fleeing in helicopters from the roof of the U.S. embassy in Sai Gon. This was a shameful, murderous, illegal war carried out by my government for over a decade. I didn't do enough to stop it, and I don't know anyone who did.

On that morning of September 11 everything before seemed suddenly far away, long ago, and lost, everything in the hours and days and weeks after, broken or brittle, frighteningly off-balance. Images of falling bodies and falling buildings, of airliners turned into human-filled terrorist bombs slamming into buildings, played over and over and over until they had their toxic effect, dulling and sickening, less and less illuminating as time passed, and the result, predictably, was pure poison. The military geared up—even in the immediate murky aftermath it was dead certain that the U.S. would exact a colorful, public revenge against someone, somewhere.

On September 12, an editor from *Newsday* called and asked me to write an op-ed about terrorism. Why me? I asked. What do I know of crazed fundamentalists murdering innocents in the service of an incredibly arid ideology?

Then a Chicago paper wanted me to do a story about life underground. Before long I was besieged by reporters and editors wanting my take on Al Qaeda, on the psychology of fanaticism, on getting ID and maintaining false identities, on hiding out in American society off the radar screen. I declined every request—I don't possess any particular insight into any of those matters, I explained. Further, I had no interest in being held up as a token representative of some subspecies of "them"—in this case, "terrorists."

I got one anonymous phone call at home on September 11: "Do you support the bombing of the World Trade Center?" a man's voice asked angrily. I was astonished that I needed to reassure anyone. I said that it was a monstrous crime against humanity, and he replied in a suddenly subdued tone, "Okay, thanks."

My eighty-six-year-old dad got anonymous calls, too, from individuals who berated him for raising me. "I just listen calmly," he told me later, "and when they run out of steam I say, 'You're wrong,' and I hang up on them." Good old Dad—I felt rotten that he had to go through all this again. And my mother-in-law's caregiver—a lovely, patient woman—left meticulous messages on our kitchen counter: *Bill, someone called at 8:40 and told me you are a murderer, but didn't leave a name or a number.* Nuts! I wanted that number. But seriously, I felt bad for her too.

Fugitive Days was the focus of controversy, but at the same time the object of a campaign. Not surprisingly, the propaganda campaign—with all the modern tools of opinion making and image building—overpowered the controversy so that any possibility of a serious discussion of complicated issues was shouted down and, for a time at least, lost. The campaign seemed to have several specific goals—one was surely to suppress the history of the U.S. war in Viet Nam, a catastrophe still too vivid in the minds of people the world over, still raising the most troubling and terrible questions, not just about foreign policy but about the nature of U.S. power and the corrupting force of privilege and empire on ordinary people; another was to ignore the content and garble the meaning of the Black freedom movement, a movement that was explosive, large, and threatening to the institutions of white supremacy in its time, that shook the country to its foundations, and that set the moral agenda for a generation—and almost certainly will again—placing issues of justice, equality, and human rights in the foreground.

The noisy upheaval surrounding and then overwhelming the book came on with a swirling force, and the book itself was rather limited by comparison, and so, soon enough, the campaign was all there was. I remembered Ralph Ellison writing, "These white folk have newspapers, magazines, radios, spokesmen to get their ideas across. If they want to tell the world a lie, they can tell it so well that it becomes the truth." Any normal person was expected to already know and accept that being a Weatherman was synonymous with fanaticism, violence, and murder. There was no need for a normal person to read the book—others would read it for them, tell them what it meant, and save them the trouble. The campaign around the book pushed forward, and the book itself became a footnote: any normal person skips over the footnotes.

Day in and day out I go about my business, hang out with my wife and our kids and grandchildren, take care of the elders, go to work, teach, and write. I also organize and participate in the never-ending effort to build a powerful movement for peace and social justice. Now and then (and often unpredictably) I appear in the newspapers or on TV with a reference to *Fugitive Days*, and some fantastic assertions about what I did, what I said, and what I believe. In 2008 there was a lot of chatter on the blogosphere about my relationship with Barack Obama: we had served together on the board of a foundation, knew one another as neighbors and family friends, held an initial fund-raiser at my house, where I'd made a small donation to his earliest political campaign. Obama's political rivals and enemies apparently saw an opportunity to deepen a dishonest narrative about him, that he is somehow un-American, alien, linked to radical ideas, a closet terrorist, a sympathizer with extremism. One night I heard Sean Hannity on Fox News tell Senator John McCain that I was an unrepentant terrorist who had written an article on September 11, 2001, extolling bombings against the U.S. and even advocating more terrorist bombs. Senator McCain couldn't believe it at first, and neither could I.

My e-mail and voicemail filled up with hate once again, mostly men, all of them venting and sweating and breathing heavily, a few threats—"Watch out!"; "You deserve to be shot"; and from satan@hell.com, "I'm coming to get you and when I do, I'll waterboard you." The police lieutenant who came to copy down the threats told me in classic gallows humor that he hoped the guy who was going to shoot me got there before the guy who was going to waterboard me, since it would be miserable to be tortured and then shot.

The more serious point is that Obama was asked once more to defend something that ought to be at the very heart of democracy: the importance of talking to many people in this complicated and wildly diverse society, of listening with the possibility of learning something new, of speaking with the possibility of persuading or influencing others. It's more than guilt by association, a deep and ugly tradition in our political life; it's the assumption that one must apply a political litmus test to begin a conversation. In a robust and sophisticated democracy, political leaders, indeed, all of us, would seek out ways to talk with many people who hold dissenting, even radical, ideas—indeed, without that simple and yet essential capacity, we'd likely be burning witches and enslaving our fellow human beings today. Open talk and free association are necessary to resist the eclipse of the public and to expand the public space as we search for a more vibrant and participatory democracy. What's at stake finally is the right to think at all.

The last decade has been a time of fear—both real and manufactured—of patriotic sentiment—both authentic and fake—of the hollowing out of democratic institutions and the throttling of the spirit of democracy, of promiscuous and fatalistic growth, bread and circuses and widespread distractions—a period similar to the days I describe in *Fugitive Days*. We might now welcome a time of searching for the new, as we did when the country was so torn by another illegal war. We might think of ourselves not as passive consumers of politics created elsewhere but as fully mobilized political actors. And we might think of our various efforts now, as we did then, as more than a single campaign, but rather as a movement in the making.

We might find some hope in the growth of opposition to war and occupation worldwide. Or we might be inspired by the growing reparations and prison-abolition movements, or the rising immigrant-rights movement and the stirrings of working people everywhere, or by gay and lesbian and queer people courageously pressing for full recognition and rights. But mainly, hope resides in a simple self-evident truth: the future is unknown, and it's also entirely unknowable. History is always in the making, and we are—each and every one of us—works in progress. It's up to us—nothing is predetermined, and we are all acting largely in the dark, with our limited consciousness and our contingent capacities. This makes our moment here and now both hopeful and all the more urgent—we must find ways to become real actors and authentic subjects in our own history. We may not be able to will a movement into being, but neither can we sit idly waiting for a movement to spring full grown, as from the head of Zeus. We have to agitate for democracy and egalitarianism, press harder for human rights, learn to build a new society through our self-transformations and our limited everyday struggles. At the turn of the last century Eugene Debs told a group of workers in Chicago, "I would not lead you into this promised land if I could, because if I could lead you in, someone else would lead you out." We must figure out how to become the people we have been waiting for.

Min-Chuan Sung

William Ayers is Distinguished Professor of Education and Senior University Scholar at the University of Illinois at Chicago (UIC), and founder of both the Small Schools Workshop and the Center for Youth and Society. A graduate of the University of Michigan, the Bank Street College of Education, and Teachers College, Columbia University, he writes about social justice, democracy and education, the cultural contexts of schooling, and teaching as an essentially intellectual, ethical, and political enterprise. His articles have appeared in numerous journals, including the *Harvard Educational Review* and the *Journal of Teacher Education,* and he has written or edited fifteen books including *A Kind and Just Parent: The Children of Juvenile Court, To Teach: The Journey of a Teacher, Teaching Toward Freedom: Moral Commitment and Ethical Action in the Classroom,* and *Race Course: Against White Supremacy* (in press). He blogs on billayers.org. He lives in Chicago with his wife, Bernardine Dohrn.